ROBERT TALLANT

Mardi Gras
...As It Was

PELICAN PUBLISHING COMPANY
GRETNA 2007

LCN: 79-103475
ISBN: 0-88289-722-5

First printing, January 1948
Second printing, January 1976
First Pelican paperback edition, January 1989
Fourth printing, December 1994
Fifth printing, January 2001
Sixth printing, February 2008

ISBN-13: 978-0-88289-722-6

Printed in the United States of America

Published by Pelican Publishing Company, Inc.
1000 Burmaster Street, Gretna, Louisiana 70053

Mardi Gras
...As It Was

Other Books by Robert Tallant

THE VOODOO QUEEN, PELICAN, 1983

VOODOO IN NEW ORLEANS, PELICAN, 1983

THE PIRATE LAFITTE
AND THE BATTLE OF NEW ORLEANS,
PELICAN, 1994

EVANGELINE AND THE ACADIANS, PELICAN, 2000

With Lyle Saxon and Edward Dreyer

GUMBO YA-YA, PELICAN, 1987

This book is dedicated

to all who have been to the Mardi Gras,

to all who plan to come,

and to all who want to come.

CONTENTS

INTRODUCTION   ix

Part One — Let's Go to the Mardi Gras!

1. MARDI GRAS IS MANY THINGS   3
2. LET'S GO TO SOME BALLS   13
3. HERE COMES THE PARADE   29
4. NOW MARDI GRAS BEGINS   47
5. UNTIL MIDNIGHT   69

Part Two — Here Is How It Began

6. EUROPA AND THE BULL   83
7. CARNIVAL AND THE CREOLES   96
8. THE LORD OF MISRULE   115
9. REX AND THE ROMANOFF   129
10. KINGS, KREWES, AND KLANS   139
11. ANOTHER CENTURY   157

Part Three — This Is What You Do

12. HOW TO GET INTO A BALL   173
13. HOW TO BE A QUEEN   185

Contents

14. SCANDAL, SKULLDUGGERY, AND SCUTTLEBUTT   198
15. YOU GO WHOLE HOG OR YOU GO FISHING   219
16. KING ZULU AND THE BABY DOLLS   230
17. MARDI GRAS IN OTHER CITIES   250

A MARDI GRAS CALENDAR TO THE YEAR 2000   259

BIBLIOGRAPHY   261

INTRODUCTION

*M*ARDI GRAS IS A SPIRIT. I BELIEVE IT IS AN immortal one. It is certain that it is at least as immortal as Man's ability to make believe, to escape the dreariness of the everyday life that is most men's portion, to have fun, to laugh, and to play. I doubt that many of us want more immortality than that, not if we have much sense.

In our generation we seem to be at the end of an era. We are told that tomorrow there will be another kind of world and that it is highly probable it will be even less pleasant than this one. We are warned, with dire solemnity, that not many of us can even hope to survive the change. We are comforted in regard to that with the assurance that if we do live through what is coming we will be sorry, unless we are monsters with paranoiac tendencies or unimaginative and humorless human automata.

That does not promise Mardi Gras much of a future. Yet

Introduction

I am not inclined to worry. I think if there is any world left in which human beings still laugh and still, even on rare occasions, have fun, there will be a Mardi Gras, and that it will live through whatever catastrophes occur, as it survived the perishing of Greece, the destruction of Rome, the centuries of pain and plague we call the Middle Ages, the perilous journey to the end of the earth that turned out to be America, and all the wars. Men cease to laugh only when they are very ill or when they have become beasts. When men are that ill they die. As for the beasts, they cannot laugh, and I do not imagine they have much fun. That is why Mardi Gras is not a trivial matter but a very important one. In a way it is a symbol of the art of being human, and wherever people are still human, wherever they enjoy living, it will exist in some form.

No book and no pictures, however excellent, can take you to the Mardi Gras any more than a travel book or film conveys you around the world. At best, books and pictures are substitutes for living experiences. But they are the best substitutes.

I offer here a record, a history, a portrait in words (supplemented by photographs I consider both charming and realistic), a guide, and, in a slight way, a commentary. For those who have been to New Orleans to see and experience the most gay, exciting, and unrestrained revel of people at play that the United States can offer, I hope reading this book will be a pleasant way of recalling the fun they had. I hope it will help those who are coming, that in it they will find guidance as to what to expect, what to see, what to do. I hope, too, that for others it will be the beginning of an intention to visit New Orleans and the Mardi Gras, that to them it will also give, whether they actually see it or not, some of the fun of being part of the celebration.

Here and there I have been critical. Nothing can be perfect —not even Mardi Gras—and it is my opinion that there could be small changes. But these are minor, and those who resent my criticisms will not do so only because I have pointed them out.

Mardi Gras is very old, but it is also very young. It belongs to the past, yet also to the present and to the future. The face it wears now is not necessarily its last. It will exist in other forms, in other times, in other places. It would be wonderful if the clown in the grinning mask should appear on all the Main Streets of the world, if the blazing flambeaux and the rocking floats were everywhere, if everywhere there could be a season, or at least a day, devoted to laughter. And, besides all the other virtues of Mardi Gras, it also keeps a lot of men and women busy for a long time each year, preparing for play and for having fun, and thinking of these things, instead of devoting their time, their labor, and their thoughts toward ends more sinister.

A number of people have helped the progress of this book, with encouragement and advice, with information, with stories and anecdotes. I want to thank, first of all, Tess Crager, whose encouragement, suggestions, and aid have been most valuable. I wish, also, to express my appreciation to Olive Leonhardt, Dr. George Raffalovich, Grace Raffalovich, Robert Kushner, Heda Kock von Meysenburg, Sue Thompson, Joel Harris Lawrence, Alberta Kinsey, Arthur Charbonnet, Weeks Hall, Rebecca Sclater of the Mobile Chamber of Commerce, and to numerous others, with whom I have talked on one Mardi Gras or another, or about one Mardi Gras or another.

Most kind and generous assistance has been extended by Edward Seghers and Mrs. E. D. Friedrichs and their staff at the City Hall Archives; by Miss Essae M. Culver and her staff at the Louisiana Library Commission; by John Hall Jacobs, librarian of the New Orleans Public Library, Miss Margaret Ruckert and other members of the staff; and by

Introduction

the staff of Dr. Garland Taylor, librarian of the Howard-Tilton Memorial Library of Tulane University.

Donald Clive Hardy, Maude Chambers, Edward Dreyer, Hazel Breaux, Ines Vila Masia, and Le Salon de Pierre contributed the photographs.

R.T.

PART ONE

Let's Go
to the Mardi Gras!

CHAPTER ONE

MARDI GRAS IS MANY THINGS

THE OLD HOUSES IN THE FRENCH QUARTER OF NEW Orleans were all dressed up in the carnival colors of purple, green, and gold. It was the Tuesday night that precedes the Tuesday that is Mardi Gras; Cynthius, God of Music and Song, leading the first street pageant of the season, was expected at any moment; the ancient buildings smiled like merry crones repressing a humorous secret.

A woman walked out into the narrow middle of Bourbon Street and shouted up to another woman two stories above, "Honey, throw your head out the window and see if the parade's coming yet!"

"It ain't even on Canal Street," replied her friend. "I'll let you know."

"How you gonna dress Mardi Gras?" a man asked the woman in the street.

"That's something I ain't telling nobody," she screamed. "When you see me Mardi Gras, you gonna see something— only you ain't gonna know it's me."

The balconies, banquettes, and windows of Bourbon Street were filled. Patrons and employees of the night clubs

3

and bars that line the street kept running to doors to peer out, then to vanish inside again, announcing to those within that "it ain't coming yet." Even in the Convent of the Holy Family at the corner of Orleans and Bourbon streets lights burned behind drawn blinds as if the little Negro nuns and their charges were waiting too.

Farther uptown, closer to Canal Street, the wide and brilliantly lighted principal business street of the city, the crowd was thicker, the impatience of waiting more evident. Vendors with baskets suspended from cords about their necks hawked candy, peanuts, and popcorn. At every corner men held aloft billowing bunches of brightly colored balloons. Pitchmen were doing a noisy but brisk business selling carnival souvenirs—buttons from which hung streamers of purple, green, and gold, tiny pink and blue umbrellas, masks of every type and every color, vivid red Spanish dancer hats, whistles, horns, false mustaches, noses and eyebrows, bunches of artificial violets, artificial red roses for lapels, bright pink cotton candy, and candied apples on sticks. In each block rough wooden sidewalk stands sold hot dogs, hamburgers, and cold drinks. In true New Orleans tradition several of these stands had signs that offered "Creole Hot Dogs," which were no different from any other hot dogs, except that Creole mustard was smeared on each one.

At the corner of Bourbon and Canal streets a young boy was selling real camellias—delicate pink, deep red, and pure white, from a low flat basket. A pitchman with a large scale and a display board covered with masks, funny hats, canes, and cupid dolls challenged passers-by to let him guess their weights. "A free souvenir if I miss by two pounds!" he offered. Five feet away another man offered to guess ages. Crowds encircled them, munching candied apples and peanuts, and urged each other to "go on and do it." Banjo Annie, one of the best-known New Orleans characters, leaned

4

against a showcase near by, strumming her instrument and singing in a low, husky voice. She wore a skeleton mask.

Canal Street was its noisiest. The traffic lanes were cleared and no automobiles or streetcars were permitted to enter it now that the time for the parade was near. Polite but adamant police kept the crowd from spreading from the sidewalk to the street. The banquettes were so jammed that any movement was difficult. There were quarrels, arguments, near fights, but almost everyone maintained his good humor.

Many persons leaned against the strained cables, some having stood there for hours, determined to retain their places and have an unobstructed view of the parade. Now they were six and seven deep, and when a late arrival managed to squirm in front of someone who had been there earlier there were indignant remarks. "What you trying to do, you!" Fathers held small children on their shoulders, or they held them high above adult heads in peculiar contrivances that appear in New Orleans only at Mardi Gras time—boxlike seats at the tops of long poles. Here and there a youth held his girl on his shoulders.

Behind these spectators surged the great fluid mass of those too impatient or too lively to stand still and wait. Young boys and girls formed chains by holding hands, and wormed their way through the crowd, shouting at each other, sometimes singing. Beggars were everywhere—blind men singing hymns and inching along slowly, slowly, as the boisterous gradually recognized their blindness and one by one stepped aside to let them pass and to make little clinking sounds by dropping coins into their tin cups. A legless man on a contraption made from roller skates was pulled through the crowd by a bull terrier wearing a little purple, green, and gold sweater and carrying a cup in its mouth. On one corner a group of adolescent boys bunched together, seized one of their number, and tossed him high into the air. He went straight up, feet first. ten. fifteen feet, above the heads of the mob, landed safely in his friends' arms, yelling with animal glee.

Groups gathered in front of show windows to admire the decorations. Every window was festive with purple, green, and gold. Mannequins in many of them wore Mardi Gras costumes; in others chic female dummies wore little half masks and smart spring suits and dresses. In the window of a clothing store a life-sized mechanical man in a clown's suit rocked back and forth, releasing continuous peals of hysterical laughter that was so contagious that anyone who stopped to watch and to listen found himself laughing too.

Several windows displayed the jewels of the kings and queens who would rule over the organizations due to parade in the week ahead—brilliant crowns and tiaras and scepters, the jeweled cup and the headdress of ostrich plumes that Comus would wear, the exquisite necklaces and bracelets of Venus, the traditional magnificence of the crown of Rex. A jewelry-store window held a gigantic open book in which were inscribed all the names of the rulers of Carnival since its beginning.

Over the banquettes of Canal Street were wooden grand-stands holding seats from which a fine view of the parades was offered. Some of these were open to the public, and ticket sellers stood at the bottom of the wooden steps leading to the tiers. Others, like the huge one in front of the Boston Club, were privately owned and barred to everyone except those having special and precious invitations. Above the Boston Club stand huge letters blazed in white electric-light bulbs, KOC—Krewe of Cynthius. Each night for the week to come the letters would change in honor of the krewe that was parading. Nearly every building, from the beginning of the second story to the roof, was a blaze of electric lights— sometimes white, sometimes in the carnival colors, some- times in the pattern of huge crowns or other designs, some- times simply in strings of lights.

Canal Street grew more boisterous with every minute now. The din was a dull roar at times. At other times the whole street seemed to be convulsed in laughter, in song, in wild shouting. Above it all was the hum of an airplane that streaked back and forth, flashing on and off an immense electric sign that read: "Carnival Visitors—Welcome to New Orleans." Beneath it all were a thousand little sounds—the rustling of paper bags, the crunching of peanut shells underfoot, the crying of a baby, the piping voices of the blind beggars, the pleas of the vendors and pitchmen, the whistles of sailors at pretty girls, the raucous laughter of the mechanical man. A drunk shouted, "Hey, Mardi Gras!" from a window above and other people yelled, "Mardi Gras!" at anyone who passed wearing a funny hat or a false mustache, for when you're in any sort of costume in New Orleans at Mardi Gras time you become *a Mardi Gras*. Policemen blew their whistles and little boys blew toy whistles, and it was impossible to tell the real from the false. There were the odors of hot popcorn and peanuts, of weiners and mustard, of whisky and chewing gum.

Active or inactive, everyone awaited the first carnival parade of the year—the Canal Street crowds, the entertainers of Bourbon Street, the socialites sitting in the balcony before the Boston Club, the boy being tossed high into the air, the policemen, the children, the dark little nuns in the convent in Orleans Street—and while they waited they had a good time. In that fact may be the real secret of New Orleans and its people. They always have a good time. And it is infectious. Those visitors who come to New Orleans, especially if they come for Carnival and Mardi Gras, have a good time too.

Perhaps only in the Rome of the Caesars did people love holidays as much as do the citizens of New Orleans. At times this passion for playing startles visitors a little. It seems to them that almost any day they arrive in the city is marked by a celebration of some kind, or it is the eve of one, or the yesterday of one. "When do people work?" they sometimes ask.

The answer is that people work in New Orleans as much as they do elsewhere, but that work is not the whole of their lives, as it too often seems to be to Americans elsewhere. It is a necessity. With work they buy the time and the money for the more pleasurable things of life. Orleanians, in general, have an instinct for the enjoyment of life that is rare in other parts of the country. This is the core, the real secret, that makes the city different from any other in the nation.

Mardi Gras is the most important date on the city's calendar, and it is then that New Orleans is at its best. In Rome a long period of gaiety began in December and lasted until March. Courts were closed, little business was conducted, and most of the time was devoted to pleasure. In New Orleans law and business do continue, except for some minor interruptions, but having a good time is the principal objective of most of the citizens during this season. And, as a matter of fact, the rest of the year may almost be said to exist for the purpose of preparing for the weeks of balls and pageants preceding Mardi Gras itself, that Shrove Tuesday, or Fat Tuesday, when the city becomes for a day like no other place still existing upon this earth.

Even before Christmas there are stirrings and signs pointing to its approach. The first official ball takes place on January 6, which is Twelfth Night, or Ephiphany, when the Krewe of Twelfth Night Revelers hold their ball, but even before that, during the past few years, other organizations have held balls. There is little time in which to recover from New Year's Eve celebrations in New Orleans.

Mardi Gras in New Orleans is many things. Primarily, Mardi Gras is the last day before the beginning of Lent, the feast before the fast, the Tuesday before Ash Wednesday. Sometimes it is in February and sometimes it is in March; thus in some years there are more than sixty days in which to hold the several dozen balls of the season, while in other years there are less than thirty days, this depending upon what date Pope Gregory's calendar has established as the beginning of Lent in a given year.

One of the important things to understand about it all is the difference between Carnival and Mardi Gras. Carnival is the entire program of balls and parades; Mardi Gras is but one day—Shrove Tuesday. The terms, however, are used rather indiscriminately, even by Orleanians, and people frequently call Mardi Gras "Carnival Day," and the entire Carnival "Mardi Gras," despite the fact that they are referring to a period of thirty to sixty days as "Fat Tuesday." One thing you must never say is "Mardi Gras Day." Would you say "Fat Tuesday Day?"

Aside from the fact that the day after Mardi Gras is Ash Wednesday and the beginning of Lent there is almost nothing religious about Carnival. New Orleans was once an entirely Latin and Roman Catholic city, but for a long time now this has not been true in a literal sense. It is true that the city is still Creole in moods and manners and morals, but it may be doubted that very many Orleanians any longer attach much religious significance to Carnival. People of every religion—and people with no religion—enjoy it together, without a memory or a thought of its meaning.

Carnival in New Orleans is the social season, or at least the better part of it. This is important to remember, for no American city has a "society" that takes itself more seriously even now. Debutantes may be going out of fashion in many places, but in New Orleans young ladies view their debuts with as much concern as did their mothers and their grandmothers. Their self-esteem is high, and the prestige they achieve during the season they "come out" is largely measured by the balls over which they may be chosen queens, or those at which they may serve as maids.

Mardi Gras is also good business, but this is a factor that is definitely incidental. Other cities in the United States may offer certain activities for the sole or the prime purpose of attracting tourists who will spend money in their community. Tourists as well as natives do spend large sums of money in New Orleans during Mardi Gras, but he who imagines this has anything to do with the purpose of the celebration is very much mistaken. Hotels, restaurants, and shops do a thriving business, but if New Orleans were isolated from the rest of the world Mardi Gras would still go on. It is not a commercial enterprise in any way. Strangers may imagine that the festivities are in some way connected with the city government. The city of New Orleans, as such, has nothing at all to do with them. Neither has the Association of Commerce. Carnival organizations are private clubs with strictly limited memberships, and all the parades and all the balls are paid for by the dues and other contributions of these members. Thus, despite its Latin flavor, Mardi Gras, at least in its psychological implications, is a very American institution. It is free enterprise.

However, this does not mean that the city does not offer encouragement and aid. The city builds grandstands, donates the protection of the police force, and does everything possible to make each Carnival more successful than the one before. It also decorates the streets through which the parades will pass, and these decorations alone are an invaluable contribution.

To some visitors to New Orleans it seems that Canal Street is always decorated. Even in Lent there is something hanging from the light standards and cables above the broad thoroughfare; perhaps it is Red Cross flags. Immediately after Lent comes the Spring Fiesta, which calls for palms (artificial) and potted azaleas. It continues all through the year until Christmas, when giant Santa Clauses and Christmas trees and candles line the street. Then, right after New Year's, the decorators are again at work, not only in Canal Street, but in St. Charles and Royal and Bourbon and any other streets through which Mardi Gras parades will pass.

Each year there is a central theme that is applied to Canal Street. New Orleans is the only city in the United States that has an official decorator, who is employed for the whole year, and under whose direction the streets are dressed up for Mardi Gras. In 1947 "The Ghost of Christmas" was the theme chosen. The huge red candles into which some Canal Street light standards had been transformed for Christmas were covered with silver paint, then further adorned with masks and balloons in carnival colors. Other standards were topped with small fir trees sprayed with purple, green, and gold paint and strung with lights in those colors. Still others became gigantic clowns, each with a different face and costume from the next. Strings of electric lights were looped from standard to standard. Then the grandstands went up.

The sound of hammers and the smell of cypress are always two of the most cheerful signs that Mardi Gras is coming. Later those mysterious iron lids marked "Carnival" that dot the edges of Canal Street banquettes disappear and into the holes go freshly painted green posts, and cables with white cloth covers are strung, blocking the banquettes from the street. It is then almost time for the parades to begin. It is Mardi Gras again! In 1947 signs, purple letters on gold backgrounds, at the bottom of each light standard on Canal Street, gave the program of the parades to appear during the week before Mardi Gras and on that day. Only the major parades were listed, for there are many smaller parades, some confined to residential sections far from Canal Street. There are marching clubs and wonderfully decorated trucks filled with maskers; there is King Zulu, the Negro

11

monarch of Mardi Gras, and his entourage; and many others, some of which provide more amusement than any of the big pageants.

Too, long before any parades appear, there are the balls of the krewes and clubs who do not parade. The street activities are the climax and the end of Carnival. It has been going on for a long time.

CHAPTER TWO

LET'S GO TO SOME BALLS

*C*ARNIVAL ORGANIZATIONS ARE SECRET SOCIETIES. Members are not supposed to reveal their membership. The clubs are closed affairs with rosters that seldom exceed two hundred persons, a limitation that is adhered to so strictly in most cases that it is necessary to await the death or a very rare resignation of a member in order to join one of them. In some, membership is actually willed—to a son, a relative, or a friend. Dues are paid yearly, these averaging about $125 per year, and out of these come the costs of the annual ball. A ball may cost $2000 to $35,000, now and then even more.

Nearly all are men's clubs. Only in recent years have women organized their own krewes, and these are still much in the minority. At most balls only the men who belong to the club wear costumes and masks—the king, the dukes, and the other members who will "call out" the ladies of their choice for dances. Except for the queen, who will wear the mantle and royal jewels of the krewe, and her maids, whose gowns may in some way distinguish their positions, all other women attending the ball wear evening dress, as do their male escorts who are not members. In the case of a ball given by a feminine organization, everything is, of course, in reverse, and then the ladies of the krewe wear the costumes and masks and the king, dukes, and male dancers wear full-dress suits.

When Carnival was revived after World War II—for it has always been suspended during wars—more clubs than had ever existed before appeared in New Orleans. For that season of 1946 there were thirty-six balls. In 1947 there were more than forty, and it is likely that they will continue to grow in number.

At present practically all the balls are held in the Municipal Auditorium, which divides into two sections, so that often two balls are going on within the same building simultaneously. At other times, while a ball is taking place in one side, a symphony concert or perhaps an opera is being held on the other. That the sections are not entirely soundproof, with the result that the orchestra playing the grand march for the ball sometimes drowns out the tenor who is performing on the other side, is a matter that does not too seriously disturb Orleanians. In a way it just makes everything seem gayer and more appropriate to the season.

Orleanians await the receipt of invitations to balls with feverish anxiety. It is quite true that there are people who loathe balls, but no one, especially the female portion of the population, will admit it, for by the number of invitations received do many of them measure their popularity, and by the quality of the balls to which they are asked may be judged their social position. Invitations may not be used by anyone other than the person to whom they are issued, but many an otherwise honest New Orleans woman is known to have begged, borrowed, or stolen one so that she may be seen at a particular ball. Only once in a while is she caught, but now and then some fashionably and expensively dressed lady is forced to depart, red-faced and trembling with shame, from the entrance of the Municipal Auditorium, because one of the gentlemen at the door happened to glance at the invitation and recognized the fact that the name upon it and the lady were not the same person.

Various ways of avoiding this have been attempted by the krewes. It is a rule with some that if a person receives a card and cannot attend the ball he must return it to the organization or else be dropped from the invitation list. Nevertheless many of the uninvited, with fur coats drawn high and heads swathed in tulle, do continue to crash the gate with the card of a sick, out-of-town, or previously engaged friend. Many have been doing this for years.

Invited or uninvited, those who get inside the Auditorium for a ball find it considerably altered in appearance from its usual, somewhat gymnasium-like appearance, and for each ball it is, of course, an entirely different scene that meets the eye. Nearly always the stage has vanished and the seats in the parquet have been removed. In the rear and on the sides only do some boxes remain on the ground floor, the rest of the space being reserved for tableaux and dancing. In the boxes usually sit the season's debutantes and other young women of social position, if the krewe is one of high social prestige, who, together with their invitations, have received call-out cards. When the tableaux are finished they will be called out by the maskers for dancing.

In nearly all balls these are the only persons who dance. All other guests are spectators and must sit upstairs. There are many differences in customs among the various krewes, but certain procedures are standard in most of them. There is a kind of court etiquette, for Carnival is a mock revival of monarchic rule. The king and queen come first in importance, then the dukes and maids, next the nobles of the court —the maskers—and, last, the spectators at the ball, who represent in a way the population of the king's mythical kingdom. And, mockery or not, it is all viewed as an affair

15

more serious than anyone other than an Orleanian may be able to comprehend.

Much money and artistic effort go into the plans and preparations for a ball, which begin nearly a year ahead of time; the councils of most krewes meet in April. Dues often do not cover all expenses, so extra money is often contributed by members. In some ways balls are not now so lavish as they once were, in other ways—and in other cases—they are improving. Some manage to approach wholly unintentional high comedy.

Rivalry between krewes is serious. Twelfth Night "officially" begins the season, but this calendar determination in no way prevents other organizations from preceding the Ball of the Twelfth Night Revelers.

Actually, Harlequins has long held the first ball of the season. After the return of Carnival when World War II ended, Harlequins held their ball of the 1946 season in what was really still 1945. It took place on December 28—just three nights after Christmas! Harlequins has a tradition of long standing. Each year, following the presentation of the court, the season's debutantes, wearing veils over their faces and plumes upon their heads, are presented. The pretty foolishness has begun.

Much more was offered in this first postwar ball. "On with the Dance" was the theme, and the curtains rose on a setting of multicolored bubbles rising and floating about musical notes embroidered upon heavy draperies of varying shades of blue. Then, one by one, the queens and courts who would have ruled over balls during war years, when Carnival was suspended, were presented. The court of the current year represented the "Desert Song" and were dressed accordingly. The queen was a harem beauty in sequins, beads, and golden fabric. The maids wore similar costumes in red and blue. After that the year's debs were introduced, and then the ball began.

Twelfth Night Revelers, who always hold their balls on January 6, also have their particular traditions. The queen and court of the previous ball are always presented at the current one. In 1946 it was the court of 1941, the year of the last prewar Carnival, who were presented. In 1947 it was the court of 1946. Thus it goes.

At Twelfth Night Reveler Balls the king cake custom is utilized, and as soon as all guests are seated and upper lights are dimmed a huge facsimile of a cake is rolled out upon the ballroom floor by young boys, dressed as chefs, who are known as the "Little Cooks." Then members of the court known as "Big Cooks" cut into the cake. The men on the floor committee then go to the boxes and call out the names of the debutantes selected for the first dance. These march around the tremendous cake, and each receives a small box in which there is a bean. The young woman who receives the one golden bean in the lot is queen, and the others, who receive silver beans, are maids. The queen is then presented with a bouquet, a mantle of white satin and silver cloth is fixed to her shoulders and a crown of jewels set upon her head. Twelfth Night Revelers is the only organization that chooses its queen and maids in this way, and as the king and dukes lead them to the dais from where they will view the rest of the ball, fluttering female spectators in the tiers are always deeply stirred.

Following the selection of the court, Twelfth Night Revelers proceed with a tableau in several parts, such as begins most balls. In 1947, for instance, Twelfth Night Revelers' subject was "Father New Orleans," and the theme was developed through scenes that depicted early colonial days in the city. The captain of the krewe wore a Louis XIV suit of bright silver, and other maskers were soldiers, firemen, bootblacks, gamblers, and policemen. After the tableau the call-outs continue.

Call-outs are noisy affairs at all the balls. The gentlemen

of the floor committee go about literally bellowing the names of the ladies with whom the maskers wish to dance. This takes time, for no dance begins until each pair have been brought together. The result is a little disjointed and a little discordant, but each time everything is at last arranged, the music begins, and the dancers circle the floor, at least for a few minutes. Then it all begins once more.

Feminine spectators in the balconies keep careful watch over each call-out. Mothers, friends, enemies, or simply curious, they listen closely for familiar names and peer downward excitedly, often jealously, and keep every sense sharp and keen in order to see who received how many, and who did not. They whisper among themselves behind cupped hands or fans, or, if they're sufficiently angered, sometimes make loud and uninhibited statements. These, together with ejaculations of pride and praise for favorites, can be heard at every carnival ball.

"That's the Tussey girl. She's going to be *fat!*"

"It is ridiculous, I tell you. Her mother wasn't even from New Orleans, that one."

"Doesn't Heloise look *gorgeous?*"

"When *I* came out *we* wore some *clothes.*"

"Sometimes I wonder if it is really like it used to be. It seems as if just anyone now can . . ."

"They're so common they're *aborigines.*"

"Her mother was a friend of my mother's, you know. I think we're slightly related. Nice? Oh, *charming!*"

Not only debutantes receive call-outs, of course, although in some organizations it is arranged that they receive the bulk of them. Older women, married ones, are also so honored.

"That *must* be her brother," says a balcony whisper. "She would see to that. She's had that same call-out for *years.*"

It goes on and on. This is the real reason why many of

the ladies upstairs have come to the ball. There is, too, always much speculation upon the identity of the king, the dukes, and the other maskers, who are all supposed to remain anonymous. In reality, their intimate friends often know who they are, but efforts are made to keep their secret.

After the Ball of the Twelfth Night Revelers the other balls come so fast that even the most intense of carnival ball devotees begins to weaken. Nearly every night until Mardi Gras there is at least one, and if the season is a short one, with Mardi Gras due early in February rather than in March, the pace is swift and hectic. But popular ladies insist on going to as many as possible, so for many of them life becomes a matter of little more than sitting under the ceiling of the Municipal Auditorium night after night. Their days are divided between the beauty parlors, shopping for new gowns, and attempts to catch up with their sleep.

The society columns of the New Orleans newspapers carry calendars showing the balls to come and their dates, listing the exotic, mythological, strange, and sometimes fantastically concocted names of the krewes: Olympians, Neobians, Orpheus, Fantasy, Eros, Iris, Bards of Bohemia, Alhambra, Virgilians, Athenians, Nereus, Caliphs of Cairo, Osiris, Elenians, Iridis, Hypathians, Dorians, Aparomest, Alpheus, Prometheus, Mystic Club, Mithras, Sonians, Krewe of Mystery, Marionettes, Cynthius, Babylon, Momus, Hermes, Venus, Midcity, Carrollton, Proteus, Rex, Comus —and many others.

Most of the balls follow the same pattern—the tableau, the grand march of the king, queen, and court, the call-outs, and in a few some general dancing. At midnight the court always departs for a supper in some exclusive restaurant or home or a hotel, where royalty and nobility amuse themselves until nearly dawn. There is food and champagne and dancing, and here, in secret, the masks of the king and his dukes come off.

Themes and titles of the balls are of infinite variety. A considerable amount of liberty is taken with history, legend, and literature, but this only lends zest to the tableaux. In recent years themes have included the American Indian, the history of the dance, Monsieur Beaucaire, Peer Gynt, numerous ones concerned with Louisiana and New Orleans, Napoleon Bonaparte in Warsaw, various Asiatic settings, including Persia, Arabia, India, and Siam, Marco Polo in Venice, Aladdin and his lamp, the life of Victor Herbert, ancient Egypt, ancient Greece, medieval England, France, Spain, and Italy, seventeenth-century Russia, eighteenth-century Vienna, and nearly every century something else.

The Krewe of Osiris presented one of the most spectacular balls of 1947. Using as a theme the 1911 coronation of King George V of England, the New Orleans debutantes, wearing white dresses and ostrich plumes on their heads, each led by her father or a close male relative, were "presented." All was conducted with as much dignity and seriousness as if the young women were actually being presented at the Court of St. James's, and the girls were nearly as thrilled. The queen, who represented Queen Mary, and her maids wore tiaras, and the effect was very elegant. The identity of "King George V" was, of course, kept a secret.

In a recent year the tableau at an Olympians Ball depicted a quite credible representation of "Faranta's Tent Show," a colorful New Orleans amusement center that flourished in the French Quarter during the last century. Outside the huge tent Negro women vended *pain-patate, calas, bière douce,* and *sucre brut.* There was a *mais tactac* vendor with his basket of popcorn balls and a *marron* vendor offering his roasted chestnuts. There were children with their mammies and a balloon man offering his wares in a loud voice. Inside the tent were clowns, strong men, acrobats, and minstrels. It was one of the most original balls New

Orleans had seen for years, and of a sort done much too seldom.

The story of Peer Gynt was enacted by the Krewe of Mystery with only slight variations on the theme. Peer ran away from his nagging mother to avoid marrying the neighbor's daughter. He returned and kidnaped the girl as she was about to marry another man and carried her off to the hills. Then he met the troll princess, resisted temptation, and married the first girl after all. All roles in these tableaux are usually enacted by persons other than those in the courts. Kings, queens, dukes, and maids stand by until they are completed, then take over the show.

A Prophets of Persia Ball, using the theme "Monsieur Beaucaire," was especially elaborate. The entire ballroom was transformed into the home of Beau Nash. Beaux and belles were awaiting the arrival of the ambassador of France when the curtain rose. English drinking songs were rendered by a quartet, and twelve young women performed a stately minuet. The queen wore a gown of slipper satin embroidered in rhinestones and trimmed with silver lace, a mantle of slipper satin edged with scarlet roses, a five-pointed crown topped with ostrich plumes, and carried a five-pointed scepter. The krewe's traditional gift to the queen, a pearl necklace with a diamond clasp, was presented to her after the tableau. Each maid received a fan, each lady in waiting in the tableau a silver bracelet. The call-outs were given handsome lapel pins. At nearly all balls the queen and her maids receive gifts from the krewe, and each call-out still receives a favor of some kind at the completion of each dance.

Hollywood might envy some of the settings and effects achieved by the decorators for carnival balls. For the Caliphs of Cairo's Marco Polo Venetian Ball a canal and gondolas appeared before the entranced eyes in the tiers. Marco Polo, his father, and his brother brought home Tartars, Chinese, and Persians. Chinese dancers—"a gift from the great Khan"—performed exotic dances. The costumes of those taking part in the tableau and of the court were magnificently adorned creations of silver and scarlet satin, of gold and silver lace, of sequins, rhinestones, and pearls.

At other balls trees and flowers come to life. Omardz presented one in which the curtains parted to reveal a flower garden being eaten by caterpillars. The caterpillars were feasting delightedly until Omardz arrived on the scene. He changed all that. The flowers turned out to be humans, and the caterpillars changed first into butterflies, then into debutantes, who were the maids in the court. In this case the court did take part in the tableau, contrary to the general rule.

Redskins whooped and howled about a blazing fire at an Atlanteans Ball. One given by the Krewe of Moslem depicted the "Loves of Men," including "Love of Home," "Love of Music," "Love of Food," "Love of Science," "Love of the Theater," "Love of Wine," and "Love of Money." The maids represented the loves, and, naturally, the queen was the "Queen of Love."

Carnival balls have not usually paid too much attention to contemporary events, at least as far as the subjects of their tableaux are concerned, but just after World War II several used themes relative to peace. At the Ball of Apollo the queen was costumed as the "Dove of Peace," and the maids represented Russia, England, France, China, and other Allied countries. The king dressed as Uncle Sam and carried a staff surmounted by the American flag. The men in the tableau dressed as soldiers, the dukes as officers in the Army Air Corps, and the captain and lieutenants as brigadier general and majors, all in proper accord with the army caste system. United Nations flags decorated the ballroom. Mystic Club used much the same theme one year, under the title "A Time for Rejoicing."

Mystic Club differs from the other krewes in that its queen and court are not members of the younger set, but mature and married women, some of whom years ago took part in other balls. In 1947 Mystic Club commemorated its twenty-fifth anniversary. The old French Opera House, destroyed by fire in 1919, was reproduced in the Municipal Auditorium. Tier upon tier of boxes mounted on each side of the proscenium arch, and there was a reproduction of the famed French Opera House curtain. Wearing costumes of the late nineteenth century, the court in the boxes looked, as the curtains parted, into scenes of other years, as other balls were depicted with as much accuracy as possible. Supposedly looking forward, they actually saw, in review, the balls of the past, as court scenes of 1923, 1926, 1927, and 1929 appeared. After the tableaux the 1947 queen led her court in the grand march.

The women's krewes have not departed very much as yet from the general procedure of the balls given by the men's organizations, except for the fact that the ladies wear the costumes and masks and remain as anonymous as possible in some instances; they are not, however, quite so successful as the men. For one thing, feminine vanity prevents them from wearing costumes that are too concealing or in any way grotesque, or even, in most cases, from covering the entire face. A woman in a lovely and often revealing costume and wearing a fetching half mask is by no means entirely disguised.

The themes chosen by the female organizations are usually pretty ones. Flowers are popular, and at one recent ball the king and queen sat in an Easter egg and members of the court represented baby chickens, bunnies, and Easter lilies. At another "The Garden of Titania, the Fairy Queen" was presented, with Queen Titania's maids dressed as "Springtime," "Twilight," "Glowworm," "Butterfly," "New Moon," and "Dewdrop." Still another depicted a Mexican masquerade, with the queen and maids all dressed as lovely señoritas with mantillas and fans.

Just after the end of World War II the women's krewes, resuming their balls, were still imbued with an affectionate regard for the uniform, and many invited young soldiers and sailors, still stationed in training camps near New Orleans, either to take part in their balls or to attend as guests. This was commendable and was, in general, appreciated, except in perhaps one case. In this instance a young soldier was invited to reign as king over a ball. He accepted with great pride and on the night of the affair arrived at the Municipal Auditorium determined to do his best and to save newspaper clippings and photographs of himself to send to his best girl back home.

When he reached the room in which he was to dress he received a severe shock. Until now he had not been apprised of the subject of the ball or of the type of costume he was to wear, but he suddenly discovered that the title of the tableau was "The Garden of Eden," that he was Adam, and that his costume consisted of only a silver fig leaf and, for some unaccountable reason, a flower to wear behind one ear.

He was a modest boy, and his first impulse was to escape. This was, however, impossible. Dukes, committeemen, and other male attachés of the krewe crowded around him, eager to make his evening as pleasant as possible. He refused flatly to be Adam. This, they said, was ridiculous. He had nothing to do but to pose briefly with the serpent beneath the apple tree and then to chase Eve around a bit. He fussed, he swore, he nearly wept, but they were adamant. They would not allow him to ruin a carnival ball. Eve, the queen, attired in a sort of sarong of silver cloth, appeared to add her pleas and arguments. This was the big moment of her life, and where was his gallantry?

The gentlemen in attendance undressed him. In self-defense he donned his fig leaf, but the flower he steadfastly refused to wear. Then, pulled, pushed, and prodded, he was driven out into the maze of scenery in the ballroom, the orchestra struck up some stirring music it thought appropriate for the Garden of Eden, the floodlights blazed down, and he stood naked and blushing and trembling before several thousand pairs of eyes. When Eve appeared he was a few minutes working up courage to give chase, but, once started, he pursued her with gusto. Later he remarked that what he had really wanted to do was to catch her—and bash out her brains.

The Krewe of Virgilians, a new feminine organization, gives balls as spectacular as any New Orleans has ever seen. Their most lavish effort perhaps was in 1947, when, with much enthusiasm and heroic effects, they presented "The Great Deluge."

Most carnival courts include six or seven maids. That year Virgilians had twelve, which necessitated a double grand march, instead of the usual single one, but which also made twice as many young women happy. All the girls represented either animals or birds Noah took into the Ark or the colors in the rainbow, the animals including a deer, a zebra, a panther, and a mountain sheep; the birds a pheasant, a parrot, and a dove; and the colors being violet, indigo, blue, yellow, and red.

The curtain rose to reveal Noah kneeling in prayer in a forest. God walked from between the trees and told him to build the Ark. The next scene showed the animals and birds preparing to enter the vessel. Lightning flashed, thunder roared, winds blew, and the rain came. In the final scene the maid portraying the dove appeared waving an olive branch, and then the maids dressed in the colors of the rainbow made their entrance.

Outside the Auditorium that night there was another sort of storm. Virgilians had been very generous with their invitations that year and thousands of persons were turned away at the entrance because the 4700 seats were filled and fire regulations in New Orleans forbid any standing in aisles or blocking of exits.

It was a very genuine catastrophe for those barred from the ball, and some of them were determined to get in regardless of any law. Extra police had to be summoned to prevent many from forcing their way, and then they remained at the doors, clamoring and arguing and pleading. But only those women with call-out cards were allowed entry, since seats had been reserved for them. The other ladies, dressed to the eyebrows, swished about furiously in their velvet and silk and taffeta, demanding of their male escorts that they "do something" and swearing vengeance against the police department, the fire department, and the management of the Municipal Auditorium.

"Not since the French Revolution," said a newspaper reporter the following day, "was high society so cut up!"

"A superbly gowned dowager," said another, "walked off a little, then turned and tore her invitation to shreds, raised her other hand to her lips and emitted an ear-shattering raspberry."

Virgilians was not the only ball from which guests were barred because of the issuance of too many invitations. At the Ball of Apollo a stout lady, wearing velvet, pearls, and a small tiara, slapped the face of a doorman because he refused her admittance, then lifted her skirts and fled toward her waiting car.

Carnival balls are by no means given or attended only by persons of high social and financial position. The krewes vary a great deal and almost every social layer is represented. Some are quite fashionable. Some others are composed of professional men, still others of businessmen and merchants. There are young men's krewes and those whose membership is made up of older ones. And besides the genuine krewes, balls are given by many business houses and department stores for their employees and friends. A ball with paid admission is given each year aboard a pleasure steamer that operates each night on the Mississippi River at the foot of Canal Street. Political groups hold balls, and recently a number of navy veterans organized to hold an annual carnival ball.

Besides all this, there are many children's balls, held usually in schools. There is even one very exclusive children's club that holds an impressive ball every year. At all the children's balls the more important procedures and traditions of the adult affairs are followed. The small kings and queens wear robes of satin, mantles embroidered with rhinestones and sequins, and jeweled crowns. They present tableaux and some even have call-outs. At one children's ball the mayor of New Orleans welcomes the young king and queen, and then the season's debutantes are presented by the royal pair.

For all the weeks between Twelfth Night and Mardi Gras, New Orleans blazes with lights and jewels, brilliant costumes and dazzling evening gowns and the dignity of white ties and tails, as the balls go on night after night. There are a few individuals, usually male, who tire of it all, but for most Orleanians and their visiting friends it all accumulates into the biggest show on earth, for where else in the world is there left such concentration upon the spectacular? Where else can one move from court to court, from land to land, to be welcomed each night by different royalty in an entirely different setting? Where else can one perhaps become royalty, even if only for a single night? Where else can one so completely escape into another world and another age? In most Americans there lurks an atavistic affection for monarchy.

And all these weeks are, of course, only preparatory to the really big show, the final week of the festivities, when

Mardi Gras

the parades appear in the streets of New Orleans, each to be followed by a huge ball, and then at last, at the climax, will be the big day, Mardi Gras, when all who wish may don costumes and masks and be anything they ever wanted to be and do *almost* anything they ever wanted to do.

CHAPTER THREE

HERE COMES THE PARADE

*L*IFE IS NOT WITHOUT ACCIDENT AND TROUBLE even for the kings of Carnival. While the crowd downtown awaited Cynthius the unforeseen occurred. The parade left its secret den in Calliope Street promptly at the hour of seven that evening. A few minutes before that a ladder had been set up beside the king's float and His Majesty climbed aboard. His pages took their places on either side of him, his magnificent mantle of emerald green was arranged behind his throne, His Majesty adjusted his mask, and the Negroes in white hoods and robes led the mules drawing his float into the street. Behind him each of the twenty-one floats, carrying out the theme of "The Land of Oz," filled, one by one, with maskers, and the procession arranged itself to begin the night's pageant that would end at the Municipal Auditorium, where the ball would take place. After the floats were lined up in proper sequence, the captain of the krewe seated himself in the horse-drawn carriage that would lead the parade, the dukes took their positions on their horses, the title-bearers, each one a Negro carrying a large sign on which was inscribed the title of a float, took their places, then the flambeaux and gasoline torch carriers lined up on both sides of the street. Finally the bands, already in place, struck up the famed Mardi Gras song, "If Ever I Cease to Love," and the procession rocked slowly out Calliope to St. Charles Avenue. The God of Music and Song, resplendent in green velvet, with bright green ostrich plumes attached to his shoulders and a crown of green jewels upon his head, waved his scepter of simulated emeralds and nodded and bowed, greeting the subjects already lining the street through which he passed.

"The Land of Oz" was a fine parade, but scarcely had it begun when an accident occurred. The pair of white horses drawing the captain's carriage bolted, and the captain was off at breakneck speed. They were captured almost immediately, and the horses replaced by two mules. Again the parade was set in order, and those watching as it turned into St. Charles Avenue agreed that seldom had a more beautiful pageant been seen in New Orleans. Behind the emerald-green float of Cynthius came the title float, constructed in the form of a gigantic and gorgeously colored rainbow, bearing the words "The Land of Oz." The third, "The Wishing Horse of Oz," held a huge white horse apparently in motion, surrounded by maskers in costumes of green and white satin, who threw trinkets, including strings of beads, bracelets, whistles, and many other small articles into the crowd as the float passed. Next came "The Sea Serpent of Oz," decorated with a monstrous, slithering serpent encircled by smaller snakes and maskers in green and yellow costumes. The maskers aboard "The Palace of the Red Jinn of Oz" wore costumes of flaming red satin covered with brilliants and rhinestones. Other floats included "The Diamond Swan of Oz," "The Monster Spider of Oz," "Ozma's Magic Carpet," "The Wizard of Oz," "The Winged Monkey of Oz," "Scraps, the Patchwork Girl of Oz," "Glinda's Magic Book of Oz," and all the rest of the fabulous people and places, animals and monsters of the fairyland of Oz, each float filled with maskers in costumes appropriate to the theme, some of these wearing fox, spider, and similar costumes and faces. And as they passed all threw trinkets generously into the yelling crowds, who leaped into the air, arms and hands thrust out to catch them, and sometimes ran beside or behind a float, for to catch trinkets from the floats is one of the particular satisfactions of Mardi Gras time.

At St. Charles and St. Philip Street the second accident of the evening occurred. One of the Negro flambeau-bearers accidentally touched the float of "Glinda's Magic Book of Oz," and the papier-mâché burst into flames. The maskers leaped and climbed to the street, the mules were unhitched, the police surrounded the float and held back the crowd, and then all stood and watched the beautiful thing burn down to the truck. Fire engines, sirens screaming, entered the scene as the final spark sputtered out. But the maskers who had been on the float had not departed without saving the stock of an improvised bar that had been concealed among the adornments, and as the only slightly singed gentlemen were assisted aboard other floats many of them clutched bottles of bourbon and scotch to their brilliant, be-spangled breasts.

Under way again, the parade continued up St. Charles to Washington Avenue, and here the third catastrophe of the night took place. As the parade turned one of the floats crashed into a traffic signal. No real damage was done, but the mules had to be unhitched from this float, "The Wishing Horse of Oz," some minor adjustments made, the mules petted to relieve their excessively nervous state, and again time was lost. But finally all was in order, the pageant completed its turn and started the thirty-block journey to Canal Street.

But before Canal Street was reached the parade had to

stop at City Hall to greet the queen and the mayor of the city. As they neared the City Hall the spectators became much more numerous and more crowded together, as the street narrowed. People crowded about, yelling and shouting and blocking the path. Little accidents occurred. A flambeau-bearer stooped over to pick up a trinket that had fallen into the street, and the flambeau behind him touched him lightly; he bounded ahead of the parade, afire and screaming. Another flambeau brushed the head of a youth in the crowd and set his hair on fire and a policeman burned his hands slapping the scared boy on the head. But all this was only a normal part of the excitement, and the parade continued in good order, slowed somewhat by the stubborn mob in the street, more than an hour late, but making gradual progress toward their destination and their queen.

Cynthius, as are all carnival parades, was escorted by a multitude of police on motorcycles and on horseback, who not only added to the effectiveness of the parade, but served to force a way through for the God of Music and Song, and the parade was led by a white car equipped with a speaker system, through which an officer, in firm but polite terms, cajoled, pleaded, and advised the crowd to move back. "Come on, folks," he kept saying. "Get back now. Let the parade through. We don't want anybody hurt. Come on now. How you expect them to get past? Hey, you, get out of the way there. Get back now. Get back! Get back! We're coming through now!"

The crowd moved out of the way for the sound car, but were again in the street immediately. Then came the motorcycles, noisy and screaming, cutting right into the curbs. The crowd surged back, mothers dragging their offspring to safety, uttering little shrieks of terror. Next came the horses, dancing and prancing to the blaring music of the twenty bands in the parade. the police on their backs smiling proudly. The horses always inspire sheer terror amongst the spectators, for they seem intent on stomping to death as many citizens as possible. The mob presses back. Children and women scream. Toes are smashed and tempers flare because in the excitement many spectators lose their places in the front of the others.

But as soon as the mounted police had passed, the crowd watching Cynthius was back in the street. Now came the dukes on their steeds, their satin mantles, encrusted with sparkling stones, spread over the animals' haunches, flashing in the bright light of the flambeaux. Next came the captain of the crew, then the first band of music, and then the emerald-green float of Cynthius, the king-god bowing and sweeping his scepter toward the people in the immense grandstand before the City Hall.

Here the parade halted and the bands—one between each of the floats—again burst into "If Ever I Cease to Love." Then, when the music stopped, a ladder was raised beside the float and a gentleman ascended it and served the king a glass of champagne. The queen and her maids, beaming with smiles, bowed and waved at His Majesty. The toast was completed and Cynthius, after a final clink of his glass against his queen's, threw his to the street, shattering it into tiny pieces. The bands began another tune, and the parade rolled on.

Canal Street banquettes were packed for their entire width as the parade entered the broad thoroughfare, but here no one was allowed to enter the street. The parade passed grandstand after grandstand of applauding, waving spectators, the maskers dispersed their favors. People yelled and called. Children, on their parents' shoulders, howled with glee and slashed the air with small fists, trying to catch a string of beads or a whistle. Peanuts and popcorn and cotton candy were forgotten and dropped and crushed underfoot, and even the vendors ceased trying to sell their wares to watch the pageant as it moved quickly and musically out Canal for a dozen blocks, circled and returned on the other side, paused for a moment at the Boston Club, then turned again down Bourbon Street, entering the French Quarter.

Bourbon Street was nearly as difficult to traverse as St. Charles had been. Customers and entertainers rushed from the night clubs. Patrons of bars ran outside, drinks in their hands, followed by bartenders. But the police were again at work, clearing the way for floats and bands. Maskers hurled trinkets to the packed balconies that line the street and were almost on a level with the tops of the floats. The bands blazed with jazz music, drum majors and majorettes strutting and dancing and hurling batons into the air and performing all their stunts as if they had just started out, instead of approaching the end of several miles and several hours. A bartender raised a siphon of soda water and squirted it at a duke who roared with good humor. No one gets angry in a carnival parade.

The parade turned at Orleans Street, in front of the convent where the Negro nuns were watching, and proceeded out that street toward the Municipal Auditorium and their ball, to which the queen and her maids had already been transported through back streets in limousines with police escorts. At the Auditorium, first the king and his pages, then the other maskers, disembarked, by ladder, at a side door and went inside to begin the ball and the tableau of "The Land of Oz." Inside the ballroom had been transformed into the brilliant green wonderland of Oz, and every seat all the way to the roof was filled with those fortunate enough to have received invitations to the Ball of Cynthius.

Outside, the streets of New Orleans started to clear rapidly. The honky-tonks of Bourbon Street began to fill again with customers, and more kept coming, for after a parade a drink is generally sought. On Canal Street people stood in great crowds awaiting the streetcars that would soon resume service. Taxis did a record business. Feet began to hurt. Children began to cry. The vendors continued to sell their wares and the price of hot dogs immediately dropped. There was still the mingled aromas of peanuts and popcorn and whisky in the air.

But in one grandstand, which alone was not emptying into the street, there was a great excitement, as more people tried to fight their way past the police who were doing their best to restrain them.

"It ain't nothing," explained a sergeant, sweat streaming down his face, "but you all can't come up here, that's all. It's just a lady having a baby."

Nearly all the parades begin at the same place—the secret dens on Calliope Street, where for nearly a year the design and construction of the floats have been going on. But Babylon gathered for its procession on Wednesday night, the night following the pageant of Cynthius, before the St. Ann Street entrance of the Auditorium, the same spot at which it would eventually disperse for its ball.

Babylon was very prompt. At seven o'clock the king, His Majesty, Sargon, and the other maskers took their places on the seventeen floats, the dukes mounted their horses, the captain climbed into his carriage, the bands took their places, the Negroes lighted their flambeaux and torches, the police sped to the fore, and the parade proceeded toward North Rampart Street, turned and moved quickly toward Canal, only a half-dozen blocks away.

The crowd on Canal Street had not long to wait to see Babylon's parade, but the same tension and excitement of the night before were in the air. Groups of boys tossed one of their number toward the sky now and then. Chains of young people writhed through the mob. The blind beggars tottled along, singing their old songs in their weak, tired voices. The pitchmen bellowed, the peanut vendors hawked their little white bags, the mechanical man continued his eerie, hysterical laughing, whistles and horns blew, the same plane hummed above the broad street, and there was a fresh (at least the customers hoped so) batch of hot dogs for sale.

The white car of the broadcasting police came first, as it had the night before, then the motorcycles, then the mounted police, and after the dukes and the captain, Sargon, on a float lighted with neon lights and decorated with huge shimmering butterflies and flowers, swept into view.

The Krewe of Babylon's theme was "The Arts," and after the title float came the "Art of Dining," holding a table laden with a roasted turkey, a roasted pig, platters of seafoods and yellow and green vegetables, all looking very edible, but all much larger than such delicacies could ever be. Next came "Dramatic Arts," on which there was a stage, with the figure of a woman stretching her hands yearningly toward it, and with maskers dressed as great actors and actresses in roles that made them famous. One "actress" already sat dreamily upon the edge of the float, waving a limp hand at the spectators and trying to straighten "her" mask with the other. There is always a passing of bottles in the dressing rooms, despite the efforts of the captain to prevent it.

"Black Arts" was a spectacle of demons and spirits and witches, "Comic Arts" depicted court jesters, the first comedians; then came in succession "Art of Writing," "Art of Painting," "Music," "Glass Staining," "Dancing," "Poetry," "Sculpture," "Pottery Making," "Spinning and Weaving," "Jewelers' Art," and "Art of Dueling."

Each float was a blaze of color, nearly every one making use of neon lighting and ingenuous design. "Art of Writing" was covered with Chinese banners, at its rear were towering obelisks, and in the center was a huge lamp, a symbol of knowledge. "Jewelers' Art" was all gold and flashing jewels of every color. "Music" had a large twisted horn in the foreground, with majestic organ pipes vanishing into billowing clouds at the back.

Babylon stopped at the City Hall en route uptown, where Sargon toasted his queen and then smashed his glass. After that, throughout the unusually long route, extending up to Jackson Avenue, and then turning to return to Canal Street, the police had much trouble. Spectators climbed up on galleries and balconies, even on lampposts. Some perched like gargoyles on the roofs of houses and buildings. On the way back to Canal Street one woman stood in the middle of St. Charles Street and defied the police to run her down. It was necessary for an officer to dismount his horse and argue with her. "I come two thousand miles to see this," she said indignantly, "and I'll be damned if I'll get back where people will get in front of me!" Gently but firmly, her elbow in his hand, the red-faced policeman led her back to the curb, requested everyone around that no one "get in front of her," then remounted his horse. The parade then continued. "I'll never forget that lady who held up the parade," that officer said later.

As Canal Street was approached again, real trouble ensued. A group of boys, apparently angry because they had not caught any, or enough, of the trinkets the maskers were throwing, picked up stones, sticks, pieces of slate, and anything else handy, and began to pelt the maskers on the floats. The parade halted again and the police chased the youths, who vanished quickly after one final assault at the dodging, cringing, and perfectly defenseless men on the floats. "It's them Communists!" yelled a female bystander as the parade moved on to Canal Street, where most of the crowd remained to view it for a second time, then out to North Rampart Street, and down to the ball.

Once more Canal Street began to clear of people, leaving behind much debris and many odors, straggling drunks clinging to show windows for support those still sober searching for uncrowded bars, and parents dragging their children in and out of drugstores, talking still about the "py-rade," which is what many Orleanians call them, and ordering passers-by who brushed against them to "Watch the baby!"

"How you gonna look at the py-rade with your behind sticking out your pants?" asked a mother of her small son as she knelt in the mob awaiting Momus the following night, Thursday, and tried to adjust his trousers.

The Krewe of Momus, a relatively old organization, had an even larger attendance at its parade than had the two preceding it, and the crowd was a particularly gay one, nearly everyone acting as excited and happy as if he had never seen a parade before.

"Join hands!" a leader would cry, and swiftly another chain would form in Canal Street.

They were out on the street even before dark, suggesting to each other, "Come on, you, let's find us a standing place!" or "See if you can find us a crack to get in."

Momus, God of Mirth and Mockery, Son of the Night, celebrated his seventy-fifth anniversary in 1947. The krewe is very high in the social scheme of New Orleans and maintains all the traditions of earlier years, not yet having adopted many modern innovations.

No neon lights decorated the floats as they moved out of the Calliope Street den, but they needed none. King Momus sat under a canopy of gold, blue, and white, while about and beneath him fluttered doves and butterflies, foliage and flowers. The title car bore a crescent moon cradled in pink and white and golden clouds, and a scroll announced the theme "Anniversaries." Consisting of fifteen floats in all, "Cotton" was represented by heaping bales about which giant spools of thread unwound; thus began a procession that included "Crystal," "Pearl," "Ruby," "Silver," "Gold," etc., and ended with "Diamond." There were perhaps more comic touches in the Momus parade, as there usually are, than in any of the previous ones. The third float, "Leather," was adorned with some of the silliest-looking moose imaginable and one foolish-looking cow. All were brilliantly illuminated by flambeaux.

Few people ever saw "Silver." The parade had gone only a few blocks when one of the mules pulling the floats slipped and fell flat, breaking the wagon shaft. The maskers climbed aboard other floats, after giving the spectators lucky (or unlucky) enough to be around the added exhibition of some fancy capering and dancing in the street, for Momus maskers are always the friskiest of the year, as befits the knights of the God of Mirth.

Momus took the traditional route—up St. Charles Avenue to Washington Avenue, then down, into St. Charles Street, past the City Hall, where the mayor was toasted, and on to Canal Street.

The queen of Momus always sits in the Boston Club grandstand instead of before the City Hall, as do Cynthius's and Babylon's feminine rulers, and this is supposed to mean something in New Orleans, a subtle thing that has to do with social prestige, of value to those who care. Here the king's float was halted, the toast to the queen was drunk, the glass dropped and smashed. Just as the parade moved away a capering masker also dropped and fell off his float. Fortunately one foot burst through the papier-mâché side of the float, and there he hung, head downward, for at least a half block, until the other maskers could help him back aboard. Many maskers have fallen from floats during the years, and a few have been killed, so the rescued young man, his mask disarranged and his face exposed to the public view, leaned for a few minutes upon the arms of his rescuers, breathing sighs of relief and feeling very fortunate. As the parade turned down Royal Street another unseemly incident occurred, although this was not quite so serious as the first.

One of the maskers began to lose his pants. Try as he might, he could not fix them and maintain his position on the rocking float until he removed his mask and thus brought upon himself howls of glee and catcalls from the merciless mob below him.

There were only a few other catastrophes before Momus reached the ball. A youth took a roundhouse curving swipe at a motorcycle policeman as the parade passed the Royal Street antique shops, a drunk knocked another officer down in Orleans Street, and just outside the Municipal Auditorium a horse stepped on a lady's foot, an accident that brought forth such a volley of abuse mingled with shrieks of pain that police and maskers cowered with embarrassment. The New Orleans police force always takes a terrific beating during the carnival season, which they bear with incredible patience and which they face with much dignity and politeness. But if anyone hates Carnival it is the cops. Waiters in restaurants and bartenders in saloons don't like it very much either, but even they don't have to endure the torments of the police.

The Krewe of Hermes, although not so new as that of Cynthius, who held their first parade in 1947, is nearly as new and as modern as Momus is old and traditional. Hermes, an organization of businessmen and civic leaders, first paraded in 1937, and from its first appearance has staged lavish pageants and balls of great beauty and cost. Never fearing the new, Hermes was the first, for instance, to use neon-lighted floats, and now each one is a swirling mass of brilliantly colored tubes of the most intricate designs.

In 1947 Hermes's theme was "Operas," and the God of Commerce and Travel led sixteen floats through St. Charles and Canal and Royal streets. All the most popular operas were there—the heavy Wagnerians and the delicate Verdis and Puccinis. "Carmen" was perhaps the most popular float of all, even for the maskers who rode upon it. The bull's tail offered something substantial to which toreadors might cling. All maskers on all floats yearn for something to which to cling.

When Hermes was over on Friday night there was a brief respite from parades, for none have taken place on Saturday in recent years. Saturday is a day on which Orleanians—except for attending a ball or two that night—rest and visitors tour the town and the bars, or inquire why there isn't one. Optimistic strangers have been noted standing in perfect bliss for hours, waiting at curbs for a Saturday night parade. Finally some Orleanian who doesn't think it funny stops and disenchants them.

Until the beginning of World War II there was a long and pretty children's parade on the Saturday afternoon before Mardi Gras, when King Nor, a small boy selected from the elementary grades of either a public or a parochial school, led through the streets a procession of miniature floats, each designed and constructed by a school. Nor always stopped at the City Hall, toasted the mayor in hot chocolate or lemonade, depending upon the weather, then greeted his tiny queen on Canal Street with another toast. The queen would then say, "Sire, the Royal Household of Nor is assembled to greet you on your visit to the city. Never have we witnessed such an outpouring of the masses." King Nor would then reply, "We feel deeply the homage of the grownups." A ball was always held that evening, and the royal couple wore crowns and jewels and magnificent mantles, just as do the adults. The Krewe of Nor did not resume its parade after the end of the war.

As if to compensate for the lack of parades on Saturday, on the Sunday before Mardi Gras there is not one but three lavish pageants. The Krewe of Venus, the only carnival parade in which women instead of men ride on floats, and the Krewe of Midcity, an organization of merchants and businessmen in that section of the city Orleanians always refer to either as "back of town" or "toward the lake," both parade on Sunday afternoon.

A little before, starting at twelve-thirty, the Old Reliable Carnival Club of Algiers, which is that part of New Orleans on the other side of the Mississippi River, stages a river procession of gaily decorated barges, tugboats, and a ferry or two. Led by a ruler known as Chief Choctaw, it is, especially on a bright and sunny Sunday afternoon, with the gray waters of the old river bronzed by sunlight, with the banners and flags and carnival colors of the boats picking up the river breeze, and with the whistles and sirens and other river noises in your ears and the multitude of river smells in your nose, one of the pleasantest features of the entire Carnival. After the river pageant Chief Choctaw and his krewe, who dress as American Indians, board about ten floats and parade through the streets of Algiers for the rest of the afternoon. They do not, however, hold their ball until the night of Mardi Gras.

The Krewe of Midcity begins their parade at about two o'clock, and starts from the head of Canal Street, in the neighborhood where most of the members live or work. In 1947 there were ten floats in an elaborate procession with the theme of "Toyland," the floats after the one upon which His Majesty, King Midcity, was seated and the title float representing various children's toys and playthings. Obviously less expensive than the other parades, Midcity is among the cleverest, presenting many novelties, such as wheels that spin around throughout the parade, other kinds of mechanical objects, intricate designs, and a usually more spontaneous and less inhibited behavior on the part of those aboard the floats. Unlike the other parading krewes, the identity of the king is kept no more a secret than that of the queen, for the king and queen of Midcity are always husband and wife and the court of dukes and maids is always composed of married couples.

Venus is the only lady among all the carnival parades. No other krewe has ever allowed a woman to set foot on a float—if they knew it, for there are as many tales of a woman slipping aboard in costume and mask as there are legends about Pope Joan—and the krewes have always been proud of this male paradise. Venus, whose first parade appeared in 1938, allows no man on any of her floats, and there is not even a rumor that any ever dared to attempt riding upon one.

The krewe begin their parade at three o'clock, so as not to risk a humiliating collision with King Midcity, should the two parades reach the business section of Canal Street at the same time, for on occasion this has almost happened. Too, Venus follows what might be termed the traditional route, rolling from their Calliope Street den to St. Charles Avenue, then uptown for a number of blocks, then returning via the other lane on St. Charles Avenue to Canal Street, while Midcity parades only in Canal Street, then proceeds down through North Rampart Street to the Auditorium.

Venus offers quite as lavish a spectacle as do the night parades, with Queen Venus, exquisitely gowned and wearing all her jewels and an elaborate mantle of satin and ermine and brilliant stones, riding the first float and looking much lovelier, even though her features are concealed behind a mask, than any of the carnival kings, who almost invariably have bellies and pipestem legs.

"Jewels" was the theme chosen by Venus in a recent year, and each float was a glittering representation of a precious gem—the rich yellow of the topaz, the fiery red of rubies, the quiet, misty blue of turquoises, the bursting, sparkling blue of sapphires, the mysterious, soft glow of opals, the vivid green of emeralds. There were fifteen floats, and on each not only the colors and appropriate settings for the jewels were used, but the women wore costumes in the color each represented.

Aboard the floats the women behave like women. No matter how cool the day, nothing bulky goes under their lovely, clinging costumes. Men will usually stuff themselves beneath their colorful outer garments, but the devotees of Venus do not risk spoiling the outlines of their figures, even to avoid pneumonia. Masks cover their entire faces, but they are pretty masks, not the grotesque ones worn by the males. Hair is carefully curled and arranged, and during the pageant the ladies spend no little time adjusting their coiffures and asking each other how they look. Like the other parades, they also throw trinkets, but fortunate is the bystanding friend capable of judging their aim.

In all other ways, however, they conduct themselves exactly as do the men. Now and then there are little quarrels, but they are really *little* quarrels that never amount to anything much. There is jealousy among the krewe members, but there is also jealousy among the members of male krewes. And, somewhat surprisingly perhaps, the ladies of Venus retain their krewe's secrets, including the identity of the queen and the maids and the others riding upon the floats, quite as well as do the men, only telling their most intimate friends, who, in turn, only tell their most intimate friends.

Usually wearing rather meek expressions, the king of Venus and his dukes, wearing striped trousers, morning coats, and no masks, wait with the mayor in the City Hall grandstand. There toasts are exchanged in a reverse of the traditional custom. (The next day the newspapers publish a picture and the name of King Venus, but conceal the identity of his queen.) After the toast the parade moves on to Canal Street and the huge crowds who are awaiting it, after having viewed Midcity.

Venus, throughout her route and particularly from the

dense crowds of Canal Street, always receives tumultuous ovations. Perhaps curiously, there is little trouble with male spectators, few whistles and wolf calls, almost no remarks of an impertinent or insulting nature. This may be due to the fact that the ladies are always completely even if thinly covered, their skirts usually reaching to their ankles, for this is no parade of bathing beauties or scantily clad sirens. Many of the ladies are rather large and of uncertain age.

Both Venus and Midcity hold their balls that Sunday night, one on each side of the Auditorium. Both are large and lavish affairs, with grand marches and tableaux, in the manner of all carnival balls.

Proteus, God of the Sea, leading a krewe that has a long history and great social prestige, appears on Monday night and is the last parade before the day that is to be Mardi Gras.

The themes of Proteus are always carefully chosen and are presented with much simple beauty. The year that "Strange Stories from Foreign Lands" was offered the parade was greeted with shouts of glee from enthusiastic revelers in a demonstration of appreciation that few pageants have ever received. This kind of reception is not precisely unusual, but Proteus's subject was rather intellectual and no doubt most of the crowd in the streets of New Orleans had never heard of the tales the floats illustrated; yet they loved it. Too often, it must be admitted, Orleanians in general seem more concerned with the trash thrown from the floats than with the beauty of the parades. In this case that was not true, for Proteus usually throws fewer articles than any other parade, and howls of "Stingy!" and "Tightwads!" always follow it, along with applause and shouts of approbation.

"Strange Stories from Foreign Lands," like all Proteus parades, was one of exceptional quality. The royal float was formed like the crest of a wave sweeping up behind the throne of the sea god. Three prancing white steeds were mounted on the front of the float, and His Majesty's throne nestled in the trough of a wave. The floats following the title car each depicted some classic tale or fable—"Perseus," "Children of Ler," "The Three Pomegranates," "The Stag and the Hammoack," "Puss in Boots," "Aladdin and His Wonderful Lamp," and many others, twenty in all.

Proteus always takes the traditional route, stopping, as he does every year, at the City Hall and again at the Boston Club to toast his queen. Always on time, moving swiftly, the parade reached the Auditorium at a few minutes before nine o'clock. Proteus, a haughty monarch, always hurries toward the sanctity of his court and wastes little time upon the populace in the streets. And even while the ball is in progress thousands of people gather about the building, hoping to catch a glimpse of the royalty within. There are those who hang around outside each ball that follows a parade, but the Proteus fans are usually the most avid, for a reason that is a mystery even to the members of the krewe.

This is the last parade before the big day, Mardi Gras, toward which everybody, no matter how tired, looks forward as the most exciting occasion of all. It makes no difference how exhausting and hectic the season and particularly the past week have been, even though many have been through ball after ball, parade after parade, then to the balls following the parades. Many others have taken their children to the parades night after night. All have walked and run and played and danced, but there is energy left in all for tomorrow. After that they can rest, but Mardi Gras is a time for fun.

CHAPTER FOUR

NOW MARDI GRAS BEGINS

*F*OR A LONG TIME BEFORE MARDI GRAS SOME CURI-
ous advertisements appear in all the New Or-
leans newspapers; they differ little from year to year. These
are as typical of New Orleans as the strange "personals" that
also appear regularly in the newspapers, and have attracted
some national attention.

It's easy to be an angel! I have two dozen pairs of angel wings
to rent for Mardi Gras. . . .

You can make a jackass out of yourself. If you don't care to be a
jackass, we can provide goat masks, cat masks, bunny rabbit masks,
cow masks with horns, and wolf masks for young men with whis-
tling tendencies. Phone . . .

Visit Costume Headquarters. You can find artificial snakes, very
realistic, from nine inches long up to five feet. We have eight thousand ostrich plumes in stock, piled up like mountains of spaghetti,
and twelve thousand colored quills for Indian braves' bonnets are
always on hand. We have one rooster suit which will make you
look like Maude Adams in *Chanticleer*, which has five thousand
feathers hand-sewn on it.

Man's rayon, gold-braided, Prince Carnival costume, size 37, $7.

Mardi Gras

There is no end to them. And there is another type that makes you wonder:

Queen's gown of silver cloth, embroidered with gold beads and trimmed with rhinestones and sequins. Also gorgeous mantle, heavily encrusted with brilliant stones. Cheap.

What debutante of another year, who once was a queen, is willing to sell what must be a precious possession? Why is she selling it?

As the carnival season advances and Mardi Gras grows near, the advertisements increase. Large ones offer carnival favors of all kinds, by the dozen or by the gross. Steel bleacher seats are for sale, to be set up for those who want to sit down to view the parades. Folding chairs and camp stools are for rent or for sale. Flags and pennants and banners, to decorate the fronts of homes or buildings, are offered. There are advertisements for pitchmen, peddlers, and vendors. People want to rent their trucks, their horses and mules, their front rooms, their front galleries, and their front yards, if these are on the route through which the parades and maskers will pass on Mardi Gras.

Jazz bands advertise themselves for hire for the many truck rides that are a part of Mardi Gras, and often the crowds who will be aboard the trucks that follow the parade of Rex, the real King of Carnival, advertise for additional maskers to ride with them.

"We need fifteen more couples," said one advertiser. "We are dressing as red devils, and we will have aboard lots of sandwiches and soft drinks, as well as a jazz band. Fifteen dollars per couple."

"Would you like to ride with the Trojan horse?" asks another. "We're wearing Greek togas with golden belts, and we're calling ourselves Greek Myths and Misters."

There are many carnival kings, but there is only one King of Carnival. He is Rex, who leads his parade through the

48

streets of New Orleans on Mardi Gras, the pageant beginning at about eleven o'clock in the morning. All the rulers
of the other krewes are secondary monarchs compared to
Rex, royal cousins who supposedly journey to the city
throughout the season, but who must all step aside for the
King of Carnival.

And for weeks before Mardi Gras the newspapers publish
"radiograms" from Rex and his "regal entourage of Ministers, Sycophants and Jesters," in which His Majesty and
his appointed scribes give, in vivid detail, descriptions of
their travels from the summer palace of Rex in Araby the
Blest to visit the Mardi Gras. Until 1947 this journey was
usually supposed to be made by sea, aboard the royal yacht,
but that year Rex became very modern, and it was announced that His Majesty and entourage were coming by
air on His Majesty's plane, named *"Consternation,* one of
the Imperial Triphibians."

These dispatches are always filled with the names of the
New Orleans men who make up the executive staff and
committees of the Krewe of Rex, all faintly and humorously
disguised as Arabic names and titles, but all easily recognizable to most Orleanians. The Krewe of Rex is less secretive
than most other organizations, although the identity of Rex
is not revealed to the public until announced in the morning
newspapers on Mardi Gras. Sometimes a dispatch will
touch, jokingly, upon the difficulties that have occurred
within the krewe that year, so, although all the humor is not
good, each is read with considerable interest by many
people. A typical "radiogram," appearing in the *Times-
Picayune* on a Sunday a few weeks before Mardi Gras 1947,
read:

To Bathurst, Lord High Chamberlain,
Greetings and Salutations:
    What a week we had here in Araby, my dear Bathurst, you will
never know. My fingers have been worked to the bone, my eyes are

49

red and rheumy from lack of sleep and overwork, my poor feet slew themselves at right angles when I walk. One more politicking, conniving, intriguing, double-dealing and backbiting seven days like this and I doubt if we will ever get to our beloved Winter Capital in New Orleans in time for Mardi Gras.

Why, do you know for a while it looked like we were going to have two Kings? Everybody wanted to get into the act. The first argument started over the Royal Route our plane should follow. Each member of the regal retinue seemed to have a favorite port or a favorite in every port which he wanted us to touch at so he could show off. Shah Lee Mak Lell wanted to stop at Marrakesh, where he knew a little Ouled NAIL. Mutapha El Is remembered a girl at Nice who was nice. Young Willah Wallah wanted to stop at Upsand Downs in England and he had fair grounds for his reasons. Each potentate had a potent date in a state that wouldn't wait unless our great plane paid a courtesy call at each of these famous places.

The Star Chamber session was in its sixth day; we were getting nowhere fast. The Khan Rajah Jim and Wal Tur Ser were running two filibusters at once when His Majesty Rex held up his scepter for silence:

"Enough is enough and too much is as good as a feast. I have a special announcement to make. The name of our giant plane is Consternation. It is made by the Takeheed people, and judging by your actions it is well named. This year our Voyage is by Air— par avion, as we say in French—and our triumphal journey to the Air Hub of the Americas partakes of some of the aspects of a commercial trail-blazer. Here is our route: We go first to Muscat for muskrats, Alexandria for a ragtime band to play at our Ball, Malta for malted milk, Gibraltar to see the biggest Prudential billboard in the world, the Canary Islands where I am to be given the bird, Bermuda for a shipload of onions, and thence to New Orleans, where we shall present our cargo as a gracious gift to the people of that fair city. . . ."

Thus at one fell swoop did Rex bring order out of chaos and restore to normalcy the confusion into which we had fallen.

The forceful manner displayed by our Imperial Majesty on this occasion was the source of great pleasure to our Chief Executive and Flight Commander, Abou Pat Tur Sun. This peerless leader and his assistant, the Grand Vizier U-Ben Roun, had been inclined to let the Royal Retinue talk itself into exhaustion or into such a state of inanition that they would readily listen to the plans which

Now Mardi Gras Begins

Abou Pat and U-Ben had decided on long ago. But the King's assumption of His Royal Prerogative saved them both the trouble.

It also put the quietus on an alternative plan of conveyance that Abou Pat had had secretly in mind for some time. The truth of the matter is that Abou Pat Tur Sun really wanted to make the annual pilgrimage by Bus, but he had covered up his tracks so well that few knew of this. When confronted with the charge he made light of the whole matter and said it was a lot of gas. He maintained his grounds were neutral, that he was for progress and modernization and stood upon his record, so the up-to-the-minute Triphibian, Trimotored, Try Anything Takeheed plane "Consternation" is to be our mode of transportation. . . .

My next dispatch to you, dear Bathurst, will find us, I hope, en route on our glorious pilgrimage, perhaps in the neighborhood of the Canary Islands. Until then, I remain your most humble and obedient and worn-out servitor,

ERB HAMIL
Scribe

Succeeding "radiograms" told of other difficulties, of imaginary accidents and near disasters, and of mythical adventures, all in a double-talk as elaborate as can be imagined.

But all went well, and when New Orleans awoke that Mardi Gras there was the picture of King Rex and his queen on the front page of the morning newspaper, unmasked and wearing ordinary clothes, with their real names beneath their pictures. The royal plane, *Consternation*, had arrived safely.

It was a beautiful day that Mardi Gras, which was good news, for weather is important on Mardi Gras, and both Orleanians and visitors worry about it for days ahead of time. Usually, however, it is warm and rainless, and there is sun. This one was no exception.

It was early, but already it was easy to tell what day it was. New Orleans seemed to chuckle softly as it stretched its arms. Outside the window there seemed to be the faint tinkle of little bells, and from far, far away came the sound

of a jazz band. From somewhere around a corner came the
shrill voice of a child, singing the old-time chant that has
been heard in New Orleans for many a generation:

> *"Mardi Gras!*
> *Tickle a paw!*
> *Catch behind a street cah!"*

"They gets it wrong," said an old Negro, leaning against
a post near the French Market, watching the early maskers
already beginning to pass. "It goes like this:

> *"Mardi Gras!*
> *Chic la pas!*
> *Run away, tra la la!"*

The French Quarter was wide awake, although it was
scarcely eight o'clock in the morning. The operators of the
stalls in the market stood patiently beside their neat, tall
mounds of green and yellow and red and white vegetables,
broad smiles on their dark Sicilian faces, or moved about
baskets of glistening apples or plump purple eggplants; but
there were few customers. A little boy with damp curls and
huge black eyes, wearing the beaded costume and feathered
headdress of an Indian, crouched behind towering crates of
live, squawking chickens and fired an arrow from his bow
at a little girl dressed in a hoopskirt and bonnet, who ran
screaming to a woman who was busy cleaning carrots with
a knife. "You all behave or you ain't gonna see no pyrade
today, no!" the mother bellowed. A clown with a chalky
face and wearing a costume covered with immense orange
dots came out of the bar on the corner opposite the French
Market, caught the arm of a masked gypsy, who was all
dazzling crimson and spangles. The gypsy pulled away from
him, laughing. He went his way, playing leapfrog by himself,
jumping over the tall garbage cans that stood here and there
along the curbs.

Now Mardi Gras Begins

A few blocks farther uptown, in Chartres Street before the St. Louis Cathedral, trucks filled with maskers were beginning to pass. Each truck was differently decorated and the maskers in each wore identical costumes or else carried out a particular theme or subject by the variety of their costumes. Here was one filled with red devils, male and female, all with tails and horns and pitchforks. Cardboard flames rose on every side, the devils waved at those they passed from between the writhing scarlet flames, and the Negro band aboard was playing "There's Gonna Be a Hot Time in the Old Town Tonight." The devils were passing around a fifth of bourbon, drinking from the bottle.

A truck adorned with old-fashioned gas lamplights came next. The young men and women aboard wore costumes of the 1890 period, the band aboard was playing, and two couples were endeavoring to dance in the straw that covered the bottom of the truck. Then came a truck filled with boys and girls dressed like farmers, in overalls and straw hats and red and white bandannas, another in which the occupants were all pink and white rabbits, and another filled with pirates.

Each truck had its band and its title, the latter printed on large signs on both sides of the vehicle. The pirates called themselves "The Cutthroats," those in overalls had titled their truck "God's Little Acre," and the rabbits were "The Woozy Wabbits." Each had a number, too, for all were a part of an organization called Krewe of Orleanians, and they were on their way to Calliope Street, where they would eventually fall in behind the parade of Rex, and would follow that parade when it appeared later in the day.

Now there was excitement before one of the Pontalba Buildings that flank Jackson Square in front of the cathedral. A truck filled with pink elephants had stopped for passengers who lived in one of the Pontalba apartments, and three more pink elephants were emerging from the building.

53

"I can't get my head right," complained one of the three, whose voice was feminine.

The other two, who were male elephants, worked carefully about her neck until it was at last adjusted.

The lady elephant waved her limp trunk at the noisy, giggling crowd on the truck. "How you all like my navel?" she screamed as the other elephants helped her aboard.

Everyone stopped and inspected her pink front. "Oh, Mellie, that's darling!" squealed another lady elephant.

Mellie had pinned a bouquet of pink tea roses and white bridal wreath to her navel.

The truck of "The Pink Elephants" rolled away.

A woman in costume stopped a man who was not in costume.

"Who am I?" she asked.

"Leona," he said bluntly.

"Goddam you," she said. "Okay, what am I?"

He looked, scratching his head. Her costume was silver, the skirt falling to the ground. Silver wires were twisted about her waist and formed a spiral pattern across her breasts, then encircled her throat. Her headdress was a silver cap from which jutted more silver wires, and she wore a silver half mask from which silvery lace dropped to her chin. She spread her arms wide and he saw that they were attached to her sides by silver threads that gleamed in the sun.

He coughed.

"Go 'head," she said. "Guess."

"You look mighty pretty," he said.

"You sure stupid, Albert," she said. "I'm a spider."

"A beautiful spider," he said.

"All that worries me is these damn threads breaking," she said. "I can't hardly move without popping one, and we're gonna be on a truck, and you know how that is. You keep jumping on and off. Good-by."

The banquettes of Royal Street were crowded with the masked and the unmasked, almost everyone moving slowly uptown toward Canal Street. The bars on the corners were already filled. Decorated automobiles rolled past, and now and then more trucks. There was a truck filled with hillbillies, with a little outhouse in the center of it, entitled "Dog Patch," and another filled with boys and girls in striped suits called "The Prisoners of Love." Two voluptuous blondes in pale lavender taffeta gowns of the Gay Nineties, wearing no masks, but with their faces heavily painted, came swishing down the banquette, each carrying a bottle of bourbon, from which they took drinks from time to time, and conversing in deep bass voices. They were men.

A carriage pulled by two snow-white horses moved slowly up Royal Street, keeping close to the curb. Inside were two gentlemen in tall hats and the attire of a century ago, wearing small black masks, and a masked elderly lady in an ante bellum costume and holding a small, pale blue, ruffled umbrella over her head. The carriage stopped before a house and another lady emerged. She was stout and her green hoop skirts took up so much of the banquette that everyone stopped to allow her room to enter the carriage. Her gown was ruffled and trimmed with lace, her shoulders were bare, and so was most of her immense bosom. Between her various chins was a green satin ribbon, and the face beneath her green mask was heavily powdered and rouged. She wore a wig that was a violent red and which included curls that cascaded over one of her shoulders, and she carried a green parasol and a huge fan embroidered with bluebirds and seed pearls. "I'm Scarlett O'Hara," she informed her friends in the carriage as she took her seat and adjusted her parasol.

A young woman in the door waved as the Negro driver guided the carriage away from the curb. "Good-by, Mamma!" the young woman, who wore a hula skirt and several leis, called out.

Mardi Gras

"Good-by, darling!" shrieked Mamma.

"I'm so glad we got her *out*," said the young woman to an unseen person within the house behind her. "Poor Mamma! She sure does love Mardi Gras. If she just don't drink too much now."

A half-dozen young men, wearing nothing but long woolen underwear, their faces blackened with soot, passed on the banquette, singing the Mardi Gras song:

> *"If ever I cease to love,*
> *If ever I cease to love,*
> *May the moon be turned*
> *Into green cheese,*
> *If ever I cease to love.*
>
> *If ever I cease to love,*
> *If ever I cease to love,*
> *May fish grow legs,*
> *And cows lay eggs,*
> *If ever I cease to love."*

Mardi Gras was off to a good start. The weather was fine, the people were happy, the old songs were being sung, and it was all as it had been on Mardi Gras for as long as any living Orleanian could remember.

The banquettes, the traffic lanes, and the neutral grounds of Canal Street were all crowded, for today all traffic and streetcars were rerouted from an early morning hour, and the entire width of the street was turned into a playground for the population and the visitors, and, as they are not permitted to do during the night parades, masses of people walked and danced and cavorted in the street itself.

And never for any night parade had there been so many people in the street. Some patient and conservative citizens, many of them with children, were lined against the cables to watch the maskers who preferred to walk in the street. Jazz music blared from windows and here and there couples, some in costume, some in ordinary clothes, stopped and danced for a few moments, then moved on. The vendors screamed even louder than during the preceding nights. Beggars were everywhere as usual. The mechanical man still laughed. The chains were forming, increasing in numbers and in lengths, and those young people who formed them were either masked or wore overalls, or slacks, or had painted their faces with lipstick and ink, for much of the dressing up for Mardi Gras is of the simplest sort.

Yet here and there, in the middle of Canal Street, were maskers so elaborately dressed that they literally stopped the entire flow of humanity, as everyone gathered about them to admire or to laugh. Cameras snapped their photographs as they posed three times every twenty feet for the scores of amateur photographers about. There was a group dressed as a colored "shotgun wedding," all their faces blackened, the bride wearing a veil made from a lace curtain and carrying a bouquet of large red and green paper flowers, the groom in a garish, checkered suit and wearing an immense green rose in his lapel, the preacher in doleful black and a white cotton wig, the father carrying a shotgun. They struck pose after pose. There were a couple dressed as East Indian potentates, the girl in a sari that sparkled with rhinestones, her hair bright yellow beneath her thin veil, her bare midriff powdered and delicately rouged. Her companion had darkened his face with grease paint, and his eyes burned fiercely through his half mask. His magnificent white turban and his chest were covered with brilliant decorations that only slightly resembled costume jewelry. Twenty young men and women, dressed as artists in red and white smocks, ran through the crowd holding hands, encircled the East Indians. and laughed uproariously as the pair tried to escape.

Mardi Gras

A group of five red devils passed—red devils are always very popular at Mardi Gras—which consisted of a mother, father, and three small children of various sizes, all their costumes and masks identical. One of the little devils seized his mother's tail playfully. "Hey, watch out, Leon!" yelled the lady. "You want to ruin me?"

There was no end to the variety of costumes, although most of the maskers wore the more commonplace kinds—clowns, devils, pirates, jockeys, various black-faced minstrels and mammies, Indians, and the dress of other eras—ante bellum, the eighties, the nineties. Two young women were flappers, in short, beaded evening dresses that ended above their knees in the style of the 1920s.

Some of the groups used vehicles of various kinds. A large woman in a mammy costume pushed her husband about in an immense baby carriage, his feet dangling over the sides, a bottle of whisky clutched in his arms against the chest of the white nightshirt that served as his dress, his protruding feet clad in ordinary brown shoes, a cigar in his teeth, his face nearly concealed beneath a flossy baby cap. Many parents pushed their children along in decorated wagons made from wooden boxes. Other parents held tiny rabbits, angels, and devils in their arms, for even babies as young as seven or eight months were in costume, and although they usually slept, their parents glowed proudly at the attention they received.

At the corners the vendors helped those who had no costumes to fix themselves up. Many buyers bought masks and funny hats, false mustaches, rubber noses, and artificial teeth. They pinned on badges that bore such inscriptions as "How About a Kiss?" "I'd Like to Take You Home for a Pet," and "You're My Type." Pretty young girls wore monkey faces. Old ladies giggled as they adjusted baby-doll masks, with pink, pink cheeks, pursed red lips, and golden curls attached to the side. Well-dressed and dignified gentlemen put on false noses and protruding teeth that gave them silly expressions.

People were getting hungry, and crowds formed around the stands selling sandwiches, where vendors cried their wares: "Hot dogs! Come'n get 'em! Steaming hot! Hot dogs with chili! Creole hot dogs!" Maskers raised their masks to eat the popcorn and peanuts, the pink cotton candy and apples on sticks, and all the other delicacies that are traditional parts of Mardi Gras. Some contented themselves with drinking soft drinks, but many men carried bottles, for no Orleanian minds carrying around his fifth of bourbon and drinking from it in plain view of everyone on Mardi Gras.

Here and there along the banquettes of Canal Street radio interviewers were stopping the maskers who passed and asking them to say a few words over the microphones. Groups of colored boys in costumes played jazz music on homemade instruments, while one of their number shuffled and wiggled in a dance that brought forth loud laughter from those watching, and, following each brief number, a shower of coins into the tin can that was always passed around. Some white couples paused to embrace and kiss, leaning against one of the decorated posts in the neutral ground. Sailors from a visiting ship in port roved about trying to pick up masked girls, and usually succeeded with no trouble at all. A gigantic ape leaned out of an upstairs window and yelled, "Hey, Texas!" at a youth in cowboy garb who was attempting with difficulty to ride his horse through the mob in the street, now so thick that it was almost impossible to move even on foot. He ignored the ape, but he reached down and scooped up a passing girl in a Spanish costume. She kicked and squirmed, her yellow skirts whirling, but when he set her before him on the horse's back she was giggling.

It was nearly eleven o'clock now and as many people as possible were jammed before the grandstand and the entrance of the Boston Club, where the Queen of Carnival and her maids would await Rex and the parades.

The court arrived in shining black limousines, escorted by motorcycle police. Sirens shrieking, the police inched through the crowd, the automobiles creeping behind, and curved up to the entrance where a path from street to door had been roped off. These were the elect—the queen, the maids, a few dowagers in hats with plumes, a scattering of male escorts in morning clothes. The court wore suits and dresses and floppy hats and carried flowers. Their ball costumes and jewels would not be worn until that night.

As they tried to enter the club the crowd surged forward and the police had difficulty clearing a path for the personages. The spectators gaped and made critical and sometimes crude remarks as the ladies and their escorts swept by. At last the chauffeurs cleared the runningboards of the limousines of the people who had climbed aboard them to get a better view, and drove the cars slowly away.

A few minutes later the queen appeared in the center of the front row of the grandstand, her maids on either side of her. She smiled down and waved a hand regally, as she had been trained to do. From the street she looked very lovely. Behind her dowagers beamed, and the men in morning attire moved about, ushering late arrivals to seats. Soon the grandstand was filled. The queen continued to stand, to smile, to wave, to try to hear the words shouted up to her from the street now and then. Often it was fortunate that it was impossible for her to hear everything that was yelled out.

The streets leading above Canal Street were nearly as crowded now as was the big street. Great masses of people chose St. Charles Street, by which the parade would enter Canal Street, as their playground. Phonographs set on balconies and in second-story windows provided music for dancers. A one-man band, who played five instruments at once and who wore a costume made of sacking entirely covered with playing cards, also helped.

There was a constant flow of people and liquor in the bars lining the first few blocks of the street, and to get in and out of any of them required football tactics. The bartenders sweated, trying to hear the orders called out by the men and women lined up six and eight deep in front of the bars. "I don't never want to see another Mardi Gras as long as I live!" vowed one, passing a highball over the heads of people in front to a customer in the rear. "This is too much, man. Next year I'm gonna go to the country!"

"I wanna go to the Sazerac!" yelled a lady who was dressed in slacks, a fur coat, and wore a heavy black false mustache in which there was beer foam. "Come on, you all, let's go to the Sazerac!"

Situated one block off St. Charles Street, where there were not so many people in the streets, the Sazerac Bar was the most crowded of all. Alone of all bars in New Orleans, the Sazerac, a bar that has long been famous for that cocktail, does not admit women upon its premises except on Mardi Gras. On that day every woman in New Orleans and every woman visitor determines to get into the Sazerac. From early morning until late at night women, escorted or unescorted, fight their way into the rather small saloon, anxious to put their feet on the brass rail, to drink a real Sazerac and to have something to talk about. The crowd outside was thick to the curbs of the street, as one by one the ladies fought their way inside, never surrendering hope.

Some of the best maskers were in St. Charles Street. As crowded as the street was, there was more room than on Canal Street, and the chains of young people ran like streaks, screaming with laughter, joking, encircling, and capturing many a lone masker or perhaps a dignified and elderly couple who were not masked, but who always laughed with good humor when caught. People sat on curbs, on campstools, on wooden boxes, some of them holding their children in their laps, some chewing on hot dogs or on lunch they had brought from home, or drinking from bottles. In front of the St. Charles Hotel a fat pig was handing out cards that read: "I'm a dirty hog!" Beside him Circe, with grapes in her green hair, proffered cards that read: "I make swine of men!"

A stout lady in an oriental costume hugged a werewolf. "Who are you?" asked the werewolf.

"Why, I'm Madame Butterfly!" squealed the lady.

"You look like Madam Goddam," said the werewolf. "How about a drink?"

But the lady fluttered her fan before her face and disappeared into the crowd.

Farther uptown on St. Charles Street the grandstand before the City Hall was now packed with spectators, and the mayor and other city officials stood in their box bowing and waving to people passing in the street. Here the crowd thickened and maskers danced and cavorted for the edification of those watching from the tiers of benches. Three huge gorillas, their costumes made entirely of Spanish moss, pretended to try to climb into the mayor's box, to the amusement of the mob in the street below. A Spanish dancer, all scarlet and black, ruffles and lace, clicked her castanets and her heels and danced in the street for His Honor. A masker whose headdress was an artificial birthday cake fled past, pursued by three clowns who were determined to light the candles on his head. A young man in blackface, a suit with loud stripes, an immense red bow tie, and another man, wearing an old suit to which beer and pop-bottle caps had been sewn, chose the spot to indulge in a heated argument which almost resulted in a fight. A strolling jazz band, colored, all its members dressed as daisies in costumes made of yellow and green paper, stopped to play for the City Hall crowd and were rewarded with a shower of money from those above.

Now a little girl appeared in the City Hall grandstand and was assisted to a seat beside the mayor. She was dressed prettily in a long ruffled dress and a ribbon about her hair. She was the orphan selected each year to present Rex with the key to the city and to receive from him a gift, usually a wrist watch. "I was so surprised when they selected me," she said, "that I just shivered all over." She waved across the street to a grandstand on the other side of the street, in which were seated hundreds of children from orphanages throughout the city.

At last the people in the street heard a band of music. Everyone became excited, and many ran about telling each other, "The parade is coming!"

It was the first of the marching clubs that finally forced its way through the mob, with difficulty but with determination. This was the Zele Carnival Club, a group of men dressed as American Indians in feathers and war paint. They danced about to the music of their band, which played hot jazz music for the war dance. Close behind them, headed by another Negro band, came the Garden District Carnival Club, whose theme was "Aladdin and His Followers," and who were all dressed in turbans and rich and garishly colored costumes, their faces red and perspiring, cigars jutting from many mouths as they strutted along and jazzed it up, swinging the bright canes they carried with a jaunty air. Things quieted for a few moments and the street filled again, but another marching club appeared, this group all wearing rompers of pale blue and pink, long golden curls, and carrying dainty parasols. After that there was a small parade every few minutes, each group in different kinds of costumes, each having a different theme. The Arabi Club were cowboys and cowgirls, the Lyons Carnival Club (a group of veterans of World War II) Indians, and the

Jefferson City Buzzard, the oldest and most famous of all
these small organizations, many of which are quite old,
represented "King Memmon and His Happy Warriors" in
blackface.

The marching clubs had caused considerable excitement,
for each time the people in the streets and in the grandstands heard music they thought it was Rex approaching.
But at last there was a scream of glee from a young boy
who had climbed a lamppost and the news spread around
that Rex *was* coming at last. Some of the spectators ran to
the banquettes, acting upon the theory that the parades can
be seen to better advantage from a little distance, but most
behaved as if the best place to see it was to get on top of it.

What followed was slightly more hysterical than what
had occurred at all the night parades. Most of the crowd
blocked the street and there remained until nearly ground
down by the motorcycles and stomped to pulp by the
horses. Shrieking, they tumbled backward on their heels as
the motorcycles bore down upon them, then surged forward
until the fine steeds of the mounted police were on top of
them, and again they fled. But after the horses were gone
they did their best to prevent the parade from progressing.
At last, however, a way was cleared, and the captain and
dukes of Rex moved serenely past the City Hall, their bright
silks and jewels sparkling in the sunlight, their plumes and
capes and mantles billowing gently in the breeze that rustled
through the street to greet His Majesty, the King of
Carnival.

Seated atop his swaying, churning float, all gold and scarlet, with a gigantic crown above his head, Rex bowed
graciously, first to the left and then to the right, waving his
jewel-encrusted scepter. His robes were white satin and
silver cloth, covered with brilliants, and upon his head was
a dazzling crown of jewels. Behind him for the entire length
of the float stretched his royal mantle of silver cloth bor-

dered with wide bands of ermine. As usual Rex did not wear a mask, but he wore a deep chestnut beard and curls that fell to his shoulders, and his face was painted and rouged and jolly. On each side stood a page, resplendent in white satin trimmed with ermine, capes of silver cloth embroidered with jewels, and plume-topped silver caps over long golden curls.

The first band in the parade, marching in front of the royal float, was playing "If Ever I Cease to Love" as they reached the City Hall. But now they and the float stopped. The little girl in pale blue ruffles presented His Majesty with the key to the city and received in return a small box that was without a doubt the traditional wrist watch, which she accepted with a squeal of delight. Then Rex and the mayor exchanged toasts, and His Majesty smashed his glass. The bands struck up music, and the floats moved on, the drum major of the first band whirling his baton and strutting and dancing and whirling about to the amusement of those watching.

The shimmering rainbow topping the title float announced the theme of the parade as "What Is the Sea Shell Saying?" and the floats that followed, numbering twenty in all, were manifestations of Rex's royal interpretation of the mysteries whispered by the murmur of a sea shell when held to one's ear. Aboard the "Portals of Oceana" huge hermit crabs, their great claws bright red in the sun, guarded the entrance. On another float gigantic sea spiders were poised to spring. A giant lobster clipped the web imprisoning sea shells on a third float. The coral reefs of Vanikora were depicted, and a dark green submarine forest, with all branches growing downward, passed into view. There was a heap of lustrous pearls, poised, it seemed, to roll into the outstretched hands of the shouting spectators. The "Lost City of Atlantis" was a submerged city in ruins, its temples fallen, its arches broken, and its acropolis shattered at the base. There was a float showing the ice blocks of the South Pole, with the maskers aboard dressed as penguins, and others depicting the mermaids who swim in the great depths of the sea, man-eating sharks, octopuses and starfish, and writhing, tooth-fringed dragons, locked in a death struggle upon an ocean bed. The final float, titled "The Shores of America Are Singing," told a story of factory whistles and industry, with a golden eagle flapping its wings in the background. And, as each float passed, the maskers aboard tossed their trinkets into the crowds lining the path of the pageant—a crowd who constantly yelled and begged, arms outstretched and hands waving for more and more of the bounty of King Rex, a crowd who struggled and fought with each other, sometimes sprawling to the street in an effort to seize a whistle or a string of beads, as often as not breaking and smashing and tearing apart the souvenir before any one person captured it, and behaving in general as if the junk were booty beyond price.

Rex reached Canal Street at last, encircled it, and stopped before the Boston Club. A stepladder went up, a gentleman in striped trousers and cutaway coat climbed gingerly upward, bearing a napkin-wrapped bottle of champagne. There was a hiss and a pop, and champagne bubbled into the king's glass, and the King and Queen of Carnival exchanged toasts. Again Rex smashed his glass. The parade moved on, the queen, her maids, and the others before the Boston Club waving and smiling and bowing to their friends aboard the passing floats, and applauding the bands and the strutting, prancing drum majors and majorettes, who put on a performance worthy of the royalty and nobility above.

Immediately behind the last float moved the trucks, who are divided into two organizations—the Krewe of Orleanians and the Krewe of Crescent City—each with its king, a small boy chosen from an orphanage or the convalescent ward of a hospital, each composed of many beautifully decorated trucks filled with maskers, many of them representing fraternities, sororities, and clubs of various sorts, each one different from the next. The Krewe of Orleanians usually boasts more than seventy trucks, the Krewe of Crescent City more than eighty, so they seem almost endless as they pass in procession. Little Marcus Speed, who had lost both feet a few months before, was king of Crescent City during their 1947 parade.

Each group seemed to be trying to outdo the next, and they really do compete for prizes later in the day. Nearly every one had a four- or five-piece jazz band, usually Negro, grouped around a small piano, and their music and colorful costumes offered as much amusement as had Rex, with every conceivable type of costume represented. There were the archers of Sherwood Forest, the Arabian Nights, a group representing the Bowery, various ones depicting farm life and hillbillies, a crowd in nightshirts who called themselves "The Gay Nighties," another in bustles and top hats and swallow-tail coats entitled *"Vieux Nouvelle Orléans,"* Irish lads and lassies, bunnies, Indians, devils, ghosts, East Indians, Turks, Greeks, Russians, and nearly everything else that can be imagined.

Simultaneously with the passing of Rex and the trucks, there was excitement on the river near the foot of Canal Street. On the other side, at Algiers, King Alla, Monarch of the West Bank, led a large flotilla of river craft, decorated gaily with flags and carnival colors, up the Mississippi from just below Algiers to the uptown section of New Orleans and back to the starting place on the west bank portion of New Orleans. There King Alla, his robes and jewels nearly as splendid as those of Rex, disembarked along with his entourage and all climbed aboard ten floats representing "The Songs of Latin America," and paraded through Algiers' streets, which, like those on the other side of the Mississippi, were thronged with maskers.

A little later in the afternoon, far uptown in New Orleans, in the section called Carrollton, there was still another parade, led by another king. The king of Carrollton led ten floats through the streets of this uptown district. The theme of the parade was "A Fantasy of Fairy Tales," and His Majesty, wearing robes of silver and gold, behaved in true Mardi Gras tradition, pausing at Palmer Park to toast his queen in bubbling champagne before the grandstand where she awaited him.

Most of the day parades were over then, but there was still much to do and much to see, and for both the maskers in the streets and the unmasked spectators the fun of Mardi Gras had only begun.

CHAPTER FIVE

UNTIL MIDNIGHT

A SLIGHTLY INEBRIATED CLOWN, PERCHED ON the edge of one of the emptying grandstands, chewed at a fried chicken leg he had removed from a paper bag, and watched the crowd beneath him. "You know something," he confided to a stranger who had joined him for a breathing spell. "I bet I could walk on their heads. I think I'll try it when I get through eating."

It was true that it looked as if anyone could have walked across the street simply by stepping from one head to another, so many people were packed into the blocks which compose the principal business section of Canal Street. The next day the newspapers estimated that at least 500,000 persons were in that space while Rex was passing.

But now they were thinning a little. There was still a lot to see. Later King Zulu, the Negro ruler of Mardi Gras, and his cohorts might be along, but whether they would ever reach this far downtown was debatable—some years they do and some years they don't. Many of the crowd had already seen Zulu early in the morning. Some now started out to see him in the Negro sections through which he wanders in his lackadaisical fashion all day long on Mardi Gras. Others decided to visit the various neighborhood festivities going on in all parts of the city, or departed Canal Street for private parties in homes or offices. Almost everyone was going somewhere, for if you want to see everything on Mardi Gras you have to move fast. Yet, before anything, many people thought about food.

Eating is always a real problem on Mardi Gras. No matter how well prepared, no matter how thoroughly doused with mustard and chili gravy, no matter how *Creole*, hot dogs become monotonous. A few stalwart beings do get into the restaurants, of course, but not many people care to waste time standing in the line that inevitably is in formation before nearly all of them. Many people, especially family groups, solve the problem by bringing along picnic lunches, which they either leave in their locked automobiles or lug about with them. There are traditional Mardi Gras foods, too. Ham, potato salad, and doughnuts are the most famous of these, with fried chicken also enjoying popularity.

Many persons, particularly those living along the route through which the parade will pass, maintain open house in the afternoon, inviting their friends to drop in for food and drinks whenever they become too exhausted or too famished to proceed with the activities of the strenuous day. This custom is also followed by some offices, where employees and their friends—and strangers who wander in and out—gather after the parade. Others rent dining rooms in hotels and serve buffet lunch and liquor all day long, while the invited come and go. For many years, until just before his death in 1946, the most famous of these was the open house Lyle Saxon, the noted and beloved New Orleans author, held each year at the St. Charles Hotel, to which everybody was invited, the only stipulation being that they come masked. There, all day long, food and drink were freely dispensed, many people making it their headquarters for the day, returning whenever they were hungry or needed a drink or were tired, while Saxon himself, always in costume and mask, went back and forth, to frolic awhile in the street, then returning to see how his guests were enjoying themselves.

There are people who never leave their own neighborhoods on Mardi Gras and claim there is as good a time to be had at these small festivities as in the crowded business section of the city. Each neighborhood has its celebration. Maskers mount stands set up in squares or before markets to compete for prizes awarded to those wearing the best and most original costumes. In many places there is street dancing and small processions of maskers who form their own parades, and jazz bands playing for dancing and marching.

It was these affairs that many of the people in Canal Street visited after they had eaten and rested a bit. Often they went home to their own neighborhoods, where they would amuse themselves until it was about time to return for the parade of Comus, the last Mardi Gras parade, which was due to begin at seven o'clock in the evening. But others traveled from one part of the city to the other, determined to see everything.

Many spent the rest of the afternoon in the French Quarter, feeling perhaps that there is no place more suitable to Mardi Gras than the Vieux Carré with its narrow streets, its faded old houses, its overhanging balconies—and its many bars and cafés. It has known Mardi Gras longer than has any other part of the city, and no other part enjoys it more.

Royal Street began to fill as soon as the last truck had completed its passage through Canal Street, and here in Royal Street there was a quieter and softer atmosphere, as gay as that anywhere else, but mellowed a little, as if the maskers who strolled down the banquettes or in the middle of the street, as many of them did, had taken on some of the gentleness of the buildings they passed.

And here, where the crowd was thinner, it was possible for everyone to perform whatever tricks might occur to them. The "Saturday Nights of the Bath," with signs identifying them as such on their backs, strutted by in bath towels, and, insofar as could be seen, nothing else, except for washcloths tied about their heads. A "Pin-up Man" pranced behind them, attired in countless clotheslines and clothespins. A man dressed like Daniel Boone went about giving raw carrots to baby rabbits. A buxom girl walked slowly past, alone, her costume consisting of a grass skirt and two halves of a coconut. Out Bienville Street, crossing Royal, rolled an old-type horse-drawn hearse, filled with maskers dressed as skeletons. There were many carriages filled with maskers in the streets of the French Quarter.

A half-dozen black cannibals with gold rings in their noses, but their white skin now showing through the grease, merrily chased a bevy of girls dressed in Japanese kimonos and high pompadours into a bar, and then came running out ahead of a group of sailors who had, evidently, been awaiting their girls in the saloon. Then from around a corner came three highly creditable gorillas, their knuckles brushing the banquette and their fierce postures and snarling expressions bringing screams from two cancan dancers who were performing in the middle of the car tracks. "Where the cannibals go at?" asked one of the gorillas, standing upright. "You all see any cannibals around?" The gorilla removed his heavy head. Several "men from Mars" then stopped to converse with him. The strange visitants wore red and black costumes, yellow rope wigs, and their faces and hands were painted bright blue. "This thing is too damn hot," said the talking gorilla, sighing. "Let's go get us a beer. To hell with them cannibals." The other gorillas unmasked, too, displaying sweating brows.

Until Midnight

In a Bourbon Street nignt club, which, like almost all Bourbon Street night clubs, remained open all day Mardi Gras, Mr. and Mrs. Frankenstein Monster were dancing together. The make-up of Mrs. Frankenstein Monster was identical with that of her husband except that a hank of red hair was knotted on top of her terrible head and she wore a dress. They danced woodenly, with stiffened legs, to the amusement of those about them. Dancing alone, his frightful black cape whirling about him like the wings of a bat, was a top-hatted, chalky-faced Dracula. When the dance was over, Mrs. Frankenstein introduced Dracula to some red devils at a corner table as her "brudder-in-law," removed her mask, revealing a soft and pretty blond face, and yelled for an absinthe.

A group of young women and men dressed in the fashions of sixty years ago went from club to club in Bourbon Street, walking in and out rapidly, then moving on. On the back of one frock-coated gentleman was a sign that read: "Basin Street." Evidently they represented denizens of that famous red-light district that went out of business years ago. This group were looking for somebody named "Charlie," for every time they met anyone they knew they inquired about "Charlie." It is more or less commonplace for a member of a group to become lost on Mardi Gras. Individuals jump or fall off trucks, or enter the front door of a bar and vanish out a back one, not to be seen again until Ash Wednesday, having had mysterious adventures that they have either forgotten or pretend to have forgotten.

"Where's Charlie?" one of the young Basin Street women kept asking. "Anybody seen Charlie?"

There was bedlam in a St. Peter Street establishment. It was almost four o'clock, and now most of the trucks had unloaded their riders, who were seeking refreshment. They piled into the place in crowds of six and eight, noisily greeting acquaintances, uproariously ordering drinks, and dancing in postage-stamp spaces to the music from the juke box. A few very drunk ones slumped over tables and the bar, and these their friends would attempt to revive by yelling at them continuously, or beating them on the back, or by dropping pieces of ice down their necks. Outside there was a fight between a large rabbit and a hillbilly. A police patrol banged out the street, scooped up the bloody battlers, and swept noisily away. Their dates decided to have a few beers before going over to the precinct station to see what could be done.

Masks began coming off now. According to a city ordinance, masks must be removed by six o'clock on Mardi Gras, but in reality most come off before that, as the maskers begin to tire and turn their attention to food and liquor. Now most sat or stood around with their masks in their hands or in their laps, relaxing, resting, making love.

Down in Café Lafitte the costumed, but unmasked, sat around the roaring fire that always burns in the center of the old place that is supposed to have once been the blacksmith shop of Jean and Pierre Lafitte, the pirates, and relaxed, too, admiring each other's costumes and stories of the day's adventures. Here the proprietors were dressed as pirates, the beautiful girl cashier was, she said, "the mistress of Jean Lafitte," and almost everyone was garbed as someone they were not in this haunt of artists, writers, bohemians, and visiting celebrities. A number of the ante bellum maskers from the truck "Vieux Nouvelle Orléans" were about, behaving in an extremely modern fashion now. An artist dressed as a witch doctor sat quietly in a corner, playing with a small pile of white bones, sipping now and then from a highball he kept on the paved floor beside him, and ignored everybody. A columnist of national fame strolled about in the disguise of a frontiersman. A writer explained carefully to a group of friends that he was not in costume because he had sprained his back that morning while brushing his teeth. Two movie stars dressed as clowns sat in quiet conversation at the bar, not mingling with anyone, but watching the scene with wide and disbelieving eyes.

The neighborhood of Jackson Square and the St. Louis Cathedral, a few blocks away, had been the scene of stunts and whimsies all day long, but shortly after five o'clock it began to clear of most of those who had spent the afternoon dancing in Chartres Street or in the paved walks of the old square. Ladies in hoop skirts stood about on lacework iron balconies looking strangely correct in their surroundings. On the other side of the square many persons crowded into the outdoor café of the French Market to drink coffee and eat doughnuts. Some couples then strolled about through the stalls of the market, stopping to examine whatever produce was offered in the stalls now open. Others began heading for Canal Street and trolleys and buses, for their cars parked near by, or stood on corners signaling for taxicabs. It was time for those who had invitations to either the Comus or the Rex Ball to go home and change their clothes, especially if they wished to be back in the vicinity for seven o'clock, in time to see Comus as this last parade of Carnival and Mardi Gras entered the streets of the city.

A tired—often rather drunken—crowd awaited Comus in Royal Street, although it was a crowd by no means devoid of enthusiasm and zest for the end of the big show.

Royal Street seemed a good place to see Comus, and the parade would be on time, for it is always very prompt. The oldest of all the krewes and one of the most aristocratic, the pageant left its den at seven sharp, followed the traditional St. Charles Avenue route, reaching Canal Street without delay, accident, or mishap, stopping at the City Hall and again before the Boston Club.

In front of the Boston Club was enacted one of the most important of Mardi Gras traditions. There on the grandstand stood the queen of Comus, wearing her ball gown, her crown, and all her jewels, and beside her stood Rex, King of the Carnival, with his queen and his pages, all of them in the lavish, sparkling robes and jewels worn during the day and to be worn at the balls about to begin, and grouped about them were the mingled courts of the two krewes. All toasted King Comus.

Back in Royal Street, ladies and gentlemen in evening clothes recoiled a bit from cannibals whose black grease paint had but half vanished from their bodies. Tired children set up howls of fatigue. All masks were off, but animals with human heads and devils with grinning faces ran about playing their tricks upon the unwary. People sat on curbs eating the last of the lunches they had brought out early in the morning or drinking the last drops from their bottles. Here and there a bedraggled masker sat holding his head. Now and then someone fell down.

The vendors were making the most of this last chance. Peanuts had dropped to a cent a bag, hot dogs, somewhat stiff and cold, were two for a nickel, and warm cold drinks were back to a normal price of five cents each, instead of the doubled and trebled prices obtained earlier in the day. You could name your own price for some of the souvenirs offered by pitchmen, although a few were wrapping and packing up their wares to save them for next Mardi Gras.

Visitors discussed it all.

"What do you think of it?"

"It's crazy. Like a nightmare, you know what I mean? But a good nightmare."

"It reminds me of New Year's Eve in Philadelphia," said one lady, obviously from Philadelphia. "Only more and worse."

"I don't see how anyone could live through more than one," commented another lady.

And one startled stranger, evidently a very late arrival

in the city, emerged from a taxicab at a corner—because the driver could not take him to the entrance of his hotel in Royal Street—glared about him with disbelieving eyes, and inquired in a trembling voice, "Say! What the hell's gotten into these people?"

A fan dancer began performing in the center of a group just as the first motorcycle siren reached the ears of the people waiting in Royal Street. She stopped in the middle of a kick and joined the others on the banquette.

Now it came. First the white police car, with the booming voice coming through the speaker. "Get back, folks! All right now! Get back! We're coming through, folks!"

Then the motorcycles began grinding through, and, after them, the horses, the patient police smiling, perhaps happy that this was the end of it, at least for a year. The captain and the dukes pranced by, glittering, magnificent, and more beautifully costumed, it seemed, than those of any other parade, although each group always seems the most beautiful.

At last the flares and flambeaux came, the white-clad Negroes, weary but happy, dancing and strutting under the heavy weights of the old-fashioned standards, the flames coloring the whole street with deep rose and scarlet and burnished gold, casting intense light and grotesque shadows upon the walls and balconies, and lighting upturned faces with glowing, fiery grins, making them look like creatures of some happy hell.

Comus, Merry Monarch of Mirth, rocked high above his subjects, bowing, waving his jeweled cup, which he carries in place of a scepter, the plumes upon his jeweled crown sweeping regally with each bow, his float all white and red and gold, his throne set in a bower of scarlet satin and velvet edged with ermine.

The theme of the pageant was "Quests of History and Legend," carried out in seventeen floats depicting Jason, Marco Polo, Hercules, the search for El Dorado, Diogenes

looking for an honest man, Moses at the Red Sea, Evangeline's lifelong search for Gabriel, Jim Hawkins setting out
to find Treasure Island, and others of the famous quests of
history, literature, and myth.

As far as the crowd in Royal Street was concerned, it
might have been the first carnival parade any of them had
ever seen. Standing on tiptoe, they reached frantic, clawing
fingers into the air and screamed for the trinkets the knights
of Comus tossed them. They stood on balconies and risked
their skulls leaning far over the railings in efforts to catch
the beads and whistles and balloons. Again a float was
stoned by angry ruffians who had, apparently, not been able
to catch what they thought due them, and again the stoners
were chased by irate policemen. Sleeping children awoke
and, from their parents' shoulders, pleaded for gifts from
the maskers. A weaving bear with the head of a man
clutched a lamppost and yelled after the last float, "Hey,
Mardi Gras! Come back here!"

"Wasn't it beautiful?" people asked each other, and
began moving away. "Did you ever see anything so lovely?"

The crowd broke, going in scores of directions. Those
who were going to the balls tried to locate their cars or taxicabs, in frantic haste to reach whichever of the balls they
were attending. Others began to drift homeward, stopping to
buy one last bag of peanuts, one last balloon for the kids,
laughing one last time at some masker's antics. Still others
sought restaurants or night clubs or bars, determined not
to stop celebrating until midnight.

For the balls the Auditorium was again divided, and
through the partitions the music of the orchestras sometimes
clashed. On one side great crowds watched breathlessly as
Rex and his court held their traditional ball. On the other
side a smaller audience, feeling very splendid and exclusive,
sighed through the elegant tableau and call-outs of Comus.
Both sides blazed with lights and color and jewels and the

magnificent robes and gowns of the court performing before them.

Then, at midnight, the Ball of Rex underwent a change. With sweeping gestures of farewell, Their Majesties, the King and Queen of Carnival, departed, passed through a secret door, and then joined the court of Comus, and the thrilled spectators at the Comus Ball watched as Rex escorted the queen of Comus and Comus escorted the queen of Rex in a grand march around the ballroom floor.

Back at Rex's Ball, the people in the tiers came down to the dance floor for general dancing. At Comus the twin monarchs, their queens and courts soon departed for their royal supper.

But Mardi Gras was over long before that for most of the population who were not attending either of the balls. By ten o'clock the streets were lonely places. Debris lay about—paper by the ton, peanut shells, bits of food, empty bottles, broken glass, pieces of costumes, a strip of brilliant silk, a crumpled ribbon, a lost mask. Now and then a man or a couple plodded homeward through a street, performing no capers or antics. Here and there a drunk crouched in a doorway, fast asleep. A passing bus was filled with youths in costumes sleeping on each other's shoulders. People slept curled up in chairs in hotel lobbies.

A few individuals tried to dance and be gay in hotel cocktail lounges and night clubs, but it was forced merriment now. In most of them the orchestras and entertainers looked and sounded exhausted. In bars groups sat about talking quietly or slumped in their chairs, too tired to play, too tired to begin going home. Bartenders were cross and very weary. Mardi Gras was over.

Tomorrow was Ash Wednesday. Catholics would attend mass in the morning and have their foreheads crossed with the ashes of blessed palms. There would be services in the churches of some Protestant denominations. All who worked would return to their jobs, with or without hangovers, with or without regrets, to discuss all that day and for a long time afterward all that had happened to them on this best of any Mardi Gras anyone could recall. They would begin to talk of their plans for next year, and "How you gonna dress up next year?" would be the most popular question. Everyone would feel a little like the drunken masker clutching the lamppost, a little like shouting:

"Hey, Mardi Gras! Come back here!"

PART TWO

Here Is
How It Began

CHAPTER SIX

EUROPA AND THE BULL

*I*T MAY BE DOUBTED THAT ANY CARNIVAL QUEEN has ever had a particular desire for fecundity, at least at the hour of her reign. Certainly if one confessed such a curious wish to the ladies surrounding her in the Boston Club balcony their consternation would be considerable. It is equally improbable that any debutante reigning over a New Orleans krewe considers herself a sacrificed goat. And if Rex had to run through Canal Street before the goatskin whips of painted priests it is unlikely that many gentlemen would seek the honor of being King of Carnival.

The symbolic origins of carnivals are fairly obvious. Spring festivals in celebration of the fertility of the earth, replete with spells and enchantments to increase the richness of the soil, were widespread long before history was recorded. Later the fertility of women as well as the replenishing of food stocks was sought.

Thousands of years ago, on a date approximating Mardi Gras, fields were sprinkled with the fresh blood of an animal, usually a goat. On some occasions the sacrifice was human, a virgin or a youth, fattened and indulged for the occasion, who might be an enemy captive, or perhaps a favorite of the tribe, chosen as a great honor, who was slain and blooded only after having received every tribute that could be offered a queen or king. In other places and at different times the date was one on which men and women joined in sexual union out in the fields and demonstrated to the spirits of vegetation, the first gods Man loved, what was desired.

The old gods of storm and thunder and darkness, of punishment and pain and death, had inspired only terror. Here were positive gods, good gods, who might give men life. Winter, dreaded in the colder regions of the earth where life was precarious during its season and death from starvation was always imminent, was gone. Spring was new birth. It was indeed a time for rejoicing and for hope, a time for a carnival. Then it must not have a feast before a fast, but rather the beginning of feasting, after a lean and hungry winter.

Perhaps the first account of such a celebration that possessed a definite pattern and tradition is Ovid's description of the celebration of spring by the Arcadian shepherds, when they sacrificed a goat, ate its flesh, and made whips of its skin, with which, at sunset, priests, bedaubed with goat's blood and paint, lashed the people, male and female, naked and joyous, through the streets of their village. That was five thousand years ago, but the date of the event was comparable to Shrove Tuesday on the present calendar of the Christian Church. But even then the motive for the festival had already changed from its original one, and it was no longer fertility of the soil or an abundant crop that was sought, but the remission of sins and the fruitfulness of women.

Carnival came early to ancient Rome. The Greek priests who built their temples there were called luperci, and historians from Plutarch to Gibbon have referred to the Lupercalia, that mad carnival that soon degenerated into an orgy of lust and pain. It was now a part of a formalized religion, just as Mardi Gras is in actuality a part of a religion, with its priests, temples, devotees, and elaborate rites that lasted for months, with a climax that was Rome's most popular holiday, even as Mardi Gras is the most popular holiday in New Orleans. The *februa*—the goatskin whips—were still in use, but this portion of the rite had become so widespread that there were no longer sufficient priests to serve the celebrants, so the *februa* were distributed among the people that they might flog each other and themselves until they were purified of sin.

Gradually, as Rome became wealthy, grand, and gaudy, and as the centuries passed, all semblance of spirituality vanished from the Lupercalia. It became a time devoted to the circus, the gladiatorial arena, and to private and public debauchery of the most extreme sensuality. The priests of Galli had arrived, those emasculated worshipers of Attis who sacrificed their genitals to their god and who wore phallic images about their necks and practiced male prostitution as a religious rite. Into the Lupercalia was introduced the costume, and the first maskers were female impersonators, men who appeared on the streets dressed as women and offered themselves as women to male celebrants. The costumes and masks worn on the carnival floats in New Orleans often have a strange, sexless character. It may be wondered how many members of the krewes have given any thought to the matter of what might have been their origin.

The Emperor Claudius, with Roman tolerance and perhaps in a halfhearted attempt to slightly purify the Lupercalia, incorporated the rites of Attis into the established religion of Rome. The purification was a dream never achieved, but a kind of order was established and some of the rites took on a certain beauty.

In *The Golden Bough*, Sir James G. Frazer, who sees a

definite connection between all the festivals of fertility and the carnivals that end on Mardi Gras or Shrove Tuesday, describes the worship accorded a cut pine tree in the Temple of Cybele on the twenty-second day of March. Frazer says the trunk was swathed like a corpse and adorned with violets, and that the effigy of a youth, representing Attis, was tied to the trunk, and that certain rites, vaguely obscene, were then performed with the effigy, which some years before had certainly been a flesh-and-blood sacrifice. At dawn on the next day trumpets were blown. The third day was the Day of Blood. To the barbaric music of clashing cymbals, trumpets, and flutes, the priests whirled in a frenzied dance until, in an ecstasy of masochism during which they slashed themselves with knives and flogged each other with whips, they climaxed the orgy with self-castration on the part of those being admitted to the priesthood, and splattered the altar with their blood and severed organs of procreation. This was the mourning for Attis, which lasted two days and nights, after which those who survived were received into the terrible religious order. It was a period of weeping and pain. On the twenty-fifth of March came the resurrection, the Carnival or Lupercalia, the festival of joy.

During the Lupercalia complete and universal license was granted the citizens of Rome. Almost all laws were abandoned and a Roman might do anything, not always even excluding murder, on that one day. It was an uninhibited debauch during which every caprice was freely and openly indulged. The wealthy and the aristocratic sometimes held forth in private with conduct that in no way resembled that of a modern carnival ball, but often they took advantage of the occasion to mingle with the populace in the streets, frequently disguising themselves to avoid recognition and, apparently, the gossip that might follow during the soberer days ahead. Women of high position and fashion donned wigs and costumes and prostituted themselves to strangers.

Aging senators in female attire practiced sexual refinements. Rape, robbery, and the slaying of enemies, while disguised, were popular diversions. All social barriers were down, and slave and freedman, patrician and pauper, ran riot in the streets of Rome, hand in hand.

The next day was one of rest and recuperation. On the next, the twenty-seventh, there were street processions. Images of the gods were exhibited in wagons drawn by oxen decorated with flowers and garlands, behind which aristocrats and common folk walked in their bare feet. There was the music of pipe and tambourine. Priests in purple robes washed the images and oxen in the Almo, a stream flowing into the Tiber outside the city walls, and, again adorned with fresh garlands, the oxen and gods completed the procession. The resemblance to the Bœuf Gras, the French symbol of the Carnival, and until a short time ago a part of the New Orleans celebration, is inescapable.

The sacrifice of a bull on this occasion had already a long and ancient history and significance. Far back in the mist of time the Druids had performed the rite upon their stone altars. Now the priests of Attis practiced the same ceremony. Still decorated with flowers, a chosen animal was led into the temple. The devotee who was to be baptized was crowned with gold and wreathed with fillets, and then placed in a pit covered with a wooden grating. Then the bedecked bull, gold leaf glittering on its forehead, was driven over the grating and there stabbed to death with a consecrated spear. The hot blood flowed down upon the worshiper in the pit until he was literally bathing in it. He emerged drenched and crimson, his sins washed away, his soul cleansed by the blood, and his body purified by the great quantities of it he had consumed with cupped hands.

With the coming of Christianity, the Lupercalia fell into disrepute. Sex, drunkenness, gluttony, and all forms of extreme physical pleasure became sinful and the road to heaven hard and stony. The early fathers of the Church had a difficult time, however, convincing the Romans, or any other Latins, that feasting, fornication, and fun were unimportant to the salvation of their immortal souls, and a number of saints made their reputations by attempting it, which usually resulted in their martyrdom by death at Roman hands, when the Caesars became bored with the prophets of gloom and despair, who were so determined to strip the earthly life of all its pleasures.

But at last the Church, through sheer persistence and some fortunate coincidences, partially won. Yet they were never altogether victorious, and by the fifth century of the present era it was necessary to resort to compromise. Many ancient pagan customs and festivals were imbued with Christian names and Christian significance. Certain rites to Apollo, Adonis, and Attis, for instance, were transformed into the Christian Easter, to celebrate the resurrection of Jesus. Spring and rebirth were still to be commemorated, but with a more suitable motive. The Lupercalia, since it refused to die, was permitted existence in a modified form as a concession to the needs of the flesh, and was placed roughly just before a period of fasting and penance, Lent, the spring. At the same time it was given a new name, Carnelevamen, the consolation of the flesh, perhaps in the hope that a different name, a more respectable name, might hasten the end of all memory of the priests of Attis and at last cast upon the celebration some faint glow of spirituality. Then, about the year 600, when Pope Gregory the Great invented the calendar we still use, he fixed the present fluctuating date of Ash Wednesday as the first day of Lent and formally established the day before, Shrove Tuesday, as the day that would climax three days of feasting and festival, after which Christians were to turn from earthly delights to prayer and to repairs upon the soul.

Through the centuries that followed, the Carnival was often abused and perverted, but the Church, although its power was constantly extending, could never eradicate it, even at that period when the Vatican ruled nearly all Western civilization. At last it was conceded that a period of foolishness and folly was necessary to the happiness of men, and attempts at complete suppression gave way to more or less genial and paternal control on the part of the priests. The *Catholic Encyclopedia* admits that "It is intelligible enough that before a long period of deprivations human nature should allow itself some exceptional license in the way of frolic and good cheer." The origin of Carnival, however, is mentioned only by: "No appeal to vague and often inconsistent traces of pagan customs seems needed to explain the general observances of a carnival celebration." But the resemblance between the Lupercalia and Carnival is somewhat more than "vague and often inconsistent."

Frazer, to a certain extent, also identifies Carnival with the Saturnalia, the famous festival celebrated by the Romans from about the seventeenth to the twenty-third of December, which was another orgy of lust, even of crime, and there are similarities. The king of the Saturnalia was a young and handsome man, chosen by lot, who, as the Lord of Misrule, reigned over the revels and was, at their conclusion, burned in effigy. Probably at an earlier date the real king had been put to death. A Christian soldier named Dasius was martyred, and thus attained sainthood, for refusing to play the role of king of the Saturnalia. But the Saturnalia took place at a time that seems to correspond more with Christmas than with Mardi Gras.

The word *carnelevamen* became *carnevale* in a more modern Italy, *carnaval* in France, and carnival in England. Its definition as "farewell to meat," now commonly accepted, is a rough one and not altogether correct, but that became so because fasting from meat is a widespread Lenten practice. A better one is "farewell to the flesh," for beginning on Ash Wednesday all earthly pleasures are to be set aside. The rites imported to Rome with the Greeks and those that had come from Egypt vanished, but the love for the old holidays remained, and some of the old symbols lived on. The bull that raped Europa exists only in mythology, but the bull is still a part of European carnivals and he is butchered at the end of the festival just as he was by the priests of Attis, even if for different reasons. There are those, too, who remember when the Bœuf Gras was an integral part of the New Orleans Mardi Gras. The name of the day was often changed, and at various times was known as Shrove Tuesday, Shrovetide, Fat Tuesday, Fool's Day and Confession Day, the last being one appellation that did not endure for long, but the spirit of the day remained the same. The people occupying the Italian peninsula were no longer Romans and their ancient gods were dead, but their nature was not suppressed, and it was the Italians more than any other people who kept alive the Carnival, and some recognition of and a time for all the desires demanded by the flesh.

And there were only too often times when the Italians, Venetian, Roman, and Florentine, outdid themselves. A Roman returning to the earth, during the fifteenth and sixteenth centuries especially, might not have had too difficult a time in recognizing what had been the Lupercalia. Some of the trappings had changed, but otherwise he would have found much that was familiar.

The Roman variety during that period was probably the most scandalous. As in earlier times, the Martedi Grasso became a day devoid of all inhibitions, sexual and otherwise. Rape and adultery were commonplace. Masks lent opportunity for crimes of vengeance, spite, greed, and jealousy. Old vendettas and feuds found outlets, and political figures were often assassinated on the day. The harmless children's races on the Corso became contests between older men that often resulted in maiming and mayhem. The powers that ruled contributed the additional diversion of having all executions held, publicly, on that day, and maskers would snatch the hanged from the gallows the tortured from the wheel, and parade through the streets with bloody corpses. It was charged that even the clergy appeared in the streets in masquerade and that priests of the Church, not emasculated like the priests of Attis, but sworn to chastity, behaved in an exceedingly unbecoming fashion.

Street masking not only resulted in brawls and murders, but some rather repelling sports became universal. Confetti is a pretty thing to throw and a nice invention for a festival, but this degenerated into the pitching of ground red pepper, sand, rotten vegetables, and fruit. Containers of doubtful contents in those pre-sewerage days were emptied upon the heads of maskers from balconies and windows, and now and then the containers and other heavy objects crashed down upon skulls. Ruffians stoned maskers in the streets.

At last, after decades of the heinous practice, the authorities stopped the executions on that day. Later, bluntly and thoroughly, many of the other unpleasant sports were put to an end simply by passing laws that made the throwing of any objects, the carrying of arms, masking as a priest or any other church dignitary, and the desecration of churches punishable by death. This seems a bit severe now, but all laws were severe and cruel, and it served to render Carnival in Italy considerably less violent and orgiastic. During the seventeenth and early eighteenth centuries the celebration reached its height of pure romantic beauty in Rome, with the whole population aiding and abetting the event, with gigantic celebrations in the Colosseum and the theaters, and streets and public places turned over to the merrymaking, all with a minimum of violence.

It is often said that if Mardi Gras in New Orleans continues to expand and to grow the time may come when the Carnival will last for the entire year. It finally managed to last for half a year in Venice. There, only a few short centuries ago, the entire population wore masquerade for six months. Life was, at least for the wealthy, a continuous round of balls and pleasure. Even the housewife was masked as she went about her duties, and the merchant and the man of business conducted their affairs in costume and mask. Masks were worn day and night, to dinners, to the opera, and to the casinos. In his *Memoirs* Casanova spends nearly as much time lifting masks as he does raising skirts.

French taste and wit, incorporating the fashions of Venice, Rome, and Florence, doted upon masquerades and carnivals. The opportunities afforded by the costume pleased the vanity of the Bourbons. Louis XIV created entire courts of mythological aristocracy. The comedies of Molière and other favored writers of the period came to life, too, during the Carnival. Louis XV was pleased that his court assumed the mask as a charming accent to its fabulous extravagance, and masks became during his reign nearly as popular at Versailles and Fontainebleau as they had been on the Venetian canals. During the season French society was at its best and most brilliant, and the spectacular balls and street processions, in which the Bœuf Gras, adorned with garlands and flowers and ridden by a child dressed as Cupid, and grotesque parades of huge and fantastic papier-mâché animals and monsters took part, may have been a major factor in kindling those fires that had smoldered so long. With the Revolution came a banning of all masks, costumes, and Mardi Gras. The promenade of the Bœuf Gras and the disguise of the person and face were termed beneath the dignity of a citizen.

Monarchs love the Carnival and Napoleon found in it a complement to his grandeur. In 1805 the Bœuf Gras again was seen in the streets and boulevards of Paris, and again reveling maskers filled the thoroughfares. Urchins, blowing *cornets à bouquin*, led the way, and behind them came carriages filled with the Committee of the Butcher Shops, garbed dourly in black, but with chests that glittered with medals. Maskers followed, a motley but gay procession, and then came the Bœuf Gras in his gilded cart, with the child representing Cupid (chosen now through a school competition) astride his back. Other carts and wagons followed, variously decorated to represent numerous subjects, then more of the populace in costume. There were great balls that lasted until dawn, and then came the *descente de la Courtille*, which continued until all of Paris was a scene of drunken revel and hilarity. The fattened ox, of course, was at last butchered.

There were carnivals in Madrid, Barcelona, and other cities of Spain. Geneva and Vienna and Warsaw also adopted the practices. In German villages there were very old folk customs about which we know little until early in the seventeenth century when, at Shrovetide, two men dressed as "Wild Men," one wearing a costume of brushwood and moss, the other dressed in straw, were pursued through the streets. There was a pretense of stabbing and shooting until the men fell "dead." They were then placed on boards and carried to an inn, while trumpets were blown.

Burying the Carnival is a custom of very ancient origin. In Bohemia a man dressed as a wild man used to be pursued through the streets until he reached one across which a cord had been stretched. Here he fell to the ground and was captured. Then the executioner stabbed a bladder filled with blood that the wild man wore about his body, and the wild man "died." On the following day a straw image of the wild man was thrown into a pool. The Saxons of Transylvania used to hang the Carnival. After a mock trial beneath a tree, a straw man was suspended from a branch with a rope about its neck. A village official then made a speech, telling those who had gathered that the Carnival was guilty of some crime, such as wearing out their shoes. The effigy was then buried. A real funeral was held for the Carnival in Catalonia, in which the effigy rode in a hearse attended by maskers dressed as priests and bishops, all the mummers wearing crape and the horsemen carrying blazing flambeaux. At the place where the funeral oration was recited devils and angels burst from the crowd and tried to take captive the body of Carnival, but they were always overcome and the sham corpse was buried in a grave. This took place near to midnight on Shrove Tuesday and was the climax of days of merriment.

In the Abruzzi, says Frazer, a pasteboard figure was carried through the streets by gravediggers "with pipes in their mouths and bottles of wine slung on their shoulder belts. In front walks the wife of Carnival, dressed in mourning and dissolved in tears. From time to time the company halts, and while the wife addresses the sympathizing public, the grave-diggers refresh the inner man with a pull at the bottle. In the open square the mimic corpse is laid on a pyre, and to the roll of drums, the shrill screams of women, and the gruffer cries of the men, a light is set to it. While the figure burns, chestnuts are thrown about among the crowd. Sometimes the Carnival is represented by a straw man at the top of a pole which is borne through the town by a troop of mummers in the course of the afternoon. When evening comes on, four of the mummers hold out a quilt or a sheet by the corners, and the figure of Carnival is made to tumble into it. The procession is then resumed, the performers weeping crocodile tears and emphasizing the poignancy of their grief by the help of saucepans and dinner bells. Sometimes, again in the Abruzzi, the dead Carnival is personified by a living man who lies in a coffin, attended by another who acts the priest and dispenses holy water in great profusion from a bathing tub."

Although Carnival was never as popular in England as

on the continent and the English seem somehow to lack
the Latin love of the revel, there were certain curious Shrovetide customs until not so long ago. In some sections of the
island Shrove Tuesday was known as Pancake Day, and it
was traditional that great quantities of pancakes be made
and eaten on that day, an observance that is still remembered
in a few rural sections. During that lustiest English period
when the Tudors and Elizabeth reigned, mummers and
masquerades were exceedingly popular, but Protestantism
had for the most part eradicated the Carnival and Mardi
Gras as they were held elsewhere. In the eighteenth century
a brutal custom of stoning live cocks to death on Shrove
Tuesday enlivened the day in some parts of England, but
even here the French surpassed them. Louis XIV used to
light a bonfire under a sack of live cats on Mardi Gras. After
Victoria flounced her prim skirts about the throne, even
most masquerades became staid and proper affairs. The
English had lost their taste for the orgy.

CHAPTER SEVEN

CARNIVAL AND THE CREOLES

*T*HE TRADITION OF THE NEW ORLEANS MARDI GRAS is French and there is no doubt but that during the first years of its existence it resembled the one held in Paris more than it did any other. It was on Shrove Tuesday in 1699 that Iberville and his party stopped to rest for a day beside a small bayou about twelve miles from the mouth of the Mississippi River. The weary, homesick men must have recalled that back home in France maskers were filling the streets, for before they moved on, Iberville named the stream Bayou Mardi Gras.

About nineteen years later his brother Bienville turned over to his engineers the task of planning the streets of the tiny settlement that was La Nouvelle Orléans. We have no record that anyone remembered Mardi Gras that year or that anything was done about it, but it was not long before a fair imitation of the Parisian festival was an annual event, and although the spectacles presented during those first years must have been poor ones in some ways, it is easy to believe that the gaiety of the small population must have compensated for whatever was lacking in costumes and decorations, for streets that were only muddy lanes, and for the absence of ballrooms and theaters. By 1766, when Don Antonio de Ulloa took possession of the colony of Louisiana for Spain, Mardi Gras, though sketchy and crude, was an established custom.

The Spanish permitted it to continue for a time, but within a few years street masking on that day was banned. Even before the Spanish had taken control many travelers had written home of the wickedness and the general licentiousness of the young city, reporting a number of gambling houses, rough ballrooms of a sort, and loose women in numbers out of all proportion to the settlement's population. Attracted by these were the flatboatmen and other river ruffians, and all this, together with an increasing number of free people of color, had made of Mardi Gras masking a rowdy, even a murderous, affair.

The balls continued, and the character of these has been much debated. There were already some private affairs, to which none but a certain circle and a few distinguished visitors were admitted. There were also public balls of varying degrees of respectability which were open to everyone who could purchase a ticket, and some of these were helping to give New Orleans a reputation as a city as evil and as dangerous as Marseille, a city which was in time to earn the appellation of "hell on earth."

It is true that New Orleans was then a wicked place, a haven of much human scum from the brothels and prisons and slums of Europe. Every sort of vice was rampant and murder was so common that it has been said that the natives would step over a corpse on the way to a ball or the opera and think nothing of it.

The Creoles (and here is meant citizens of New Orleans and its environs of pure white blood) became a haughty race who withdrew into their own circles early in the city's history, partly through necessity in a port with such an

Mardi Gras

abundance of undesirables. First they were French, but
later they intermarried with the Spanish, and sometimes
with other nationalities, but they long remained an exclusive
group with a complex caste system of their own, but as a
whole surrounded by barriers through which few outsiders
were admitted.

In 1803 came the Louisiana Purchase and with it a severe
blow to Creole pride. Now the Americans, Anglo-Saxon and
Protestant, and in many cases far richer than most of the
Creoles, began pouring into the city. The Creoles found
them crude and bad-mannered and mercenary.

As a whole the dislike was mutual. The Americans did
not approve of the Creole way of life at all. There was indeed no more resemblance between this completely Latin
city of New Orleans and that of any on the New England
seaboard than there is between granite and velvet. Here was
a warm and luxury-loving people living in a society closed to
the Americans and to all outsiders, a people served by black
slaves and inordinately devoted to the ball, the theater, the
opera, the promenade, who placed an unseemly degree of
importance upon fine food, fine liquor, fine manners. The
Americans thought the Creoles superficial and hypocritical.
When an American ate he wanted to fill his belly with
beans and potatoes, when he drank he drank rum and
whisky and he drank to get drunk, when he fought he used
his fists, not a glittering rapier. On Sundays the Creoles
went to mass, but from the St. Louis Cathedral they crossed
the Place d'Armes to shop among the lush produce of the
French Market, and Sunday afternoon was devoted to the
soirée and the matinee. Life was a continuous round of
amusement, even for those who could not afford it. Whenever possible there was a party. On the slightest excuse
there was a parade. New England thought New Orleans
reeked with sin.

All this was not entirely as it looked. There were austere
Creole families who scarcely left their shuttered homes,

98

their cloistered gardens, and when they did—for mass, a wedding, or a funeral—were garbed in black and unadorned as a positive and deliberate renunciation of the bright and gay behavior and attire of the others. It was true, too, that the Creoles were a kindly and gentle people, frightened now at what might lie ahead for them, becoming, as they became a minority, almost like strangers in their own home.

But the Americans did not know this. They saw only those citizens who frequented public places, which the highest caste of Creoles seldom did, for publicity of any sort was considered distasteful, and any Creole of this stratum would have felt disgraced if his name appeared in print, as he would have starved to death in preference to working in any ordinary occupation.

The Americans saw the cafés and coffeehouses filled with fiery young gentlemen who fought duels with each other over a look, a sneer, a sigh, and sometimes just for fun. They saw the physical and moral corruption of some streets. They visited the public balls and some of the less exclusive private ones where the dancers danced until dawn. They attended the theaters and found them packed to the roofs for performance after performance. They walked through the French Market, where, among screeching parrots, gibbering monkeys and alligators in cages, Indians wrapped in blankets, and reeling riverboatmen, lovely quadroon women walked in their bright cotton dresses and their brilliant *tignons*. They saw, also, Negroes in chains, with the ripe wounds of the whip still fresh on their backs. They saw much filth, much disease, much cruelty, and, finally, much indifference to all these horrors. They learned of the little houses on the edge of the town, where Creole gentlemen kept their quadroon mistresses. They visited the quadroon balls, which were attended only by those women when very young and as yet unchosen and by white men who came to select mistresses. They saw Mardi Gras.

Mardi Gras

Street masking was revived in New Orleans in the years between Spanish suppression and the American acquisition of the colony, when the French again ruled, and the American authorities permitted it to continue until 1806. Then a report came that Aaron Burr and a large flotilla were on their way to the city, were descending the Mississippi River to capture New Orleans and there establish a base to be used by Burr in his dream of empire.

The city was fortified and there was a surging wave of panic. As a minor but important precaution the Mardi Gras that was about to be held was banned. Burr and his party of less than a hundred men were arrested at Natchez before the date of Mardi Gras, but the City Council met in the old Cabildo and decided that even though the danger seemed to be past, Carnival should not be resumed. Masking and masquerade balls were dangerous in themselves, and, besides, Burr had friends in the city.

It was not revived the next year, or the next, or for many more. The authorities explained that ill feeling between Creoles and Americans was high and that, also, there was the racial situation. Who could predict what might happen if masked men walked the streets again? Besides, the Americans had never approved of Mardi Gras. They considered it a part of the wickedness of New Orleans.

This time Mardi Gras almost died, and for years it existed only in the memory of the Creole population. In 1823, after numerous petitions, balls were at last, although begrudgingly, allowed once again, and in 1827 street masking was once more permitted.

The balls were soon more numerous and more brilliant than they had ever been. Orleanians of every race and social stratum donned costumes and masks and gathered to dance all night long, and on Mardi Gras they marched through the streets in costume, rowdy and happy once more, despite the wrinkled noses of the city fathers—wrinkled most perhaps at the number of Americans who now joined in the frivolity, but disapproving heartily of it all. What crimes, what sins might be committed under cover of a mask! reflected these Anglo-Saxons. And Ash Wednesday always proved them right, for the jails were always filled, and more than one corpse, still dressed in a ridiculous costume, lay in a gutter or sprawled across a banquette. Even some of the older Creoles did not approve now. No lady ever masked in the streets, or if she did she took the utmost precaution never to be recognized.

Many balls ended in disasters, especially some of those that attempted to keep out the riffraff. There were elements who resented the closed doors bitterly, saturated their anger with alcohol, and then set out to attend the ball anyway. Then gentlemen armed themselves. The result was shooting and stabbings galore. Gentlemen had their skulls bashed in. Ladies had their handsome gowns ripped from their backs and their faces clawed by whores. The authorities saw neither humor nor beauty in any of it.

The quadroon balls were at their best during the carnival season. Travelers and visitors to the city sometimes thought them the most shocking spectacles in New Orleans, or else they found in them much excitement and beauty. All were amazed. Here was a group of lovely girls, reared by their mothers to conduct themselves with grace and all the arts of the best feminine society for the sole purpose of becoming mistresses of young white men of wealth and social prominence. When a Creole made his selection he established his mistress in a small house on the outskirts of the city. In most cases the affair was terminated with a financial arrangement when the man married, although sometimes they continued throughout life. Creole men thought the custom ideal, and fathers often arranged and financed the affairs for their sons. Creole women saved their faces by ignoring the very existence of the women, even when one knew her husband had not forsaken his dark little beauty after marriage.

There can be no doubt that many of the girls were lovely, by any standards. According to all reports, few betrayed their Negro blood, and in most cases the word "quadroon" was one that was used loosely and as a generalization, for many of their mothers and grandmothers in the latter days of the system had been quadroon, too, while the paternal side of their bloodstream had been white for generations. They would, therefore, have had much less than the quarter of African blood the term implies. Many were probably as white as their lovers, as far as appearances were concerned. An Englishman, John Buckingham, wrote home in 1841 that they resembled ". . . the highest order of Hindoos, with lovely countenances, full, dark, liquid eyes, lips of coral and teeth of pearl, long raven locks of soft and glossy hair, sylph-like figures, and such beautifully rounded limbs, and exquisite gait and manner, that they might furnish models for a Venus or a Hebe to the chisel of the sculptor." Bernhard, Duke of Saxe-Weimar-Eisenach, "hasted away to the quadroon ball" as soon as he could escape from a Creole affair of social importance, he confesses in his *Travels Through North America, 1825–26*, and was nearly as thrilled at the sight of the quadroons as was Mr. Buckingham. He found that "The quadroons are almost entirely white; from their skin no one could detect their origin; nay, many of them have as fair a complexion as many of the haughty creole females." Many other travelers, too, found the quadroons ravishing and the balls the gayest of all that took place during the season, and compared the affairs with the masquerades of Venice and Nice.

Creole balls became increasingly exclusive. They shrank to small affairs, and as the years passed the barriers tightened, invitations being extended only to the same group of families and carefully selected friends. Most were held in private homes, where there was less chance of the uninvited forcing entrance than if they had been held in public halls and ballrooms. Every effort was made to keep out most Americans. It was these affairs that fathered the idea of the closed organizations that exist in New Orleans today, even though those of the present time may be headed by persons with names as un-Creole as Smith. For the Americans, in most cases possessing more wealth than the Creoles, settled in that section of the city above Canal Street, far removed from the Vieux Carré, built themselves handsome mansions set in great gardens which gave their neighborhood the appellation of the Garden District, by which it is still known, and molded themselves into a social group of their own, destined to finally wrest the rule of Mardi Gras from Creole hands and to at last almost drown out the last frantic cries of the Creoles for recognition as the social arbiters of the city.

It was the Americans who gave Mardi Gras its present pattern. It was they who, at least to some extent, took it away from the people and changed what had been an unorganized and informal street revel into an entire social season, a highly stylized program of balls and pageants, related to debutantes and a caste system as rigid, although in a different way, as that of the Creoles. The Creoles had formed their groups and built the walls around themselves as a last effort to survive as a social entity. The Americans, however, kept alive and increased the whole concept of imitation aristocracy and the ridiculous snobbery that still characterizes some of the Mardi Gras krewes. Only street masking remained as delightful a custom as ever, although even there many people, both Creole and American, considered it in bad taste to mingle in the streets in costume, and this unfortunate feeling continued to grow for many years.

The first formal parade took place in 1838. Until then

maskers had formed lines and chains and walked and run through the streets on Mardi Gras to the amusement or disgust of the spectators, but without real organization or plan. They romped and shouted and behaved as foolishly as possible, but those taking part were usually considered wild young men at best. Perhaps a few groups had also ridden about in carriages and wagons, but there was no semblance of order.

The very first account of what was evidently the first real Mardi Gras parade in New Orleans appeared in the *Commercial Bulletin* on Ash Wednesday 1838, and described the day as follows:

The European custom of celebrating the last day of the Carnival by a procession of masqued figures through the public streets was introduced here yesterday, very much to the amusement of our citizens. The principal streets were traversed by a masquerade company on horseback and in carriages, from the fantastic Harlequin to the somber Turk and wild Indian. A delightful throng followed on the heels of the cavalcade as it marched through our city suburbs, and wherever it went the procession raised a perfect hubbub and jubilee. The exhibition surpassed anything of the kind ever witnessed here.

The *Daily Picayune* was impressed, too, and said:

A large number of Creole gentlemen of the first respectability, went to no little expense with their preparations. In the procession were several carriages superbly ornamented—bands of music, horses richly caparisoned—personations of knights, cavaliers, heroes, demigods, chanticleers, punchinellos, &c, &c, all mounted. Many of them were dressed in female attire, and acted the lady with no small degree of grace.

One wonders if that writer knew very much about the Lupercalia and the priests of Attis!

The next year, 1839, the newspapers were apparently prepared, for *L'Abeille*, a French-language paper, invited the public on the day before Mardi Gras to gather at half past three o'clock on the following afternoon to view "the sublime and extravagant" procession that was to take place. There had been a thousand balls in the city, said *L'Abeille*, since Twelfth Night.

A thousand balls. One wonders where so many were held and by whom. Most of them must have been small and must have taken place in private homes. However, there were then a few affairs in some ways more elaborate than any held today. Now the balls consist of brief tableaux, followed by the call-out dances, and then sometimes by general dancing. But at that time a long theatrical performance or *galopade* was the principal feature of the more important balls. This lasted until midnight, after which dancing continued until daybreak.

As time went on more and more persons took part in the street pageants. Anyone in costume could fall in behind, so as the parade proceeded through the streets it grew longer and more elaborate. And in general the public's reception of the parade was most enthusiastic. They shouted and applauded the maskers as they passed, and even the city officials began to smile upon the mummers. For some reason confetti has never become a part of the New Orleans Mardi Gras, although in late years small amounts of it have been used. During the 1840s the throwing of flour or pellets of flour, which broke and dissolved, became popular, as it has long been in European carnivals. In 1843 a newspaper writer said that so much flour was thrown on Mardi Gras that on Ash Wednesday the streets looked as if they were covered with snow.

But this was not to continue. The tougher element of New Orleans, more vicious by now than they had ever been, and also very poor, decided not to waste their precious flour but to substitute dust. This caused much discomfort to the maskers. Then one year some heartless spectators threw quicklime upon them. A number were severely burned and several almost lost their sight. After that attempts began to outlaw the throwing of flour and all its substitutes, but without much success. After the Mardi Gras of 1848 the newspapers threatened the populace with a movement to suppress the custom entirely unless the rough practices ceased. That year a lady was struck on the head by a brick and knocked unconscious while viewing the parade from her balcony.

For a number of years an organization in Mobile, who called themselves the "Cowbellion de Rakin Society," had been holding elaborate parades in their city each year on New Year's Eve. In 1852 the Mobile Cowbellions journeyed to New Orleans for Mardi Gras and paraded in the streets with tremendous success. However, the most spectacular organization on the march that day was the Company of Bedouins, the largest and most extravagant pageant yet to be seen in the city. "There were thousands of these maskers," said the *Daily Picayune*, "disguised as beasts, camels, bedouins, chanticleers and Englishmen, some on foot, others on horseback, in carriages, or in wagons." They were bombarded with flour and bonbons, despite the fact that the throwing of any objects was now illegal. Happily there are no reports of the tossing of lime or brickbats.

A tragedy ruined Mardi Gras in 1854. A few nights before the balcony of the Théâtre d'Orléans collapsed while a great carnival ball was in progress, killing and injuring many persons. Only "Boys with bags of flour paraded the streets, and painted Jezebels exhibited themselves in public carriages," commented the *Bee* on that Ash Wednesday, adding that perhaps this would be the end of Mardi Gras, and admitting, "We are not sorry this miserable annual exhibition is rapidly becoming extinct. It originated in a barbarous age, and is worthy of only such." The conservative editors of the *Bee* had long been enemies of Mardi Gras.

The *Bee* was to be disappointed. On Shrove Tuesday in 1855 the largest street pageants ever seen in the city were out and there were thousands of maskers. However, it was a rough year. A woman and a child were badly injured by a masker on horseback. A "wild Indian" hit a man on the head with a club. The *Daily Orleanian* reported in a shocked tone that a masker had been caught impersonating a priest, referring to him as ". . . a scoundrel whose privileged liberty degenerated into insult." Scores of citizens were arrested during the day. Two thousand persons assembled for a ball at the repaired Théâtre d'Orléans. There were over a hundred other balls in the city during the week preceding Mardi Gras alone.

Yet Carnival continued to fall into disrepute. Other newspapers joined the *Bee* in denouncing it as having become increasingly disreputable. The Creoles blamed it on the Americans, and the Americans blamed the Creoles. It is true that the festivities were becoming more and more rowdy. There was much drunkenness and fighting and subsequent filling of jails. "Licentiousness reigned again," was about all the *Daily Delta* said of the celebration of 1856.

Most of the newspapers began to campaign for a complete abandonment of the custom, citing two major reasons. One was the constant melees between white men and boys and Negroes. The whites, of a rough order and from that riverfront section known as the Irish Channel, took advantage of the day and their masks to make open war upon the Negroes, whom they hated with all the racial animosity of the ignorant and because the Negroes were competing with these poor and hard-working immigrants for work as longshoremen and wharf laborers. Many employers preferred to hire free Negroes because they were more docile and would work for smaller wages. This rivalry went on for decades, and until after World War I it was the boast of residents of the Irish Channel that no Negro dared to set foot in their neighborhood after dark, although by then the Negroes had won out in so far as employment on the wharves was concerned. In the 1850s the Irish Channelers did not wait for Negroes to enter their section, but often went, armed with weapons of every sort, into Negro neighborhoods to "get niggers." It was their principal Mardi Gras diversion, and on each Ash Wednesday the dead had to be counted.

The other objection the newspapers and the respectable portion of the population had against Mardi Gras was that the vast numbers of prostitutes in the city poured into the streets and into the best neighborhoods on that day, some of them with their men, sometimes in groups wearing the most daring costumes and behaving in the most brazen fashions. Through the streets of the old French Quarter would roll carriages of painted ladies from Basin Street, one of the most lavish and notorious red-light districts in the country, wearing tights and bonnets with plumes, or dressed as pages with long golden curls, their fat legs bursting in silk hose, their bosoms powdered and their dresses most décolleté. Others liked to dress as men, particularly as sailors, and this was considered shocking.

They would shout gay and obscene remarks from their carriages, or stroll along the streets, mocking the ladies who quite literally and pointedly would draw aside their skirts when they passed, making sly and insinuating remarks to the gentlemen, especially if they were accompanying ladies. Mardi Gras was a paradise for whores.

Some years there were wars among them too. Just as the Creoles and Americans divided themselves into uptown and downtown sets, so was there rivalry among uptown and downtown prostitutes, which on occasion broke into open fighting among all except those very elegant courtesans whose conduct outside of bed was as chaste as that of any Creole belle. And there were such. But the others, white, black, brown, yellow, and pink, would now and then form groups and march into each other's sections to start attacks that began with verbal blastings and ended with fists, sticks, and stones. Mardi Gras was a favorite time for this, when the heart was in high spirits and the inhibitions were released by alcohol and the gaiety of the season. Whores had their ballrooms in which they held forth with their own particular kind of festivity, and a favorite trick of one crowd was to crash the gate of some affair given by another. The result was always a brawl that necessitated police interference.

Prostitution was legal in New Orleans in those late 1850s, as it was until 1917, and the better houses had the protection of the city authorities and the police. Gentlemen would often as soon as possible flee the duller but respectable Mardi Gras balls to attend the ones given along Basin Street. These were not precisely sedate, but there was no trouble, and no fighting in most cases. However, there were others that were quite different. In Gallatin Street, for instance, where the police would not venture even in the broadest daylight, the murders showed a remarkable increase on Mardi Gras, although there was always bloodshed and excitement in that vicinity. In Gallatin Street the inhabitants' Mardi Gras costumes were very simple. Both men and women would wear masks for their dances, but they wore nothing else, except perhaps a knife or a gun strapped to a thigh or an armpit.

But Gallatin Street was a country garden compared with an uptown section on and around Girod Street known as the Swamp. It was a boast of the Swamp that not for twenty years had an officer of the law dared to set foot in the section, and that the half-dozen murders that occurred every week were never investigated, never even reported. Bodies were as a matter of custom left where they fell in the mud streets or on a saloon floor until the odors drove the inhabitants to toss them into the river. A man could obtain a drink, a woman, and a bed for the night for six cents in this neighborhood, although it was certain that if he had any other money on him it would be gone when he awoke in the morning—if he awoke at all. Women in the Swamp prostituted themselves for a few pennies—often, because they possessed no real roofs, under canvas tents of a sort, or on the banquettes and in the streets. All the women were terrible fighters, brawny and battle-scarred female savages, ready and willing to gouge out a man's eyes or to slit his belly or his testicles with a razor or a knife. Some bragged about the number of men they had killed. Their male companions were river boatmen or criminals who had sought sanctuary in the Swamp, where the police would not dare to follow them.

There was really little that the Swamp could do to commemorate Mardi Gras that could be counted upon to provide additional excitement, so on this day they would often wander in large numbers to Gallatin Street to exhibit their superior prowess, to tear the Gallatin Street dives to pieces, and to maim the inhabitants. These attacks and forays were not taken calmly by Gallatin Street, and when all had quieted on Ash Wednesday mornings the law, who had not dared interfere, would notice a larger than usual number of corpses floating down the Mississippi River. (It was perhaps poetic justice that later Gallatin Street displaced the Swamp as the toughest section of New Orleans, and that both sites are now among the most harmless parts of the city, although both maintained something of their reputations until after the turn of the present century.)

These things, together with a continued throwing of lime and bricks, were threatening to bring about the end of Mardi Gras in New Orleans when, in 1857, as the newspapers were predicting this Carnival would be the last one, there appeared in the streets of the city a display such as it had never seen before. No one knew it then, but this was not the end. It was a real beginning.

Of the day of that Mardi Gras little was recorded. The

newspapers noted that decent citizens had preferred to remain indoors, even indicating here and there that going abroad on Mardi Gras was now considered dangerous. The *Daily Crescent* commented, "The street maskers were a God-forsaken and man-forsaken set."

But rumor spread during the day that a new Mardi Gras organization intended to parade that night, and after dark the streets began to fill with Orleanians who stood waiting, just as they still wait, with tense excitement, not quite knowing what to expect. At nine o'clock Comus arrived; those who waited were well rewarded, and some of them knew they could have new hope for Mardi Gras, for this was a pageant such as the city had never seen before.

"They came!" said the *Daily Crescent* the following day. "Led by the festive Comus, high on his royal seat, and 'Satan, high on a hill, far blazing as a mound, with pyramids and towers from diamond quarries hewn, and rocks of gold; the palace of great Lucifer,' followed by devils large and devils small, devils with horns and devils with tails, and devils without!"

There were only two floats in that parade: one on which rode Comus, the other occupied by Satan, the rest of the maskers walking before or behind these cars. But these were the first real floats New Orleans had ever seen and it was the first parade by torchlight to be held in the city. Negroes carrying blazing flambeaux lighted the night for blocks, until the sky above glowed like fire. There had never been such a sight.

And that night at the Gaiety Theatre there was perhaps the most spectacular masquerade ball in the city's history, in which "The Demon Actors in Milton's Paradise Lost," was presented with four gorgeous tableaux, representing "Tartarus," "The Expulsion," "Conference of Satan and Beelzebub," and "Pandemonium." There followed dancing and then the members of the krewe gathered for a banquet that lasted until morning. Thus was the precedent for all future carnival balls established.

Not all the citizens approved of it. The Creoles were resentful. Their Carnival was facing failure. They examined the names of the men who had founded Comus. Every name was American, Anglo-Saxon. The Gaiety Theatre, where the ball took place, and which advertised itself as "the most magnificent theatre in the United States," was not a favorite Creole playhouse, but was frequented by "uptown society." Some few Creoles had been invited to the ball, to be sure, but by far the larger number of the three thousand invitations went to the Americans. Even those Creoles who had attended the ball began to feel they had been patronized. Why, they had found everyone there speaking English! It had been most insulting.

The French-language press, still powerful in the city even in 1857, decided to pretend Comus had not existed or else that the innovation was a slight and temporary one. The *Daily Orleanian* described the other balls that had taken place that night at length and in the gaudiest language, but did not once mention Comus. The *Daily Creole* was so piqued that it insisted that Mardi Gras and Carnival be abandoned at once, implying that the entire event was shifting into the hands of most undesirable persons. "This one," it said, "was unusually flour-y. Nothing else need be said about it here." The *Daily Delta* concluded their description of Mardi Gras with but a few lines about Comus:

When night came on, matters were not mended by the Mistick Krewe of Comus, each man habited rather as a "goblin damned" than a human being, perambulating the leading thoroughfares with torches. They went their way to the Gaiety Theatre, and there gave a series of infernal tableaux, more startling than pleasing. Pandemonium seemed the natural home of every one of them, and we doubt not that our surmise will be verified in the course of time. Then came the ball, in which devils and citizens strangely commingled, and thus the time wore away.

Carnival and the Creoles

Most bitter of all was the *Bee*, which admitted that the pageant of Comus had been brilliant, but in the satirical language of the period also poured forth insult upon the new organization, the editors being especially caustic because Comus had paraded through the uptown streets rather than in the Vieux Carré. They said that evidently it had been the krewe's intention to celebrate Washington's Birthday (which fell two days before Mardi Gras that year) — a deliberate untruth of which the editors must have been fully conscious. They added, "Such things will serve for a twelve-month," and concluded with: "their mobile movements rather indicate a Mobile parentage."

As to the Mobile parentage of Comus, of the floats and the flambeaux, that was true. A young man named Michael Krafft, who had been born in Pennsylvania and who had nothing that was Latin in him, had organized the Cowbellion de Rakin Society in Mobile in 1831. It was this organization which first paraded with torch and float, although in Mobile the pageants appeared on New Year's Eve. (Not until 1866 did Mobile have parades on Mardi Gras.) The entire conception of the parades of the Cowbellions and of those later to become popular in New Orleans seems to have originated in the minds of Krafft and a few of his friends.

In the 1850s some of these friends settled in New Orleans. First, missing the New Year's Eve celebrations, they organized a New Orleans version of the Cowbellions, and then some of them, observing the vulgarities into which Mardi Gras had sunk, decided to regenerate the holiday by demonstrating what might be done by using the Cowbellions' type of parade and ball. A meeting was called in the rear room of an uptown drugstore some months before the Mardi Gras of 1857, and six of the Mobileans gathered and prepared a very select list of names chosen from the leaders of the "uptown," American portion of the city. A little later nineteen men met in the clubroom above the old Gem

Saloon in upper Royal Street. Charles M. Churchill was elected captain, and Joseph Ellison was made chairman of the dress committee. The name of Milton's Comus was adopted, and then Ellison was sent to Mobile to secure the costumes suitable to the subject of the initial celebration.

As the Creoles gradually learned these details they became more irate than ever. Not one of the nineteen were Creole, and on the roster of those who played roles in that first pageant there were only six French names out of the eighty-three displayed. Days later the *Bee* denounced Comus as being composed of "swine-eating Saxons." Yet when the Krewe of Comus opened its membership to a limited few in addition to those who had already joined, Creole gentlemen as well as others applied for membership, and many of these were accepted. The little war was thus ended. On June 8, 1857, these gentlemen organized themselves into the Pickwick Club, which still exists as a closed and very exclusive social club. Then Mardi Gras as it is today began to take a new form that was not French or Italian and that bore almost no resemblance to any European variety, but was the original conception of an Irish and Dutch Pennsylvania American, at least as far as its outer trappings were concerned, and that at last had found its proper setting in New Orleans.

CHAPTER EIGHT

THE LORD OF MISRULE

*D*ESPITE THE CREOLE PRESS, THE MISTICK Krewe of Comus found itself famous after that first spectacular performance, and as the Mardi Gras of 1858 approached it was upon Comus that the entire attention of the city was turned. The day seems to have been a quiet one. There were many maskers out, but few disturbances of any importance. The press reported that "the painted women were out as usual," but the Swamp and Gallatin Street seem not to have gathered for battle, and in other sections the atmosphere was calm. As if searching for something to describe, several newspapers reported the appearance of a young man whose hoop skirts stretched the width of the Canal Street banquettes.

When darkness arrived, however, said the *Daily Crescent*, "the whole city was in motion." There were masquerade balls everywhere. The Creoles were holding forth at the Théâtre d'Orléans and there was a tremendous affair at the Théâtre de l'Opéra. There were dozens of smaller affairs, in halls and theaters and homes.

But before the balls began fifty thousand persons gathered

in the streets to see the brilliant second pageant of Comus. This year the parade had extended its route to include a part of the French Quarter and the ground covered was very much the same route through which Comus still proceeds each year. St. Charles Street and Rue Royale were both ablaze with torchlight as the parade passed, and happy Orleanians of both population sections gaped and cheered with wonder and pride at this new kind of Mardi Gras.

The subject Comus had chosen this second year was "The Classic Pantheon." No one was disappointed in it, for the parade was far more splendid than the first one. Presented in thirty-one parts, some of the subjects were represented by maskers on floats, some in carriages and wagons, others walking. The float bearing Comus was followed by one on which Momus, who would one day lead his own parade, appeared for the first time, then came Janus in his temple of the four seasons. The car of Bacchus was drawn by leopards. A car of flowers showed Flora surrounded by gigantic butterflies. Oxen drew the wagon upon which Ceres rode, eagles that occupied by Jupiter, peacocks that of Juno. Apollo appeared in his chariot of the sun. Night was drawn by a bat, Aurora by a winged horse. Vesta stood before an altar of fire. There was Destiny riding his dragon, Mars in his war chariot, Minerva drawn by owls, and Diana, drawn by stags and followed by the nine muses. And all about them, before them, and behind them were the white-clad Negroes bearing the torches and flambeaux that gave the floats and figures a magical and grotesque reality and lighted the scene through which they passed to daylight brightness. To add to the merriment, bands of music played stirring marching tunes and Creole songs.

The parade terminated at the Varieties Theatre (the new name of the recently rechristened Gaiety), where the ball was being held. Four tableaux were presented before an audience so overcrowded, said the *Daily Crescent*, that "the gentlemen were obliged to content themselves with standing places in the rear." The ladies' "rich toilettes were transcendently beautiful." A pamphlet published by the Pickwick Club in 1929 stated that the parade and the ball had cost $20,000, an enormous amount in those days, and still a large expenditure for any Mardi Gras organization of today. After the ball there was the usual midnight supper for the krewe members, held in a private dining room of a restaurant, "where champagne flowed and all were merry."

On Ash Wednesday the English-language press was lavish in its praise. The *Daily Crescent* said it was the most brilliant and novel affair New Orleans had ever seen and that not within the memory of the oldest inhabitant had there been anything like it. Even the Creole newspapers were kinder, much kinder. Some of the editors had been invited to the ball and Creoles were now members of the krewe. The *Courier* shouted its praises as a thing of marvelous beauty. Only the *Bee* remained aloof, satisfying itself with a gentle smile of approval.

That the news of Comus had spread beyond New Orleans was evidenced by the fact that in 1859 thousands of visitors came to New Orleans to see Mardi Gras for the first time; until now only a few hundred had come, and these from towns or from the nearby plantations. Now began the annual visits of crowds that filled the city, which have been recurring every year since.

New Orleans either behaved well, or misbehaved well, according to how you look at it, for that first large group of tourists. Gone were the quiet and peace of 1858, which some of the residents must have thought of as a rather nice year now. In 1859 even the residents of Gallatin Street decided to see how the other nine tenths lived, or at least how they celebrated Mardi Gras, and emerged from their neighborhood to disport themselves in the streets with the more respectable citizens. All the women of Gallatin Street dressed as men and all the men dressed as women, and they paraded the streets all day long, getting thoroughly drunk and singing songs that sent many Orleanians fleeing back to their homes. They also picked a great many pockets, beat up a number of persons, and murdered four, including one officer of the law who had the effrontery to stop some of them and question their behavior.

Basin Street was out, too, better behaved, but adding their bit: great, buxom women, painted and curled and dressed as Egyptian beauties, riding by in their carriages, blowing kisses as they passed, or wiggling a stockinged leg over the side of a carriage. Others dressed as sailors, which seems to have been a favorite costume among them, and walked about Canal Street, their suggestive shaking and conduct blanching the face of many a female spectator. Flatboatmen reeled by, fighting and brawling among themselves and with others. Boys were out with bags of flour, whitening everyone who came within reach. Men on horseback, dressed as Arabs and cavaliers, dashed through the streets all day. Others, in feathers and war paint, galloped past, uttering terrible war cries. It was, altogether, a wonderful Mardi Gras. Only the denizens of the Swamp seem to have remained at home sulking, or celebrating in their own peculiar fashion.

"The English Holidays" was Comus's theme that year, and the parade again surpassed the previous one. There were, according to the *Daily Picayune*, a thousand flambeaux-bearers, which seems an incredible number. Comus was followed by Twelfth Night, represented by a masker whose costume was a gigantic cake, so large it reached from curb to curb in Royal Street. There were great papier-mâché figures, some twenty feet tall, portraying Gog and Magog, Santa Claus, and Piper Heidsieck. There was the Abbot of Unreason, Midsummer Eve, Puck and the Bear, the Lion and the Unicorn, Titania, Bottom wearing the ass's head, Robin Hood and his Merry Men, and many, many others, floats being used in some representations, wagons and carriages for others, many more walking.

Comus had a great deal of trouble that year in satisfying the demand for invitations to their ball, and finally discovered that not even all those who should have received them could be supplied. A few days before Mardi Gras notices were placed in the newspapers which warned all readers that the doors of the Varieties Theatre would open at nine and close at ten and would remain closed all throughout the affair. "The Committee of Reception," it concluded, "who will be known by their rosettes, will escort the ladies to their seats, and to and from the different parts of the house. Gentlemen will not be permitted to occupy seats until all the ladies are seated. All invitations being personal, no transfer of tickets will be recognized." And on Mardi Gras morning the *Daily Picayune* said that "men go about, taking as much pains to secure an invitation to the great ball, as if they were electioneering for some fat office: supplications, introductions, recommendations, are all put in motion, and even bribery would be attempted if it could effect the thing. . . ."

The doors of the Varieties Theatre opened at nine that evening and shortly after ten they were closed, but outside some three thousand persons stormed about demanding admittance. The police had to clear the scene. Only those invited—and not all of them—got in to view the magnificent tableaux.

Even the *Bee* acknowledged that the Mardi Gras of 1859 had been quite a success, although the editor remarked that the "conduct of a certain element was outlandish and revolting, especially with our fair city filled with visitors," and that the maskers "lacked in quality rather than quantity as compared with other years." However, the *Daily Picayune* said, "It is probable that the mysterious society known as the Mistick Krewe of Comus, by their perfect organization and brilliant and tasteful display have inspired the community with the old feeling and love of fun so long dormant." Thus did Comus receive full credit for the success of this 1859 Mardi Gras, and for a renewal of the public's interest in the festival.

"Statues of the Great Men of Our Country" was the subject of Comus in 1860, and the newspapers agreed that this would be the most splendid of all the pageants to date. But on Mardi Gras morning it seemed that there would be no chance of any parade appearing. The streets filled with maskers almost at dawn, then, suddenly, as noon approached, the skies overhead blackened and a gale of wind swept through the city. There came pelting rain and sleet that drove the celebrants into cafés and saloons and their homes. It was one of those infrequent storms that have now and then struck New Orleans. The streets flooded and there was considerable property damage. Roofs were stripped of slates, chimneys toppled. Uprooted trees and sprawling lampposts lay about. At the wharves ships broke their moorings and crashed into each other. In the cafés maskers consoled themselves with bourbon and absinthe, with wine and beer. The result was fights and brawls and orgies that smashed all records for arrests in the city's history.

Late in the afternoon the storm passed and those maskers who could still see returned to the streets. At once it was almost as if there had not been a storm at all. Out came the carriages and the men on horseback, the bags of flour and the sacks of bonbons, the latter reappearing that year in great number, to be thrown at passing maskers in vehicles. Soon the crowd was making up for the lost time, frolicking and dancing about, and feeling it was a good Mardi Gras after all. They also tossed lots of mud that year.

There were fifteen cars in the Comus pageant when it appeared that night. Each one was designed as a block of granite upon which rode figures that were living statues of historical personages in American history. Orleanians saw Columbus, Cabot and Ponce de Leon, Bienville, John Smith and George Washington, Henry Clay, William Penn and Andy Jackson. The thick black mud of the streets trapped and bogged down the cars, and before the parade was completed two of them were so stalled that the maskers had to desert them and proceed to the ball on others. But, all in all, it was a fine success. Everybody liked it but the editor of the *Bee*, who wrote, "The various characters were not worth a description, either for whom they were or for those uptown citizens concealed behind the masks," and returned to chewing his pen, or whatever it was he did in his spare time. At the ball there were ten tableaux, all illustrative of American history, a subject Creoles did not like too well.

But a far greater dissension than that between the uptown and downtown portions of New Orleans was approaching, and these petty animosities were soon to be forgotten. That storm of 1860 might have been distant cannon, and the thick mud that seized and held back the wheels of Comus might have been the gnarled fingers of war trying to stop the parade.

Since the advent of Comus nothing has suspended Mardi Gras in New Orleans except war. In 1861, the first time it came, New Orleans does not seem to have known just what to do, and despite a war that was inevitable the citizens attempted to hold their celebration as usual. Louisiana had seceded from the Union, but maskers filled the streets that Mardi Gras, and, if anything, the day was a little gayer than usual. A number of organizations paraded in the afternoon —the Young Men's Society, the Jolly Fellows, the Celestial Empire Club, all walking clubs. Boys were in the streets throwing the forbidden flour. The prostitutes were about. The *Daily Picayune* remarked that it was the merriest celebration in years. Only a small degree of political satire seems to have been noted. Men in blackface carried an effigy of Abraham Lincoln riding a split rail.

When Comus appeared that night it was evident some economies had been practiced, for the entire procession marched on foot, and the theme, "The Four Ages of Man," and all the characters, which included Vice, Virtue, Fraud, Folly, Jealousy, Murder, Gluttony, Faith, Hope, Charity, and many others had to be represented by costumes, since there were no floats. But the Ball of Comus was as costly and as splendid as ever that night, and numerous other balls were in progress until dawn in all parts of the city. If anyone felt that tragedy was now in descent it was not betrayed by their behavior. The *Bee*, even with its last breath, exhibited its customary prejudice and stated that the most elegant ball was of course not Comus, but the French Ball at the Grand Opera House.

In 1862 there was no Carnival. The war had absorbed all attention, all manpower, all money. Farragut's fleet arrived at the wharves of New Orleans on April 25, just a few weeks after the date of Shrove Tuesday. On May 1 came Ben Butler. Yet even that year the date had not been forgotten, and on Mardi Gras morning Comus had addressed his subjects through the newspapers, as follows:

Whereas war has cast its gloom over our happy homes, and Care usurped the place where Joy is wont to hold its sway. Now therefore, do I, deeply sympathizing with the general anxiety, deem it proper to withhold your Annual Festival, in this goodly Crescent City, and by this proclamation do command no assemblage of the Mistick Krewe.

Given under my hand, the first day of March, 1862

Comus

But even before the war was over some vestiges of social life seem to have revived in New Orleans, and in 1864 there was a rather feeble attempt to hold Mardi Gras. Some children appeared in the streets in costume and a few adults celebrated in the cafés. That night a hundred balls were in progress, but most of them were attended only by federal troops in uniform and the women of the town. There was a more successful one the following year. The streets filled with maskers, although there were no parades, and the theaters and ballrooms were well attended. Two Creole organizations gave large affairs, but it was whispered that only the names were the same, that it was a device of the forces of occupation, and that those citizens still loyal to the South remained at home. A few weeks later the Confederacy collapsed and the Civil War was over. Later in the year the Pickwick Club reassembled and plans for the return of Comus were begun. Yet another year passed.

Mardi Gras was on February 13 in 1866. Almost at dawn maskers began to appear, anxious and hungry to enjoy the first genuine Mardi Gras since the war's beginning. All day long informal processions of maskers, walking or in carriages, paraded the streets. Balls were scheduled at the Varieties, the St. Charles Theatre, the hall of the Young Men's Society, at the National Theatre, and at scores of other places.

Comus issued two thousand invitations and these were much sought after. Ladies again donned evening clothes and jewels, as many of them had not done in years. The male maskers exchanged their uniforms for the bright garb of the parade. Appropriately, the subject that year was "The Past, the Present, and the Future." All were on foot, but again the torches and the flambeaux glowed in the streets, again the bands of music struck up their tunes of love and laughter, again there was cheering and applause for the maskers as they passed through St. Charles and Canal streets and through the narrow Rue Royale, where, upon the overhanging ironwork balconies, pretty women, their gowns and jewels and flowers sparkling in the red glare from the

Mardi Gras

torches, waved and blew kisses at the men, many of whom bore the wounds of war beneath their satin and tinsel costumes. The Past, a large group, tried to depict the horrors of war. The Present showed the blessings of peace, with the maskers dressed as Science, Industry, Law, Agriculture, History, and Art. The Future was composed of a group who represented Peace and Plenty.

"The Triumph of Epicurus" was the subject the next year. Still on foot, the Krewe of Comus achieved effects that it is doubtful have been matched until now, in so far as originality is concerned, despite the absence of cars or floats. Through their costumes and by suggestion an entire colossal menu was worked out, the maskers marching in the following order, each man or group of men representing a certain article of food or drink:

Absinthe   Sherry   Bitters   Epergne

Oysters   Johannisberger

Soupe à la Tortue   Soupe à la Julienne

Salt Cellar

Shrimp   Crawfish

Crab   Lobster

Butter

Celery   Pickles

Horse Radish   Claret   Club Sauce

Codfish à la Jonathan   Sheepshead à la Shoddy

Westphalia Ham   Irish Potatoes   Boarshead à L'Ecossais

Candelabra

Knife   Fork

Peas   Corn   Pumpkin   Squash

BŒUF GRAS

Beets   Rice   Carrots   Cabbage

Bread   Tomatoes

Candelabra

Mutton Venison Epergne Pork Potatoes Turkey

Peacock Duck Macaroni Bird Pie Chicken Curry

Chicken Marengo Partridge Pie Snipe Sausage Epergne

Candelabra

The Lord of Misrule

Frog	Lettuce	Salad	Fork and Spoon		Coleslaw
Cauliflower		Castors		Artichoke	Asparagus
Ice Cream	Jelly	Epergne		Pudding	Strawberries
Macaroni		Champagne		Sherry	Meringue
Banana	Fruit	Pineapple	Melon	Nuts	Burgundy	Candy

Candelabra

| Omelette Brûlé | | Cigars | Coffee | Whiskey | | Brandy |

Kirsch and Curaçao

It was a magnificent pageant, with the living candelabras in their glittering golden costumes perhaps the most beautiful of all. The ball was huge, with Comus and his court departing for their midnight banquet, at which, it is said, nearly every article of food and drink upon the menu they had portrayed was served.

The occupation authorities dimmed Mardi Gras a little in 1868, although they did not suppress it entirely. The year before there had been scattered criminal acts and a United States official had been found murdered, wearing a scarlet clown's suit. All parades but that of Comus were refused permission to parade and a regulation was established that banned all after-dark masking except by those who were members of the Comus parade. The ban against night masking has become a part of Mardi Gras tradition. Even now all masks must be off by six o'clock.

The carpetbagger was a favorite costume on Canal Street during the day, and each was cheered at sight. A masker dressed as a huge ape attracted much attention by constantly chasing Negroes. On the other hand, newly freed Negroes affronted the racial feelings of the whites by their bold behavior and constant flaunting of their release from slavery.

Comus presented "The Departure of Lalla Rookh from Delhi." There were horsemen in the parade, and other maskers rode in palanquins on the backs of "elephants," each "elephant" consisting of several men under an appropriate elephant costume. Besides the usual flambeaux, Japanese lanterns strung on bamboo poles lighted the scene. A number of persons tried to force their way into the Varieties Theatre to see the ball, and a riot was narrowly averted when some of them, indignant because they were denied admittance, began cries of "Fire!" in an attempt to start a stampede. Several women were injured.

The Varieties Theatre burned to the ground in 1869, a loss to the city that was at the time thought irreplaceable. Comus was forced to present the tableaux of "The Five Senses" at the New Opera House, which would be called the French Opera House a few years hence. It is interesting that when the French Opera House burned a half century later it was considered an ancient building, a landmark of distinction and great prestige, which indeed it was, but the year Comus held its first ball there it was looked upon only as a substitute for the Varieties, then still called "the most magnificent theatre in America," and members of the krewe and their guests felt it was a poor one for the theater they had lost.

In 1870 a new organization with a costly parade and an elegant ball made its debut. This was the Krewe of the Twelfth Night Revelers, a club that lasted only seven years and had little connection with the Twelfth Night Revelers of the present time.

This pageant appeared on the street on Twelfth Night, January 6, to officially commence the carnival season, and those who viewed it had to admit that it rivaled Comus in every way. There were nine floats and many maskers on foot, these being divided into four groups representing Europe, Asia, Africa, and America. Over all reigned the Lord of Misrule. The parade was followed by a ball at the New Opera House, where after two tableaux the Lord of Misrule led Cleopatra and the court in a grand march, preceded by four court fools carrying a huge cake. This grand march was

more or less an innovation, of which the Twelfth Night
Revelers were to contribute several.

Until now no carnival krewe had ever had a queen. Male
maskers performed all tableaux and then summoned ladies
from the audience for dances, although not quite in the manner of present-day call-outs. Now, for the first time, a queen
was to be chosen, in this case by the method of receiving a
golden bean concealed in a slice of cake. The grand march
completed, the maskers cut the cake with their spears and
began the distribution. However, all did not go as planned.
They were so overwhelmed with merriment that they began
to throw the cake at the ladies, instead of serving them in a
more genteel manner. Many ladies received cake upon their
immaculate laps instead of in their hands. Other pieces fell
short of the boxes and were crushed on the floor. If any
belle received the coveted bean she evidently did not approve of the extreme hilarity, for she never revealed her identity, and that first year Twelfth Night Revelers had no queen
after all.

As a whole the year was a rough one. There were about
thirty thousand visitors in the city for Mardi Gras, among
them Dr. Mary E. Walker, who the *Times* said must have
been "badly disgusted at how she was out-Heroded" by the
women from Basin Street and other red-light districts, who,
like the famous woman doctor, were on the streets in male
attire. There were some fights, three murders, and a house
set on fire by overjubilant maskers, despite the fact that
many police were on duty, one even being assigned to each
streetcar in the city. Gallatin Street and the Swamp met in
one of their classic battles, but here the injured and dead
were not reported, and probably not even counted. At the
Comus Ball a number of ladies had most of their clothing
ripped from their backs while trying to gain admittance.
At another two socially inclined females were knocked unconscious and had to be taken to the hospital. The next day

the *Republican* complained that "society ladies need more than one or two balls, so that all may enjoy the gorgeous and jolly spectacles."

The Twelfth Night Revelers were better behaved in 1871, and Miss Emma Butler received her bean in a proper and dignified manner and with it the distinction of becoming the first Mardi Gras queen in a New Orleans festival. That year, for the first time, the names of feminine guests at balls and of those recognized viewing the parades from balconies were published in the newspapers, it having been hitherto thought undignified for any lady's name to appear in print.

Two other new customs came into being that year, too. All maskers and groups of maskers, on foot or in vehicles, were invited to meet at the Clay Statue at the foot of Canal Street at four-thirty in the afternoon. There a parade of all who gathered was formed, which marched and rode through the streets of the city until almost dark. The other new feature was the appearance of serenaders in carriages or wagons, on horseback or on foot, who went through the city playing music and singing before the residences of friends and on street corners. Both these customs were popular for many years. Comus presented "Spenser's Faërie Queene" that year in a procession of thirteen floats, the largest parade of floats yet seen, and there were the usual number of fights and disasters, including at least six murders. That year, too, the Varieties Theatre was rebuilt and reopened in time for the Comus Ball.

CHAPTER NINE

REX AND THE ROMANOFF

*H*IS IMPERIAL HIGHNESS ALEXIS ROMANOFF Alexandrovitch, brother of the heir apparent to the throne of all the Russias, grand duke of the Empire, lieutenant in the Imperial Navy, was a restless young man. Tall, dark, and elegant, with a reputation for amorous conquests that extended the length and breadth of Europe and reached into Asia Minor and the British Isles, and with fame as a sportsman that covered India and Africa, he was still dissatisfied with life. He wanted to shoot an American buffalo. So the grand duke, unable to extinguish this ambition, arrived in New York on November 21, 1871, aboard the Russian frigate *Svetland*, which was escorted by the corvette *Bogatir* and the clipper *Abreck*. It is probable that he had then never heard of Mardi Gras in New Orleans.

There was much excitement when he arrived in New York. However, the ladies on the pier were under control and the police present were not even called upon. There were some appropriate speeches, some good loud music, and then a noisy military parade to the Clarendon. Cannons were fired, New York yelled its head off, and Trinity's chimes rang out with the Russian imperial anthem.

The grand duke discovered that when a grand duke sets out to shoot buffalo there is a great deal he must do before he ever sees one. A few days after his arrival he was received by President Grant and the Cabinet of the United States, and there followed a series of receptions, banquets, balls, and newspaper interviews. His Imperial Highness then embarked upon a grand tour of this country and of Canada. He went to Boston, where the school children entertained him by singing "Wake, Gentle Zephyr," and where there was a banquet and a ball. He went to Toronto, Montreal, and Ottawa. He visited Niagara Falls, where, according to a newspaper account, the sight of the falls "made his imperial blood curdle." In Cleveland he was literally mobbed by admiring women. In Detroit he was "worshipped by the fair and young Michiganderesses." In Chicago he was taken to the stockyards, to the scene of the fire, and was entertained by the mayor, to whom he gave $5000 for those persons still in need because of the recent conflagration.

He met Buffalo Bill in St. Louis, invited him to join his party, and then proceeded, via Omaha and more receptions and dinners, to a spot on Red Willow Creek, where a "Camp Alexis" had been established, and where he spent several days hunting buffalo with Buffalo Bill, Sheridan, Custer, and a number of Indian chieftains. Here he became enamored of an Indian maiden known to posterity only as "Spotted Tail's sister," who accompanied the party when it moved on to Denver, where a mountain peak was christened "Peak Alexis," more buffalo were hunted, and the grand duke was nearly killed by two enraged bison. After that he seems to have forsaken Spotted Tail's sister, when the party left for Topeka.

Before leaving New York His Imperial Highness had met another lady, Miss Lydia Thompson, a musical-comedy star, who was playing the leading role in *Bluebeard*, and he had been enraptured by her singing of "Up in Mormon Land," "The Mandolin," and an absurd little ballad entitled, "If Ever I Cease to Love." He had entertained Lydia at a late supper after the theater and had begged her to sing that ballad over and over again, not knowing that he was selecting the famous theme of Mardi Gras and because of this that the song would attain immortality in a city he had never seen and, according to all evidence, did not then ever expect to see.

Now, his shooting completed, he inquired about the pretty actress and learned she had taken her company on tour. His Highness then decided that he had not seen nearly enough of America, and he set out to visit, in turn, Jefferson City, Louisville, and Memphis, which were the very cities in which Lydia Thompson was appearing, although he missed the show in Memphis, the company having left for New Orleans just before he arrived.

The date was one late in January, and Mardi Gras was to be on February 13 in 1872. It seemed reasonable to accept the invitation to visit the New Orleans festival that was among the large collection the grand duke had received. It might be amusing to view this mock royalty that seemed so odd in this democratic country. And Lydia Thompson was to be there. A message was sent the imperial squadron to move to the Gulf of Mexico to await His Imperial Highness's pleasure, and an elegant river steamer, the *James Howard*, was chartered for the trip down the lower Mississippi River.

When the citizens of New Orleans learned that the Grand Duke Alexis was to attend Mardi Gras there was excitement and confusion, for they seemed to have doubted that they would be so honored, despite the fact that more and more visitors were being attracted by the Carnival, including many distinguished ones. The last-minute preparations were hurried and somewhat disorderly, but at last the streets were especially decorated, reception committees and military societies organized, and Comus rushed an invitation to their ball down to the river front to meet the *James Howard.*

Some of the excitement was due to the fact that there had lately been no small amount of apprehension within the city. Carpetbaggery had reached its most unfortunate phase and a number of Orleanians were already meeting in secret and planning revolt against the current Administration. Many persons, also, viewed the approach of Mardi Gras with growing alarm. The past one had not been without acts of violence, and they feared that this time Orleanians donned costumes and masks an outbreak of terrorism might result. Yet a grand duke did not often visit the city.

It was in an effort both to render the day more placid and to welcome the visitor that prominent citizens, a group including members of the federally appointed government and those of the opposition, decided upon the formation of a new krewe and upon the selection of a "King of Carnival." A dozen days before Mardi Gras the first edicts of the first Rex appeared. These asked that the "wandering maskers" organize into a procession on Canal Street, that the governor of the state of Louisiana close his office from 3 P.M. until sunset "to refrain from the exercise or attempt to exercise any gubernatorial privilege and to disperse that riotous body known as the Louisiana State Legislature for those hours," that the courts be adjourned at noon, that all places of business shut up at one o'clock, that schools and post offices take a holiday, and, finally, that all citizens behave themselves and refrain from malicious mischief of any sort, including the throwing of flour. The mayor promised Rex the full aid of the police department. Then Rex sent His Imperial Highness the following special message of welcome:

Rex and the Romanoff

His Royalovitch Highnessoff the King of the Carnival, officia llywelc omest one worle ansh isroy alcous inth emostp uiss ant Duke Alexis Alexandrovitch Romanoff, andwi llh o ldaspe ciala udie ncef orh Isrece pti on atsu nse ton Mardi Gras.

REX

There is no record of what Alexis thought of that, but with all the other messages of welcome he received there came an invitation from Lydia Thompson to attend the performance of her company in *Kenilworth* at the Academy of Music.

The actress had played New Orleans before and she was a favorite of the city. A baseball team had been named after her, among other honors that had been conferred, and when the gossip spread that she and the grand duke were acquainted, aside from the chagrin of some female socialites with a taste for titles, her importance increased. Popular novels and plays of the period were filled with romances between actresses and royalty. Did not all New Orleans recall, too, how, some years ago, but within the memory of living persons, Lola Montez, who had also had a baseball team named for her and, who, furthermore, had been kicked by a jealous New Orleans swain—doubtless the only time she was ever kicked, too!—had gone on from such beginnings to become a countess and the sweetheart of the King of Bavaria? All New Orleans turned the eye that was not watching this new Rex and the rest of Mardi Gras upon Lydia and Alexis.

The *James Howard* arrived in the city at nine o'clock on the evening of February 11. A tremendous congregation, largely feminine, rushed to river-front wharves for a first glimpse at His Imperial Highness. Gentlemen in evening clothes waited with prepared speeches. Musicians tuned their instruments with patience and smiles. Then three of the grand duke's staff disembarked and informed those who waited that His Imperial Highness would not leave the steamer until the following morning, and that they would represent His Highness at the opera that evening, the enter-tainment planned for the royal entourage. Alexis and the balance of his party spent that evening aboard the boat dancing quadrilles. One likes to believe that Lydia was there, but we don't know that she was.

The steamer was moored to the Gravier Street wharf the following morning and the reception committee was back, including a great many more breathless ladies than had been out the night before, all of them chattering and flutter-ing about under their parasols, and asking each other if they had practiced their curtsy. Or did one curtsy to a grand duke? Was it true Alexis had stated in Cleveland that he thought American women were the most beautiful in the world? His Highness was said to be most democratic and a fervent admirer of all things American. Where was Lydia Thompson? But certainly Miss Thompson could not be *here*. Even if she and the grand duke were *friends*, with all her charms, she was an *actress* and she would be out of place.

At ten o'clock Mayor Flanders arrived. Then Admiral Poisset marched down the gangplank beside Alexis, who was resplendent in the uniform of a lieutenant in the Imperial Russian Navy. Admiral Poisset began to address the as-sembled Orleanians in French. The mayor and his commit-tee smiled and informed the admiral that those present did not speak French, that New Orleans was now governed by English-speaking authorities. The admiral was surprised, but he managed a few words in English. Next day the *Bee* com-mented with pride that few if any Creoles had been present at the arrival of the grand duke, and that thus they had demonstrated their disapproval of Mayor Flanders.

But Alexis was little concerned with politics. Smiling and gracious and as democratic as the ladies had heard, he bowed and beamed and then entered his carriage, which took him to his hotel. There, during the day, he gave inter-views, punctuated by luncheon with the city dignitaries.

In the evening he attended a performance of *Il Trovatore* at the Opera House. His later activities that night are unknown.

Mardi Gras was the next day, and it was a fine one, the weather warm and sunny, the Mardi Gras decorations more splendid perhaps than they had ever been. There were thousands of maskers in the streets before noon, and the grandstands along the banquettes were filled with spectators, most of them women, for in those days nearly all the seats in the balconies were reserved for ladies. Before the City Hall in St. Charles Street a dais had been erected for Alexis. Above was a canopy of crimson silk adorned with golden fringe and tassels. Beneath was the closest approach to a throne that could be found in New Orleans. Here Mayor Flanders and Governor Warmouth received His Imperial Highness in the afternoon, with thousands of women crowding the grandstands on either side and across the street, and even filling the street below.

Then a wholly unpredictable thing occurred. The grand duke refused to sit upon his throne. The mayor and the governor protested with smiles, then pleaded, but without success. No, said Alexis, in quite excellent English, he preferred to stand with the others. He did not really understand this at all. He appreciated their intention, but was not this a democratic country? He was amazed at this reverence for a title in a nation that had rejected titles. Had not their own Mr. Thomas Paine said something on the subject —something about titles being only nicknames at best? He was here, the honored gentlemen must understand, only as a lieutenant in the Imperial Russian Navy, and he preferred to be treated as such.

The dignitaries were piqued, but they did not further insist. The feminine admirers of Alexis were disappointed almost to the point of illness. They talked of it for years afterward. They had longed to see Alexis on his throne.

Mardi Gras

There had never been a Mardi Gras parade in New Orleans that contained so many maskers as that first parade of Rex. A conservative estimate has placed the number at ten thousand, and it is probable there were many thousand more. Composed of carriages, wagons, and marchers on foot, it stretched for more than a mile.

Rex and his assistants gathered the maskers on Canal Street early in the afternoon, but it was three o'clock before the procession started from the Clay Statue near the river front. The parade moved down Royal Street from Canal Street, with more and more maskers falling in behind as it passed, circled through the Vieux Carré, and returned to Canal, then up St. Charles Street.

Rex was Louis Salomon, a merchant and businessman. Wearing purple velvet embroidered with rhinestones and a jeweled crown, his face painted, but not covered with a mask, this first King of Carnival rode on horseback, waving a hand in a purple glove as he passed his applauding subjects. He was followed by a Bœuf Gras, a white papier-mâché figure, adorned with garlands and flowers and surrounded by butchers in white smocks and caps. Behind came carriages, mule-drawn vans and wagons, bands of music, horsemen, and marchers. At the City Hall Rex stopped his horse and drew up close to the grandstand where Alexis stood beside the empty dais. They exchanged a champagne toast. Alexis bowed stiffly. Rex waved merrily and moved on.

When the first band reached the City Hall there was a surprise for Alexis, for they were playing his favorite song, the one Lydia Thompson sang in *Bluebeard*, now transposed to march time. The grand duke did not smile and no one knows what his reaction was, but band after band took it up, as they passed, and then some of the people in the street began to sing it, adding a parody that was later said to have been written by Lydia herself:

Rex and the Romanoff

If ever I cease to love,
If ever I cease to love,
May the Grand Duke ride a buffalo
In a Texas rodeo. . . .

The grand duke stood perfectly still and said not a word to any of the dignitaries near him.

In the first Rex parade Alexis saw many things that must have seemed strange to him. There were Dan Rice's famous troupe of trained animals, carriages of Chinese merchants in magnificent costumes, impersonators of the Ku Klux Klan on horseback, carriages filled with sailors with extremely buxom figures and painted faces, satirical and bitter representations of President Grant, Abraham Lincoln, even of the governor and the mayor beside him, troupes of actors from the theaters, Arabs, American Indians and savage-looking Turks, and a stream of maskers on foot in every conceivable costume, including a few who were dressed in what were representations of himself. And, perhaps most mystifying to him, there were the vans and wagons advertising things: the Old Gem Saloon, Warner's Bitters, the Singer Sewing Machine, Mme. Tigau's Elixir for Ladies, the Old Reliable Furniture Company, and Dr. Tichenor's Antiseptic. Advertising remained a part of some carnival parades, particularly of Rex, for some years after that, but eventually went out of fashion.

Mr. Salomon endorsed many products in newspaper advertisements that year, which appeared both before and after Mardi Gras. The readers of the New Orleans press were told where Rex bought his clothes, that he ate at Mme. Begue's when he ate out, but that at home he cooked upon Buck's Brilliant Stove, that in the evenings he attended the Varieties Theatre, that he drank at the St. Charles Hotel and at the Ramos, and that he bought his poultry and eggs at Chick Lalande's Stall in the French Market. Advertising endorsements were widely popular in the newspapers during the 1870s. Robert E. Lee endorsed half a hundred articles, including Buck's Brilliant Stove, the same stove used by Mr. Salomon.

Returning to Canal Street, it was nearly dusk when Rex disbanded his parade. The maskers then danced in the streets in the fading light, and later by gaslight and without masks until it was time for Comus to appear.

Comus presented "The Dreams of Homer" that year, and Alexis was again in the City Hall grandstand to view the brilliant night procession. As soon as the parade was out of sight, he was taken to the Varieties, where a special box had been prepared for him, and here he viewed the nine tableaux and remained a little later to watch the dancers. But again His Highness was disappointing. Many of the ladies and gentlemen at the ball approached his box and extended a hand, but Alexis either kept his right hand behind him or pushed it into his jacket. He shook hands with no one. Perhaps he thought democracy had its limits. Furthermore, and even more heartbreaking in its effect upon the belles present, he sternly refused to accept any hints from the entertaining committee that he might dance. He danced with no one.

Perhaps Alexis was displeased, it was whispered next day. It may have been the parody of "If Ever I Cease to Love" which he had considered in bad taste. No one knew, but it was said he never saw Lydia Thompson again. The night after Mardi Gras he attended a play and became so infatuated with the leading lady that he remained in New Orleans for four more days, refusing most of the invitations extended to him, failing to keep at least one appointment with Lydia Thompson, and presenting his new little friend with a bracelet of diamonds and pearls when at last he departed New Orleans forever.

CHAPTER TEN

KINGS, KREWES, AND KLANS

*P*ERHAPS ALEXIS NEVER KNEW IT, PERHAPS HE DIDN'T
care, but his influence upon Mardi Gras in New
Orleans had been extensive, and because of his brief visit
the day became a legal holiday, Rex remained a permanent
addition to the celebration, and "If Ever I Cease to Love,"
ridiculous little song that it is, attained immortality. In return, although the rest of the world has almost forgotten
that he ever lived, the grand duke remains forever famous,
and in a way cherished, in at least one corner of the earth.

But Rex was not the only krewe that appeared in 1872
for the first time. On New Year's Eve of that year, when
it was almost time for another Mardi Gras, the Knights of
Momus appeared in the streets with a torchlight parade. It
was a small organization, composed of younger men than
those who took part in Comus, many of them sons and
nephews of the latter, we are told, and it was not so rich
or spectacular an exhibition. The theme of the pageant was
"The Talisman," and most of the maskers were on horseback or on foot. There had been political changes in New
Orleans that year, after which Mayor Wiltz, an administra-

tor more acceptable to most Orleanians, now occupied the City Hall, and a historical action of the first Momus parade was a stop at City Hall to present the new mayor with a badge of loyalty. Four years later, in 1876, the Krewe of Momus changed the time of their parade and ball to the Thursday night preceding Mardi Gras, at which time they appear now.

Rex had held no ball in 1872. Neither had there been a Queen of Carnival, for as yet only the Twelfth Night Revelers chose a leading lady. In 1873, however, the first Ball of Rex took place.

That year was the one in which the general pattern for Rex's entire carnival behavior was drawn. On Mardi Gras at about eleven o'clock in Front Street, along the Mississippi River, His Majesty, the King of Carnival, arrived on horseback and, attended by his dukes, bands of music, and various military organizations in the city, rode through the streets to the City Hall, where two hours were spent in toasting and drinking the health of everyone present. At one o'clock Rex and his staff joined the parade at the Clay Statue and then headed the procession through the traditional route of city streets. It was that year that the illusion of Rex's journey from a Far Eastern country was begun, which has persisted since. In 1874 Rex and his courtiers arrived in the Mississippi at the foot of Canal Street on the day before Mardi Gras and held a noon military parade on that Monday, parading again with floats on Tuesday. This custom continued until World War I. Now Rex supposedly arrives by air, but there is no daytime parade on Monday.

The 1873 parade was in six divisions, in which at least half the city seems to have participated, leaving only the other half of the population as spectators. In the first division came a wagon of the Southern Express Company, upon which a masker bore aloft a red banner that ordered: MAKE WAY FOR THE KING! Then came a squadron of

police, followed by four heralds, trumpeting the approach
of His Majesty. Mayor Wiltz and members of his staff came
next in a carriage, then a half-dozen military organizations
and some bands of music, one military detachment encircling three pages, who walked, carrying upon satin pillows
the key to the city, the jeweled crown, and the orb. Mounted
pages trailed this group, bearing the royal mace, banner,
shield, and sword. Then came Rex, and, according to the
Handbook of the Carnival, published in 1874, "His Majesty
was robed in a brilliantly-hued Egyptian frock, sparkling
with jewels and fringed about with gold, while at its front
he wore a golden breastplate, from whose burnished surface
the sun reflected its rays with dazzling brightness." Most of
the costumes of the krewe were Egyptian in motif, and
eighty noblemen, in splendid Egyptian costumes, followed
His Majesty in a long line of carriages, and behind them
came four hundred mounted Bedouins, then a company of
the 92d Lancers on horseback and also dressed as Bedouins.
Next there appeared, in a carriage, a masker, reputed to
have weighed 446 pounds, who represented the "Daughter
of the Regiment." The Royal Navy followed—twelve small
boats mounted on huge floats, with Real Admiral John
Clemens and a crew occupying the first vessel. After that
there were several bands, then about eight hundred maskers
on foot. At last came the great Bœuf Gras, a real steer this
time, his horns decorated with apples and the rest of him
draped with garlands of flowers.

The second divison was led by the "Master of the
Horse," and there followed two hundred guardsmen in suits
of chain armor, wearing gilded helmets topped with plumes
and carrying spears, scimitars, and glittering broadswords.
There were at least three bands of music, then the Ancient
Order of Oxonians, representing the meat industry. Next
came the State Lancers dressed as crusaders, then several
hundred maskers on horseback and on foot.

Mardi Gras

Seven large floats depicting the "Seven Ages of Man" were the principal features of the third division, which was led by the Lord of the Carriages, who was followed by seventy-five carriages filled with maskers.

More floats followed in the fourth division, which were trailed and interspersed with wagons, carriages, horsemen, and marchers. Many of these floats were satirical and made fun of the snobbishness of the Pickwick Club and the new Boston Club, and similar organizations.

Division five was led by the Lord High Sheriff of the Guilds, and it contained some six thousand maskers in wagons, carts, vans, and on foot. This consisted largely of advertisements, signs, designs, banners, and maskers' costumes urging the spectators to buy Pelican Fertilizer, Carter's Mucilage, Darcy's Hats, Septoline Oil, Tarrant's Seltzer Aperient, English Baking Powders, and Leighton's Premium Shirts. Others advertised Philip Werlein's Pianos, the Original Express Company, the Babcock Self-Acting Fire Engine, the Robert E. Lee Stables, Carré's Portable Cabins, the Kansas Pacific Railroad, and many other companies, products, and articles, including at least six different brands of sewing machines and nine different brands of whisky.

The final divison of the parade was of course also the longest, for here, preceded by the Lord of the Unattached, almost all the maskers in New Orleans fell in, walking and in every conceivable type of vehicle then invented. A rough, although not reliable, estimate placed the number of maskers in this last division at more than twenty-five thousand.

For his first ball Rex had rented the Exposition Hall at a reputed rental of $2000 for the night, and here the Rex Ball was held for years afterward. Four thousand invitations were issued and the tiers erected for the occasion were jammed with people in all kinds of dress, from carnival costumes to their Sunday best, although evening clothes were not much in evidence. There were no tableaux at all. The ball began by the parting of the huge folding doors between the throneroom and the ballroom and the appearance of Rex upon his throne surrounded by his court. The orchestra played "If Ever I Cease to Love," which has begun each Rex Ball since, and to the already traditional tune Rex and his nobles marched around the ballroom floor.

It was known to many persons present that a queen was to be selected, but it seems perfectly true that no one, not even the lady to be chosen, had any knowledge of her identity. Many a girl and woman, it is said, was certain she was to be the one, and waited with mounting excitement for His Majesty to send for her, receiving a terrific shock of disappointment as the court passed slowly by. At last Rex, who was in private life E. B. Wheelock, paused in front of Mrs. Walker Fearn, a young matron whose husband was in diplomatic service and would one day become United States minister to Greece, Serbia, and Rumania.

Mrs. Fearn, according to one of her descendants, was completely astounded by her selection and a little embarrassed. The possibility of her selection had been so far from her mind that she was not even dressed for the honor, but was wearing her second-best black silk and a black bonnet, the clothes that she had worn all day while watching the parades and the maskers. It is impossible to imagine a present-day carnival queen in her second-best black silk and a bonnet and without a jewel or a flower, and Mrs. Fearn resisted at first, saying that she was not properly attired, but Rex put at his feet the silk cushion he carried and commanded her to kneel. Hesitantly Mrs. Fearn untied the strings of her bonnet, tossed it to her husband, and fell to her knees with a nervous smile. Then His Majesty summoned his pages, who fastened the magnificent mantle of Rex to her black silk shoulders. His Majesty placed a jeweled crown upon her head, and, the orchestra still playing "If Ever I Cease to

Love," led her to her throne, then announced that their subjects would be received and greeted. The reception that followed lasted only forty-five minutes, the people in the tiers coming down to the floor to greet Their Majesties. There was no dancing that year, and when the allotted time was over Rex, his queen, the court, and a few selected guests departed through a rear exit for a private celebration.

That night Comus presented "The Missing Links to Darwin's Origin of Species," both the subject and the conduct of the pageant itself causing no little excitement. When Comus appeared in the streets the spectators realized at once that the entire parade was political satire and an attack upon the federal Administration, and that each of the "missing links" represented a Republican official. The Hyena wore a mask that was Ben Butler's face, the Tobacco Grub was without a doubt the image of President Grant. There were only two floats, the other maskers marching on foot and wearing papier-mâché costumes, in many cases with huge heads. Asses heading each group carried large lighted signs, then called "transparencies," each of which bore the verse of a poem, and in pointed doggerel assailed the Republicans with thinly disguised satire. It was the first parade in which all the cars, costumes, and masks were invented, designed, and manufactured in New Orleans. The designs were by Charles Briton and the construction was under the supervision of George Soulie. The firm of Soulie and Crasson have been building almost all carnival floats ever since.

The march of Comus that night was short. The police who had been promised to escort the pageant did so, even after they realized the meaning of the parade, but on Canal Street they were met by hundreds of angry men who blocked the way and refused to allow the procession to go on; some of them carried firearms. The parade was then dispersed without any attempt to enter the lower section of the city, the Vieux Carre, where thousands of spectators awaited, and the maskers went at once to the Varieties Theatre for their ball.

The next day the *Times* contended editorially that the theme of Comus had been really an attack upon Darwin and his theories, and then proceeded to blast the whole theory of evolution. This article and a copy of a souvenir booklet describing the parade and containing the verses that had appeared on the transparencies were sent to Charles Darwin, to which he replied:

DEAR SIR:
As I suppose that Comus and the newspapers were sent in good faith, I thank you for your kindness and for your letter. The abusive article in the newspaper amused me more than Comus; I can't tell from the wonderful mistakes in the article whether the writer is witty, ignorant, or blunders for the sake of fun.
> Yours faithfully,
> CH. DARWIN

In 1874 Momus offered "The Coming Races," which seems to have been in imitation of Comus's parade of the year before. Twelfth Night Revelers presented "Dolliana and Her Kingdom," and, as they had in the previous year, selected not only a queen but a maid of honor, thus keeping a little ahead of the others. Comus, still without adopting the custom of choosing a queen, which they were not to do for many years yet, used "The Visit of Envoys from the Old World and the New to the Court of Comus" as a theme. Rex made his first "arrival" by water on the Mississippi River, and paraded briefly on the Monday before Mardi Gras and, again on Mardi Gras in a long pageant containing many thousands of maskers, the organization using a Persian motif in their floats and costumes. Rex that year was W. S. Pike, and his queen was Margaret Maginnis, her choice as an unmarried girl for Queen of Carnival setting a precedent that has never been broken since. Another such precedent was established when the Court of Rex left their own ball after the grand march and a short reception to join the court of Comus in another building, a custom still followed each year.

There was an attempt to change the carnival song from "If Ever I Cease to Love" to one written by Mary Ashley Townsend, a local poet, who wrote under the psuedonym of "Xariffa" and attracted national attention for many years. This poem, set to music, appeared in the newspapers all during that carnival season, its verses describing the journey of Rex from his mythical kingdom to New Orleans. Rex issued a royal edict just before Mardi Gras, designating it as the "national anthem" of his realm and titling it "The Soldier's Song." In a further effort to establish its popularity Lydia Thompson, again in New Orleans, sang some of the verses at the Academy of Music. But it was all unsuccessful. After that year "The Soldier's Song" began to fade from memory, but decades later "If Ever I Cease to Love" was still being played in the streets and at the balls on Mardi Gras.

There was no Mardi Gras in 1875. Again there was war in New Orleans, not admitted nor declared war, but very real nevertheless. The historic street battle between the Crescent White League, composed of a military organization and civilians, and the metropolitan police had taken place on September 14, 1874, with victory for the White League. It was short-lived, for federal troops, under the command of Lieutenant General Sheridan, soon arrived and restored order. Carnival was scheduled to take place as usual. All the parades were ready and invitations to some of the balls had gone out when, on January 4, General Sheridan, fearing trouble, and knowing that many of the members of the krewes had been White League members also, banned the celebration. There had been no pageants, for that year Momus had planned to appear on the Thursday before

Mardi Gras instead of on New Year's Eve, and Orleanians and the visitors (not many yet were present, although it was said the hotels were nearly filled) were informed of the canceled events by a notice inserted in the newspapers by Twelfth Night Revelers on the morning of the very day, January 6, which explained that the krewe was compelled to "postpone their annual festival to a more fitting season," but promised that they would return.

That year was the last one in which political events ever played any major importance in Mardi Gras. Even that year children and young people attempted some unofficial and unsanctioned celebration, and Mardi Gras morning a few were in the streets in costume, as well as several thousand persons who apparently had not read the newspapers and were preparing to await Rex. Then there occurred that disaster that can ruin any Mardi Gras, regardless of anything else. It rained. The kings of Carnival smiled in their beards.

Twelfth Night Revelers held their last parade in 1876, a pageant of thirty-three floats, longer and probably more elaborate than any parade today. Momus appeared for the first time on the Thursday evening before Mardi Gras. The Queen of Carnival was Cora Townsend, daughter of Xariffa, the poetess.

Political events never stopped Mardi Gras again, but in 1877 Momus caused considerable excitement by presenting "Hades—A Dream of Momus." In this Dantesque spectacle Momus maskers appeared on their floats as denizens of hell, who bore strong resemblances to the Cabinet and other department heads of the government in Washington and to certain dignitaries and officials in Louisiana. Beelzebub was remarkably like Grant, and as easily recognizable were Adrammelech, with the features of Secretary of State Hamilton Fish; Baal, who was certainly Sherman; Lucifer, who looked like Landaulet Williams, Secretary of the Department of Justice; and dozens of others. What followed threatened for a time to be fairly serious. The most angered were the brass hats of the Army, many of whom had been depicted. Never again, they asserted, would troops of the United States take part in a carnival parade. Not even an army band would be allowed to march with one. A high-ranking army officer told the masker who had portrayed Beelzebub that if the identity of Beelzebub were ever discovered he would shoot him personally. Washington protested against a display "which insulted and professed to caricature the President, the General of the Army, the Ministers, members of the Cabinet, and leading officials of the United States." Governor Francis T. Nicholls of Louisiana finally apologized for Momus in a telegram to Washington and branded the satire as "the act of a few private individuals, entirely unauthorized and unknown, and universally condemned and regretted." But among those maskers were some of the most prominent men of New Orleans, including Edward D. White, who years later became Chief Justice of the Supreme Court of the United States, and was appointed to that high office by President Taft, whose father had been cruelly caricatured in that Momus parade.

That year Rex appeared with a parade consisting only of floats, bands of music, and military organizations. The promiscuous maskers who had formerly joined behind the parade were banned from doing so, and the advertising vans were forbidden, although some forms of advertisements trailed loosely behind, as if determined not to be discouraged.

There was consternation that year, too, when two of the invitations to the Comus Ball were stolen, or at least so it was thought. The blood of New Orleans aristocracy was curdled with wrath and indignation and chilled with horror that some outsider might get in. We learn that "every precaution against admitting the culprit or culprits was taken."

A reward of $1000 was offered in all the newspapers. The invitations were never found, but they were never used.

As Mardi Gras of 1878 approached all was quiet. Rex decided to be most elegant that year. Until now almost any kind of apparel could be worn to a Rex Ball, although Comus had already instituted formal attire as a requirement. For the first time Rex made a similar stipulation. According to the notice posted in the press, the Lord High Chamberlain now wanted "it to be plainly understood that no gentleman will be admitted unless he is in full ball dress, and that ladies must come without bonnets." As a result of the fact that many even of those who might receive invitations were not prosperous enough to possess evening clothes during that period, a great many Orleanians were angered. Rex dispersed fifteen thousand invitations that year, but only three thousand were used, and the vast majority of them by women, who needed only to go without their bonnets.

A new organization, the Phunny Phorty Phellows, appeared for the first time, following Rex, in 1878, a small krewe then, that rapidly grew in size, and, always accenting the comical, was one of the most popular parading clubs that ever appeared.

Momus was again in disfavor after their 1880 parade, but this time it was the ladies of New Orleans who were wrought up, rather than the government in Washington. Their theme that year was "A Dream of Fair Women," and their burlesque did not please many of the fair women who watched them pass. The press was also indignant and the *Democrat* commented that "it was a perfect nightmare" to see "the lot of gorgeously appareled brawny men who hid their beards and mustaches behind false faces." The *Daily Picayune* ignored the parade entirely. The *Bee* received comfort from the fact that Zenobia's throne, on one of the floats, collapsed and that "she" almost broke her brawny neck. Again it was the Lupercalia.

Eighteen-eighty was the year, too, in which Comus offered "The Aztec People and Their Conquest by Cortez," which attracted attention from writers all over the world. The visitors in the city were estimated at nearly seventy thousand, the largest crowd in the history of Mardi Gras. Rex arrived in the river aboard the famous *Robert E. Lee* on Monday, but on Tuesday was rivaled by the appearance of the Phunny Phorty Phellows with a parade as long as Rex's own, and one that was much more appreciated. Both Rex and the Phunny Phorty Phellows included the Bœuf Gras in their parades that year, Rex's a real one that was later butchered, a custom that endured for many years after that, but the Phunny Phorty Phellows exhibited a monstrous and comical animal that was actually a jackass in disguise and bull make-up.

The Krewe of Proteus, who still provide one of the most beautiful parades, appeared on the Monday evening before Mardi Gras in 1882. Joseph Shakspeare, the mayor of New Orleans, was King Rex that year, and Frances Isabel Morris was his queen. Following the brief formalities of the Rex Ball, the monarchs and their court joined the Ball of Comus, where Comus, still without a queen, led Lula Carter in the first quadrille, then danced with Queen Rex. It was 1884 when Comus first allowed women into his court. That year, seated in boxes in the French Opera House, where the ball was being held, were the girls writers of the period always call romantically the "five daughters of the Confederacy"—the daughters of Robert E. Lee, Jefferson Davis, Stonewall Jackson, and D. H. Hill. After the tableaux Comus led Miss Mildred Lee out for the first dance, and other krewe members danced with Miss Mary Lee, Miss Julia Jackson, Miss Nannie Hill, and Miss Varina Davis. Although none of these young women were then called "queen," this was the beginning of the long line of Comus queens which followed. All the other large krewes now had queens—Momus from the third ball they had presented, Proteus from the very first one.

It was after that year that misfortune knocked Comus from his throne for a while. Financial difficulties had come to the Pickwick Club, and for five years it seemed that the first of the great New Orleans Mardi Gras kings was through. In 1885, after Comus announced there would be no parade and no ball, Momus obtained permission to appear on the night of Mardi Gras in the place of Comus, which they did, offering "The Legends Beautiful" as their theme, a subject that was all sweetness and light and entirely untainted by anything that could be offensive to anyone. As if in appreciation, Rex and his court joined the court of Momus that night at the French Opera House, after their own reception.

But virtue did not seem to be rewarded in the case of Momus, for the next year Momus, like Comus, suffered some money troubles and vanished. That year, 1886, Proteus quickly changed over to parade on Tuesday night, and were also rewarded by the visitation of the King of Carnival and his entourage.

Now Proteus held first place after the King of Carnival himself as the leading monarch, and he held fast to that honor. The French Opera House was his on Mardi Gras night, and it was he who received the visit of Rex. Mardi Gras night was his time to parade. Momus reappeared in 1887, but was forced to accept the former Monday night place of Proteus, and then collapsed once more in 1888.

These Carnivals without Momus and Comus were, however, anything but dull. In 1885 Rex departed from the custom of arriving on the river and came to the city on the Illinois Central Railroad, then rode a white horse to the river front, where, together with his court, he led a water pageant on the Monday afternoon preceding Mardi Gras. In 1887 the Queen of Carnival, while being entertained by an admiral aboard the *Tennessee,* saw some sailors in the brig and indignantly demanded that they be released, a command the admiral obeyed at once. During those years, too, the men who had composed the Krewe of Comus were, without using the name, still holding lavish balls on Mardi Gras night, inviting exactly the same stratum of society as had attended Comus, but using a smaller invitation list and holding the affairs in the rooms of the Pickwick Club.

The Edison Company provided a parade of incandescent lights in 1889. The current was supplied by batteries and dynamos mounted upon vehicles, each of which required sixteen mules to pull it through the streets. From these ran extension cables, and each participant in the parade was supposed to hold aloft a lighted electric bulb or to have one or several of the lights attached to his person. This idea, taking place in the year electric lights were first used in street decorations, does not seem to have been successful. First scheduled for the Saturday night before Mardi Gras, it was canceled again and again for various reasons, appearing at last on Ash Wednesday night, when there had never before been a parade and when all good citizens were supposed to be doing penance for their sins. By now many Orleanians were thoroughly frightened of the whole thing and it was widely believed that the least of the catastrophes that might occur was the electrocution of the paraders. Some believed a terrific explosion that would raze the business section of the city was practically inevitable. So when the hour of the parade arrived less than a third of the marchers showed up and only the morbidly curious were out to witness the expected mass electrocution. Nothing happened, except that the maskers who wore electric-light bulbs on their heads and set on their shoulders and arms sweated a lot as they passed in review, and that the general effect was much tamer than that which had been promised in that year's *Carnival Edition,* the annual publication then

sold on the streets every Mardi Gras, and which was written during the 1880s by Lafcadio Hearn.

In 1888 the people in the streets awaiting the Rex Parade
were charmed or shocked, depending on their natures, by
a procession of snow-white carriages drawn by snow-white
horses and inhabited by Basin Street prostitutes dressed not
in sailor suits or any other male attire, but in all their splendid finery, including hats weighted down with ostrich plumes
of every conceivable color. Those who didn't like it protested, so the ladies were back in 1889 in larger numbers
than ever, some of them smoking cigarettes! This was the
cause of much startled comment.

It was in 1889 that a tipsy fireman, summoned to put out
a tiny blaze on the second story of a building in St. Charles
Street, turned his hose upon all in the vicinity. A horse ran
away with a parading duke that year and came to a halt
only when he had reached the interior of a saloon, an event
that so delighted the owner of the saloon that he tried to
present the dignified and irate masker with a dozen bottles
of the finest bourbon.

The throwing of flour had nearly vanished, although it
was to return, but Rex was pelted with candies, doughnuts,
and eggs in 1889. From one grandstand on Canal Street the
privileged sitting above amused themselves by throwing
coins into the crowd below. In another three young men
emptied bottle after bottle of champagne upon maskers in
the street, with results that almost caused a riot, as the
maskers fought with each other to get their mouths beneath
the golden streams. The police arrived and took the young
men to jail.

Before the year 1890 had begun it was announced that
Comus would again appear. The krewe had severed its old
connection with the Pickwick Club, and most of the former
members had decided to form a separate organization,
which would be self-supporting.

This little announcement caused much consternation among the members of Proteus. The captains met. When would they parade? asked the captain of Proteus. On Mardi Gras night, of course, said the Comus official, as they had always done. But the date belonged to Proteus now, complained the captain of that krewe. Proteus, said Comus, must return to their Monday night schedule. Ridiculous, said Proteus's captain. Then, said the captain of Comus, there would be two parades on the night of Mardi Gras. What about the French Opera House? asked the Comus captain. It was already engaged, the Proteus captain said triumphantly. They parted in humors that were not to improve as Mardi Gras grew closer.

When the date arrived each krewe, starting out, was determined to reach Canal Street first, for both were so angry that neither had revealed to the other their plan of march or any of their intentions. Comus had started first, but had suffered several minor accidents that delayed the parade, so that Proteus was first in Canal Street and had already completed its parade on one side when, torches blazing, Comus entered from the other end. It was a double spectacle that suited the people lined along the banquettes, for the entire length and breadth of the street was lighted with flambeaux, and in every direction they looked were the towering, rocking floats in their vivid colors and grotesque designs, and the two kings, covered with satins and jewels, presented one of the most splendid sights New Orleans had ever seen. But soon there was trouble. Proteus reached Bourbon Street and turned down it toward the French Opera House. A few flambeaux had vanished when Comus, proceeding out the lower side of Canal Street, came to a halt, blocked by the float on which Proteus sat glaring at him over his beard. Neither could move. The two captains came galloping up and were soon side by side on their prancing horses.

The captain of Proteus was a Creole. The captain of
Comus was an Irishman. While the two kings remembered
their dignity and contented themselves with icy stares interspersed with gracious waving at the much amused crowd in
the streets, the captains began to lose their inhibitions and
their tempers. Proteus was going through, said their captain.
The hell they were, said the Comus Irishman. They must
wait until Comus, who was the real monarch of Carnival,
had passed. Neither would give way. Proteus said it was the
fault of Comus for being so delayed, that now Proteus had
the right of way. The Comus captain declared Proteus
would proceed only over his dead body. The Proteus captain said they would love to do just that. Then they became
more personal, each telling the other what he thought of
him and his ancestors. It went on for some time, and the
rival kings were having difficulty in remembering that they
were above such bickering. A riot might have resulted, for
maskers on both sides were restraining other maskers from
leaping to the pavement and deciding the argument by combat. Then out of the bystanders emerged a mysterious
stranger in a domino, the cowl concealing his features, who
took the reins of the Proteus captain's horse and led him
away from the Comus official. At last Proteus waited while
Comus passed, the captains yelling out final jeers at each
other.

As Comus went its way and Proteus stewed about, the
police—apparently because they felt they had to arrest
someone—carried the man in the domino off to jail, where
he identified himself as the brother of the captain of Comus
and as being a member of both Comus and Proteus, who
decided to take no part in either parade, partly because he
did not wish to choose sides, but partly because he had
foreseen what might and did occur.

But this was not the end of the night's problems. Rex had,
it seems, been in a quandary for weeks. The situation was
most delicate and very serious.

Mardi Gras

For four years now the Rex court had joined that of Proteus, yet for a long time before that it had been Comus they had visited. Which was he to favor tonight? Invitations had been received from both.

A council was held and the majority opinion was that Rex should revert to the tradition of attending the Ball of Comus, Rex agreeing. But could he not visit both courts? He consented to that, too, but he would go first to the one of Comus. Thus there still remained the necessity of showing a preference, with no way to avoid it.

The Comus Ball was at the Grand Opera House that year, and when Rex and his court entered they were welcomed with applause and acclaim, and the King and Queen of Carnival were conducted to a box on the right side of the proscenium. There were toasts with Comus and his first real queen, who was Kate Buckner, and the dukes and four maids, and then with Momus and his court, who occupied a box at the other side of the ballroom. A little later Rex and his queen visited Proteus at the French Opera House. The reception they received is said to have been cool.

Comus and Proteus were rivals again the next year, again parading on the same Mardi Gras night, but this time there were no clashes, at least not in the street. Again Proteus had obtained the French Opera House, while Comus had to be satisfied with the Grand Opera House. The next year Proteus, at the insistence of some of the members and of friends who wanted to attend both balls, returned to parading on Monday night, the date on which they still appear, and both krewes were able to use the French Opera House.

Since then there has been peace. Even those captains who nearly fought it out on Canal Street became intimate friends, and many of the members of one krewe always attend the ball given by the other. Rex, at least in his role as King of Carnival, now goes only to the Ball of Comus.

CHAPTER ELEVEN

ANOTHER CENTURY

*T*HE FRIENDSHIP BETWEEN THE KREWES IS NOW, despite rivalry in some ways, quite warm. Many Orleanians are members of more than one organization, and on occasions the same man has been chosen king of several balls, although seldom in the same year. Even in the larger krewes this will occur now and then. Rex has been the Proteus or the Comus of a year or two before. Once, however, a single gentleman was king of nearly all the krewes in existence, and in the same year. He was even both Proteus and Comus, who, a few years before, had glared each other down in the torchlight that brightened the intersection of Canal and Bourbon streets, when their parades collided.

This happened in the 1890s, when so much happened, and when everybody is supposed to have been gayer than they had ever been before or will ever be again. During that decade numerous new krewes, who did not parade, were formed. Over each reigned a secret set of kings and dukes, but queens selected from the debutante ranks and also debutante maids whose identities were not only published but flaunted, although not until the day after the ball, and whose choice was—and still is—a measure of their social success.

It was Atlanteans who first invited this prominent Orleanian to be their king that year, an honor he accepted with the profound appreciation and the utter seriousness with which prominent Orleanians always accept such an honor. A few days later, at a meeting of the Knights of Momus, he was asked if he would impersonate Momus. He could not have given his reason for refusing even if he had wanted to do so, since he was bound by an oath to keep Atlantean's secret, so, smiling, he accepted with the modesty with which Napoleon received the crown of France. Some days later he attended a Proteus confab, an organization to which he also belonged, for he really loved Mardi Gras, and was there informed that he was to have the honor of being Proteus on the Monday night before the big day. There was nothing he could do but accept. He went from there to see his friends and fellow members at Comus, and there a great surprise was awaiting him. He was to be Comus. Nothing could tear carnival secrets from his lips, at least yet, so he bowed humbly before the ruling of the powers. But then came the final impressive decision that at last made him break at least one vow. A committee from Rex called upon him and told him he was selected to rule as the King of Carnival. There was nothing he could do then but confess that he was also to be Comus, and since the two monarchs must meet in the grand march at the Comus Ball, and he could not possibly manage to meet himself in a grand march, someone else would have to be chosen. He ruled well and splendidly over all the others, changing costumes and jewels nearly every night for a week, and was recognized by only a few close friends.

Carnival, always a chameleon, took on the whimsies, the manners, and the morals of the nineties. The balls and midnight suppers became more lavish. Krewe members began to present their call-outs with such expensive presents that many protested and some parents made their daughters return the costly jewelry or too personal gifts presented to them for a single dance. Real pearl necklaces, diamond pins, and combs of gold and jet were not unknown. The poverty that had followed the Civil War was gone and many of the members of the organizations were wealthy, none of them poor. One year the golden bean drawn by the queen of the new Twelfth Night Revelers, who did not parade, turned out to be a tiny gold watch. Other queens received bracelets blazing with emeralds or rubies.

The balls themselves became extremely formal. Women guests began to rival each other with expensive gowns and jewels, such as they wore only to the opera, and no one was admitted in street clothes. Men were required to wear formal attire—top hats and tails. Not even dinner clothes were permitted.

Before 1900 there were already many krewes, some of which had brief lives, others that still exist. Elves of Oberon, Nereus, Argonauts, Consus, High Priests of Mithras were some of the names they chose. Most of them adhered strictly to tradition, but others tried to introduce new ideas, most of these not receiving too enthusiastic receptions by tradition-loving New Orleans. An exception had been the call-out system, first used by Argonauts in 1900, who reserved five or six rows in the parquet for the young women who were to take part in the maskers' dances, instead of making them sit in the boxes and balconies with the other spectators. Proteus adopted the idea the same year and all the others soon followed.

In 1900 Nereus presented a street pageant of sixteen floats mounted on trolley trucks which rolled along the car tracks of St. Charles Avenue and Canal Street. It was a fine experiment, but not a successful one. Press and public complained that there were too many breakdowns, that the electric lights decorating the streetcar floats looked too artificial and destroyed the mystery and allure of a Mardi Gras parade and that they wanted no more, please. There were no more. Mules still draw the floats.

Eighteen ninety-nine was the year it snowed in New Orleans, which it has never done since in any perceptible amounts. But that year snow began to fall on the Sunday before Mardi Gras. Proteus called off their parade. Rex and Comus appeared on Tuesday, but there were not too many maskers out, although New Orleans children quickly adapted themselves and heaved snowballs at the maskers on the floats and had a wonderful time in general. The balls went on as usual, however, so society did not suffer anything beyond endurance.

The new Krewe of Consus scandalized that society, as well as amazed it, from the date of its first ball in 1897. In 1900 Consus had its orchestra play a funeral march while the tableau of the theme, "The Houseboat on the Styx," was enacted. For its final appearance in 1906 the krewe presented "The Land of Frontinback and Upondown," and the maskers wore their costumes backwards and their masks on the backs of their heads—with masks representing the backs of heads over their faces. Moreover, the padding of their costumes was so cleverly arranged that the debutantes who received call-outs actually had the sensation of dancing with someone's back, for the maskers protruded here, and, in the case of those dressed as women, as many of them did, there, too. The young ladies were somewhat indignant and their mothers, recalling the more proper affairs of a generation before, were outraged. Consus disappeared after that year, almost by popular request.

The Chinese minister to the United States visited the Mardi Gras of 1900 and attended the balls of Proteus, Rex, and Comus. He watched the maskers at the Proteus Ball giving the favors to their call-outs, which sometimes included a part of their costume, such as a jeweled badge or a mantle, the latter being a particularly prized gift. Wu Ting Fang was so charmed with the custom that he hastily removed his own mantle of heavily embroidered yellow satin and presented it to a rather startled but very pleased young woman in an adjoining box.

As New Orleans entered the new century its population was approaching 300,000, and every year at least 100,000 visitors came to see a Mardi Gras that was both the same in all its fundamentals yet vastly different from the Mardi Gras of earlier decades, and, like New Orleans, seemed very old but was also very young. The city was prosperous, with high hopes of continued growth and expansion, its health improved, with no more yellow fever epidemics, no more cholera to wipe out half its population.

There was still vice, but even it was more civilized, and the regulated red-light district known as Storyville was considered more of an asset than anything else. On Mardi Gras the women of Storyville did not often mingle with the maskers but remained in their own neighborhood, which now was spreading from Basin Street into the French Quarter, as they took over the houses left by the vanishing Creoles, who once had also possessed Mardi Gras. Now, on that day, visitors would wander through Storyville in the hours between parades, to gasp at the luxury of the gaudy establishment of Josie Arlington, "a five-dollar house," which was four stories tall and furnished with cut-glass chandeliers, ornately carved furniture, oriental carpets, huge beveled mirrors, and much gilt and satin upholstery. They would drop in at the Countess Willie Piazza's, where the girls were always in lovely Egyptian costumes on Mardi Gras, and at Lulu White's, where there were bedrooms with walls and ceilings composed entirely of mirrors. They could peep through shutters into the cheap cribs, where naked girls sat around awaiting patrons. They heard remarkable stories, such as the one about the new kind of music being played in Storyville called "jass," which was being introduced in other parts of the city but was considered rather indecent. They heard the story of Josephine Icebox, who was so cold that a prize of ten dollars in extra trade was offered to any man who could arouse her. They even heard a yarn—probably untrue, for several girls claimed the distinction—of the prostitute who had once been a member of a carnival court.

It was all amusing, all a part of New Orleans, and all a part of Mardi Gras, and the visitors enjoyed prowling through Storyville, the big brassy saloons the city offered, and the still wide-open gambling houses quite as much as they did attending the balls.

Costumers had sprung into existence all over the city, too. Visitors could buy or rent a large variety of disguises and this many of them did, the most prominent persons sometimes slipping into the city incognito and romping in the streets as a clown, a minstrel, or a flaming red devil.

More and more distinguished visitors came to New Orleans after 1900. Alice Roosevelt, as the "Duchess of the White House," occupied a special box at the Ball of Comus. In 1909 President-elect and Mrs. Taft sat upon special thrones beside the king of Oberon and Queen Laura Merrick.

Since the introduction of the floats there had not been many changes in the four major parades, Momus, Proteus, Rex, and Comus, as there have not been until now. Gone were the advertising vans and the bands of maskers who had once followed the King of Carnival, but some advertising wagons still trailed through the streets on Mardi Gras. The Bœuf Gras was still a part of the Rex parade, and he was still butchered on the following day and his haunches and the rest of his carcass divided among the members of the court, for now the queen and her maids received a good roast as well as all the other honors. Entirely missing from the parades even after 1880 was political satire or any political or racial feeling. Dissension of the sort that had existed between Creole and Anglo-Saxon and between Democrat and Republican no longer held an important enough place in the minds of Orleanians to allow it to intrude into something like Mardi Gras, which was really so much more important. There were Creoles, it is true, who still sneered at "uptown society," but they were a minority, whose children were marrying into it.

Mardi Gras masking underwent much change. Formerly great papier-mâché giants had been everywhere on Mardi Gras, monsters with huge and grotesque heads wobbling about on their necks. After 1900 they began to vanish, unfortunately, and no longer did two or three men appear in the street as a gigantic, realistic elephant, or a dozen forming a writhing serpent half a city block long. The interests of the day are always reflected in Mardi Gras costumes. Now minstrels in blackface, straw hats, and loud suits and ties became popular. The cartoons in the newspapers were favorites—Happy Hooligan, the Katzenjammer Kids, Mutt and Jeff. A little later it was Maggie and Jiggs and Buster Brown. Still later it was Dick Tracy and Lil Abner. Political figures were still impersonated, but good-humoredly. Teddy Roosevelt and his Rough Riders enjoyed years of popularity. (By World War I bitterness had returned and effigies of the Kaiser were carried through the streets suspended from a gallows. A generation later his place was taken by Adolf Hitler.)

Marching clubs were numerous in the early 1900s, some of which, such as the Jefferson City Buzzards and the Garden District Club, will probably live as long as there is Mardi Gras. Then there were others—the Broadway Swells, the Jassy Kids, the St. Roch Carnival Club, the Jan Jans, the Sons of Rest, the Vampy Vamps, and the Chrysanthemum Social Club. A rather short-lived organization of prominent Italians, who called themselves the New Era Club, paraded in the downtown section with floats and held a water pageant on the Mississippi River. The Crescent City Carnival Club also presented a small pageant of floats.

The Phunny Phorty Phellows, after disappearing in 1898 with the outbreak of the Spanish-American War, a fracas that did not otherwise suppress Mardi Gras, never returned, and their loss was probably the greatest the festival ever suffered. In 1896, for instance, they had held a parade of eighteen floats, under the title of "Phads and Phancies." The "Phad of Creation" showed Adam and Eve languishing beneath the apple tree in Eden, while a female ape tried to seduce Adam. "The New Woman" portrayed women riding bicycles and in the costumes of jockeys and baseball players, wearing bloomers and even smoking cigars.

But it was the stately and the elegant krewes that endured, and with so little change in the types of floats used and the styles of costumes that today they are almost exactly as they were a half century ago.

On the Mardi Gras before the United States entered World War I, and again on the first Mardi Gras after the end of hostilities, boys hanged the Kaiser in Canal Street and young women wrapped in American flags rode around on trucks bellowing "The Star-Spangled Banner." Otherwise the war made small change in the Mardi Gras pattern, except to suspend activities for the years 1918–19. Momus, Proteus, Rex, and Comus made no attempt upon their return to use any theme even remotely connected with it, partly as a matter of policy, but largely, also, because their floats were almost completed when war came and those used in the 1920 parades were the ones intended for 1918.

With the postwar celebration, however, came a reflection, in the costumes of the maskers, of the interests of the era and of the changes the war had begun. Many maskers depicted John Barleycorn and Prohibition, and poked fun at the advances of women and suffrage. Mah-jongg, Coué and the Teapot Dome scandal were also represented in Mardi Gras costumes and behavior as the twenties advanced.

Krewes continued to come and go. Even Alexis Romanoff was remembered, and there was an exclusive organization known as the Krewe of Alexis, over which, as in the case of Mystic, there reigned a married queen and maids who were also matrons. A new parade, presented by the United Ancient Order of Druids, a fraternal order of men of moderate means, who were not part of the top social layer of New Orleans, appeared behind Rex on Mardi Gras 1920, and continued to parade for years after that. Their floats were in the tradition of all the other pageants and were often as fine as any of the others, despite the comparative lack of wealth among those who paid for them.

Feminine krewes were becoming popular too. The first of these was Les Mysterieuses, who gave their first ball in 1900, and who had four queens, each of whom occupied a throne and had a half-dozen maids. At their balls the women belonging to the club were masked, and men occupied the call-out seats in the parquet. After an elaborate tableau the queens and maids then chose their kings and dukes. Les Mystérieuses lasted but a few years, but they had begun a new idea and they were quickly followed by such feminine organizations as Les Pierrettes, the Krewe of Iris, the Krewe of Aparomest, the Krewe of Iridis, the Krewe of Elenians, and others that came into being after World War I, some to quickly fade, but others to last until the present. It was not until the appearance of Venus in 1940 that women rode floats through the streets of New Orleans and Venus and her ladies are still the only ones who do so.

Mardi Gras

Huey P. Long did not like Mardi Gras at all when he came into power in Louisiana. Every man, said he, was not a king in so far as Carnival was concerned. Huey fumed a great deal over the snobbery of the krewes, and, frustated because of his inability to exercise any control over them, promised to eliminate the festival entirely or at least to alter it to his liking. The aristocrats ignored the dictator completely, did not include his name or the names of his supporters and friends on their invitation lists, and treated the whole matter with the indifference and disdain of Bourbons. Certainly those who composed the membership of the more elite krewes were the very persons most opposed to Long and all he represented politically and philosophically. A marching club satirized the Long promises by having every member wear a crown and royal robes on Mardi Gras and parading with banners upon which were inscribed the words "Every Man a King." And during the years of Long's rule individual maskers often dressed as the Kingfish, the title Huey had given himself.

It was the Elks who organized the Krewe of Orleanians in 1935, one of the two loosely knitted groups of maskers who follow Rex on Mardi Gras aboard the decorated trucks. Until then truck rides had been popular for years, but they had been unconnected and individual affairs that rolled haphazardly through the streets, appearing along the parade routes at unpredictable hours or confining their activities to outlying sections of the city. Now they became an integrated part of Mardi Gras, contributed much beauty and humor and merriment to the day, and, in a way, replaced the custom of decades before when most of the city's maskers had followed Rex during his procession through the city. In 1946 the Krewe of Crescent City was formed, the second of the truck organizations, which now follows the Orleanians and lengthens and enhances the parade that begins with Rex.

The Krewe of Hermes was organized in 1937 and gave its first parade that year, on the Friday night before Mardi Gras. It has been very successful, the parades beautiful and in what has become the stylized tradition, except that neon and electric lights are used on the floats, although the flambeaux and torches have been retained. Cynthius and Babylon, two other new krewes, also used neon lighting and electrical decorative effects on their floats.

Carnival was suspended for four years during World War II, the longest period during which New Orleans has been without any signs of the celebration. It was so long that many citizens worried that their young children didn't know what they were talking about when they mentioned Mardi Gras, and some Orleanians even worried that it might not return. But return it did, with new krewes and new parades and an expanding program that will increase its pleasure and its fame.

Signs of the times were plentiful when Mardi Gras was revived. In 1946 there was such a shortage of male evening attire that long before the season began New Orleans men who had outgrown or outworn their white ties and tails had exhausted the stocks of local stores and tailors and were trying frantically to purchase what they needed all over the country—through the mail, through friends in other places, or by taking special trips for the purpose. Evening shirts and collars were virtually unobtainable, so many an otherwise well-dressed gentleman was somewhat frayed and worn at collar and cuff as he escorted his spouse or sweetheart into the tiers of the Municipal Auditorium night after night. Some who had been in service solved their problem by appearing at the balls in uniforms they had otherwise discarded. Others found the situation attractive and an excuse to stay home.

The krewes themselves found the war had made a difference. The cost of everything was doubled, and many of the types of trinkets tossed from floats were not to be had. Much of this paraphernalia had come from Japan. The rest was not being manufactured. Yet trinkets were found and thrown, although sometimes it was doughnuts that were tossed or paper books of matches. There was trouble, too, in obtaining the jewels for kings and queens, but they were found at last, and krewe members just dug a little deeper than usual and contributed a little more, and, in general, all was as grand as ever.

The Negro flambeaux-bearers, previously paid two dollars a night, went on strike for five dollars in 1946. The torches and flares are the life of the night parades, and upon them depends much of the illusion of the pageants, but here the gentlemen had a principle at stake. As a result the night parades that year were almost unlighted and in some cases and places along the streets almost unseen by the spectators. After that a compromise was reached and the white-robed Negroes again strutted beside the floats, again all the brilliant colors of the lumbering vehicles made the nights magnificent, and again everybody was happy.

Since World War II, maskers in the streets have been particularly fond of impersonating Stalin and John L. Lewis. Other popular representations have been OPA and the landlord. The Good Neighbor policy has been encouraged by exchanges of visits between Hermes and his queen and the king and queen of the Carnival at Merida, Mexico, and every year more and more visitors from Central and South America arrive in New Orleans at Mardi Gras time. So many visitors come now that hotels and rooming houses cannot possibly accommodate them, so railroad companies allow many to sleep in Pullmans on the outskirts of the city, the mayor has cots set up in City Hall and in the city's fire stations and other municipal buildings, and many others sleep in hotel lobbies, railroad and bus stations, allnight restaurants, or in their automobiles; not that sleep is really necessary, for many people don't go to bed at all when they come to see Mardi Gras—or so it seems.

Some phases of the celebration do seem to be changing, too, and sometimes in directions that would have been startling a few years ago. In 1947 at least one young woman slipped out of a uniform she had worn all during the war and afterwards and into the gown of a queen of a carnival ball. Furious krewe captains arrived in a body at the mayor's office to protest against the installation of bars in the Auditorium and other places where balls were being held. Even the labor situation was evident, although in a rather cheery manner. A group of pickets before a building in the business district continued their picketing even on Mardi Gras, but they did so in costumes and masks.

PART THREE

This Is
What You Do

CHAPTER TWELVE

HOW TO GET INTO A BALL

*D*URING THE YEARS BETWEEN THE BEGINNING OF
this century and World War I, Orleanians and
visitors, usually male, although some sophisticated women
were included, sought by every means possible to obtain
invitations to the notorious Ball of the Two Well-Known
Gentlemen, the classic annual carnival celebration of Storyville. The Ball of the Two Well-Known Gentlemen had
been originated by Tom Anderson, "king of the tenderloin,"
and some of his friends, and those who participated were
the women of the district and their male friends.

Thomas C. Anderson was the undisputed dictator of the
red-light district that was Storyville, then the most lavish,
the most expensive, the most infamous neighborhood of its
kind in the United States. From humble beginnings as an
honest office clerk, Tom Anderson had risen in the favor
of the politicians who ran the city to become the political
boss of the Fourth Ward, the owner of several gaudy saloons
and a number of houses of prostitution, and to a position
where those in the City Hall obeyed his wishes almost as
completely as did the madams of Basin Street. He even

served two terms of office in the state legislature, and the ward he controlled was often called Anderson County.

It was after his service in the legislature was completed that Tom Anderson conceived the idea of forming a carnival krewe. Storyville inhabitants were already fond of mocking New Orleans society. Anderson's *Blue Book*, an annual directory of houses and women, which was first published in 1902, always used a tone and style of great elegance, referring to the female residents of the neighborhood as if they were grand ladies. The *Mascot*, a weekly tabloid devoted to the activities of the underworld, had a "society" column in which was recorded much gossip about the whores, such as, "It is safe to say that Mrs. Theurer can brag of more innocent young girls having been ruined in her house than there were in any other six houses in the city," and, "Miss Bessie Lamothe, 9 South Franklin Street, wishes her friends to understand that she did not announce that she received in a pink dress on New Year's, because she desires it to be understood that she receives every night in *un robe, blanc de nuit.*" From this sort of thing to a carnival ball was simply natural evolution.

The first ball was not too successful. Held in the ballroom of Arlington Manor, the house operated by Josie Arlington. Anderson complained later that his friends had displayed a lack of delicacy, that the tableaux were somewhat unrefined, and that the ladies drank too much champagne. The queen had herself raised her skirts and performed a dance that the queen of Comus would never have countenanced, much less performed. There had been too much intrusion of business —couples vanishing upstairs even before the ball was over. Worst of all, far too many outsiders had been admitted. His ball, said Tom Anderson, must be as exclusive as any in the city.

So the Ball of the Two Well-Known Gentlemen became more exclusive. Women who could not prove that they were professional prostitutes were seldom admitted, for above all Storyville despised amateur competition, and the day was approaching when the Countess Willie Piazza would ruefully exclaim, "The country-club girls are ruining my business!" The men invited were friends of the women or of Tom Anderson, including of course the politicians, the city and police officials. Invitations were as elaborate and colorful as those sent out by other carnival organizations. A court was always chosen and there were tableaux, which usually presented pantomimes by women in tights of the "living statue" variety then so popular.

Almost at once it became the desire of Orleanians to see a Ball of the Two Well-Known Gentlemen, and it was not easy to get in. One had to know the right people and have the proper connections.

But invitations could be bought at fabulous prices. The feminine members of the court would sell them on occasion, thus rendering Mr. Anderson's krewe less exclusive than he had hoped it would be. Both men and women from other strata of society would appear at the door of a ball with bona fide invitations and Storyville was much too hospitable and polite to deny them admittance. Then, when they were admitted, these guests did not conduct themselves properly, but remained aloof and patronizing, smiling at the proceedings behind the small black masks they sometimes wore, and which were in themselves trappings of the most utter snobbery. Thus did Tom Anderson and his friends discover that it is almost impossible to have a really exclusive carnival ball, at least without the use of very stringent methods. These were sometimes used, and ladies who had thought it a lark to attend the Ball of the Two Well-Known Gentlemen would flee into the streets, their escorts trailing them, after having been subjected to a few minutes of conversation and questions by the women who belonged at the ball. On one occasion at least, probably at Tom Anderson's instigation, the police descended upon one of the balls in a peculiar raid in which they took off to jail only the females present who did not have licenses in their profession. This was an event viewed with satisfaction by those who prided themselves upon their professional standing.

The other carnival krewes have not had to resort to measures quite so strong, and many have remained most exclusive at the same time. For instance the chances of an outsider—either a stranger in the city or a resident who does not know the right people—of wangling an invitation to a Momus, a Proteus, or a Comus ball is very slight. Visitors are often disappointed by this, but unless they have friends in the city who are members of these krewes, or have friends who have friends, they have almost no reason to hope to ever see one. Those who do not *belong*—and the word is used in its worst, most aristocratic and most old-fashioned sense—are simply not admitted. Relatively, this is also true of many smaller organizations. The krewes' side of the matter is that they are private clubs and are under no obligation to invite anyone they do not choose to include in their list, which is, of course, perfectly true.

Comus and Proteus have always been strict with their invitations. Names on invitations are carefully checked at the door. Each year Comus warns the world through a newspaper notice that its invitations cannot be exchanged and that if one is not used by the person to whom it is issued it must be returned to the krewe, or else the person's name will be permanently struck from the list. And this is done almost without hope of recourse.

In most of the krewes members are allowed a very limited number of invitations—about ten or twenty each. The demand upon each member is severe and he is compelled to make narrow choices. There are always, naturally, his relatives and closest friends, each of whom expect an invitation as a normal course, but even here he must often exercise caution, for more than sentiment must be considered. All names are submitted to an invitation committee, who scrutinize for eligibility each person to be invited and examine every detail of their social biography. In general, it is felt that this committee should in most cases know the background of every person who is to attend and the slightest irregularity is sufficient to cause a rejection. The member is then notified and he may submit a substitution. Wealth is not, as many Orleanians imagine, a requisite, nor is ancestry, although the latter undoubtedly helps and the former does no harm.

There were originally very good reasons for the severity of the committees, which was engendered during the early rough-and-tumble days of Mardi Gras in New Orleans. Without some strong barriers all the balls would have been invaded by guests who not only might have belonged elsewhere but who would have misbehaved to the extent of riot and mayhem. Now the committees have developed an almost psychic sense in this regard. Not too many years ago a coterie of prostitutes were ejected by the police from a balcony during a ball, an event that seriously disturbed the entire evening. They had been invited by a whimsical member of the krewe, who was further delighted that the girls did not go quietly, but loudly denounced the entire affair as the officers dragged them down the aisles.

Members are not often so capricious. Nearly all of them look upon Carnival as a very serious affair and their membership in a krewe of high caste as an honor. Expulsion follows at once upon the commission of any major infraction of the rules. This is considered a disgrace and is such a rare event that New Orleans gossips about it for generations.

In the case of visitors, members are allowed extra admit cards for strangers from out of town, and, if there is no way to verify their worthiness, the strangers are usually accepted upon the recommendation of the member. But even here the number is limited, and the visitor had better be certain his friend can obtain him an invitation before planning to attend certain balls.

Besides the large krewes who parade before the balls, there are many small but equally exclusive ones, those in which the debutantes compose the courts and the call-outs. It is as difficult in most cases for a stranger to view a ball of the Twelfth Night Revelers, Atlanteans, Mystic Club, and many others as it is to get into Momus, Proteus, and Comus.

Visitors are sometimes disappointed, too, because they do not have an opportunity to dance at most balls, but remain spectators throughout the evening. Krewe members are allowed less than a half-dozen call-outs each, and in the balls given by the socially elite most, often all, of these go to the season's debutantes. Influential women visitors may on occasion, of course, receive a call-out, which is considered a triumph.

Because the more important krewes are male, men are actually the social arbiters of New Orleans. At the very top, perhaps, is the Boston Club, reputed to be the second oldest club in the United States; it is composed of professional and businessmen of New Orleans and has a membership limited to four hundred, a number they consider significant.

Originally formed for the playing of Boston, an old card game, the Boston Club is now a group of rather elderly gentlemen, usually of a high financial rating, who consider themselves quite important and manage to exercise a considerable influence over Mardi Gras. For many years now Rex has had to be a member of the Boston Club, and usually the other kings of the krewes that parade are also members. It is upon the Boston Club balcony that many of the queens and their courts await the kings, and where is seated a portion of New Orleans society. It is the Boston Club, too, to a large extent, that has maintained the exclusiveness of the older krewes. It is the club members and their ladies who most deplore the fact that new krewes are being formed every year among groups who are not of their own circle, for many of them think Mardi Gras belongs to them and look upon it as the mainspring of the social season, as something nice for debutantes, and nothing more. One dowager, awaiting a parade on the Boston Club grandstand, expressed their feelings when she sniffed, "I don't think Carnival is nearly as nice since it's been taken up by the common people, do you?"

Perhaps the most serious condition existing among the older krewes, especially at this time, is their anti-Semitism. Louis Salomon, the first King of Carnival, was a Jew, but no other Jew has ever held that position. Jews once belonged to Comus, it is said, but now they are not only not allowed to join, but they may not even attend the Comus balls. Proteus is equally strict. Even the sight of a name that might be Jewish requires an investigation by the Proteus committee, and back goes the name and the question to the member who has submitted it. One visitor who had almost received a Proteus invitation was telephoned by the friend who was a member, and asked in an embarrassed and hesitant voice, "Say, your name does sound Jewish; are you? I never thought of it."

"No," replied the visitor. "But skip it."

When the Baron de Rothschild was in New Orleans a few years ago society ladies prostrated themselves *en masse*. But then came Mardi Gras. A social leader made a frantic telephone call to a Jewish friend and announced that she had heard a rumor that the baron was Jewish. It couldn't be true! The answer was that the Rothschilds had been Jewish for a very, very long time and were known to take pride in that fact. So De Rothschild, who had been received in all the real courts of Europe, was not allowed to attend the carnival courts of New Orleans, at least not those of Comus and Proteus, or those of the many smaller organizations who are also inclined to bar Jews, and which include Athenians, Twelfth Night Revelers, Mystic, Atlanteans, Nereus, and Momus, among others.

Jews belong to Rex and to Hermes. One year the king of Hermes was a Jew. They are also members of some of the smaller krewes and still others, who do not have Jewish members, will extend them invitations. The original intention in organizing the Mystic Club, it is said, was to form a krewe composed of both Christians and Jews, but the idea failed when less liberal elements gained control of the krewe and all Jews were barred. The Harmony Club in New Orleans was a few years ago the home of a carnival krewe composed entirely of Jews, which held its ball in the traditional manner, with a king and queen, maids and dukes. This organization dissolved because of lack of interest of the members themselves after a short while.

One of the most scandalous situations arose when a debutante who had a Jewish mother but a Gentile father was selected as Queen of Carnival one year. All went well at the Rex Ball, but when the court departed and arrived at the Ball of Comus, the queen of Comus snubbed the queen of Rex so thoroughly that New Orleans still talks about it. Still worse, perhaps, was the fact that the Jewish mother of the Queen of Carnival was not allowed to sit upon the grandstand before the Boston Club.

Of course those krewes who ban Jews have their arguments. Mardi Gras, they point out, is a Christian festival. Carnival begins on Twelfth Night to celebrate Epiphany, when the Magi visited the Infant Jesus. Mardi Gras itself is the final feast before the beginning of Lent. They argue, too, that twenty times as many Gentiles are refused memberships in the krewes and even invitations to the balls as are Jews. Neither of these reasons is very sound. Jews who were Christian converts and therefore must have been objected to on racial rather than religious grounds have been refused admission to certain balls on many occasions. And the Gentiles who cannot secure admit cards are barred for a variety of reasons, while in the case of Jews members inviting them are given only the one reason—that they are Jews.

Individual krewe members often deplore the situation, but there are enough anti-Semites in the organizations to prevent any changing of this tradition. These give all the timeworn arguments against the admission of Jews, the most frequent one being: "If we begin to let Jews in they'll soon take Carnival over." And of course there is always "Some of my best friends are Jews, but . . ."

The reactions of New Orleans Jews vary. Some prominent ones resent it keenly, for the most part for what it symbolizes. Others do not care, or will not admit that they do, and enjoy Mardi Gras despite it.

There is much that the visitor can enjoy, too, without attending the balls of Momus, Proteus, and Comus. Invitations to Rex and to Hermes can sometimes be obtained from the Association of Commerce, although the number is limited. Rex, however, does not present the best example of a carnival ball. There are no call-outs, and at eleven o'clock, after three maskers' dances, the ballroom is turned over to the guests for general dancing, the court departing to visit Comus. The Hermes Ball follows a more typical procedure.

Some of the smaller krewes are extremely generous with their invitations, and it is necessary only to have a friend who has a friend who has a friend to obtain an admit card, although a connection of some sort is essential for every carnival ball given in New Orleans.

Evening clothes are compulsory at all carnival balls. Men may now wear dinner coats, or tuxedos, if they are taking no part in the ball itself, although a few years ago not even these were allowed. Women wear long dresses and no hats. Most of them wear their best finery.

Many New Orleans men hate balls. One prominent citizen, whose father had been an active member of Comus, boasted that he had attended only two balls in his life. The last time was to please a friend. The gentleman did not even possess evening clothes, but at his friend's insistence he rented some. Then came the night of the ball. The son of the Knight of Comus spent several hours priming himself with strong drink and enjoyed this so much that he did not arrive at the ball until after eleven o'clock. He climbed to his seat in the Auditorium balcony and looked down, but the haze before his eyes was so thick that he could see almost nothing. Almost a few minutes later the ball was over, and home he went, feeling dejected about the whole thing. Then, determined to derive some benefit from the evening, he crawled into his bed fully dressed and slept that way. Later he said, "I had to get something out the money I spent renting those damned tails, so I slept in them."

With the exception of women with call-out cards, all guests are seated in the balconies above the dance floor by the gentlemen of the floor committee. Except for the call-out dancers, there is no mingling with the maskers and the guest is but part of an audience.

Whether or not a visitor attends a ball need not disturb his enjoyment of Mardi Gras, for he can still manage to have a wonderful time. There are even people who confess they have a better time for not attending any balls at all. However, if a ball is viewed it is required that the visitor think it is beautiful and he risks more than he knows should he dare to say anything to the contrary. There was a certain movie star in New Orleans for one Mardi Gras who received not only an invitation to a ball of great eminence, but also was honored by a call-out.

How to Get into a Ball

As the masker who had called her out floated about with her in his arms he inquired what she thought of it all.

"Lousiest thing I ever saw in my life," replied she.

The masker promptly released her, walked away, and left the astonished lady standing in the middle of the floor. Her temper aroused, the actress forced her way rudely and roughly through the dancing maskers and debutantes, and a tantrum was about to ensue when a man on the committee took her elbow politely and led her off the floor, out of the building, and into a waiting taxicab. Before morning she had left the city.

But most people like the balls, both visitors and natives. Orleanians like them so much, as a matter of fact, that they arrive at balls in wheel chairs, on crutches, on canes, and with arms in splints. They will come out in sleet and rain with double pneumonia, just to see once more the curtain rise upon some glittering, fictional court and to see the young girls in their white dresses come forward to dance with the maskers who have sent them call-outs. They will attend balls when they're in a state of pregnancy that causes concern to all around them, and they'll still be attending them when they're ninety-nine years old and never go anywhere else.

There are actually old people who never go anywhere else in New Orleans, but remain within their houses all the rest of the year. There are still a few, you see, who consider it common to go to shop on Canal Street, for instance. They employ other people to do this for them. Old ladies will tell you they consider it "bohemian" to be seen in a department store. "How can one tell who will be there?" they'll ask. On occasion they may visit each other or attend a funeral, although many are of the opinion that ladies don't attend funerals, for ladies did not go to funerals a long time ago in New Orleans.

But during the carnival season all emerge, ancient and

elegant, garbed in rusty green or black robes of untold age, bedecked with musty, slightly dirty jewels, swathed about their chins and throats and high, proud heads with yards and yards of tulle, leaning forward upon their canes in their limousines, going beyond their houses and their gardens to see once more a Mardi Gras and still another season's debutantes, going of course only to certain balls, to Proteus, to Comus, in whose courts they had a place when they and the world were young.

CHAPTER THIRTEEN

HOW TO BE A QUEEN

*S*OMETIMES A QUEEN OF A CARNIVAL KREWE IS born to her position and sometimes she is not. A New Orleans father may point to his female infant burping in her cradle and announce that exactly eighteen years hence she will be queen of a Comus Ball, and his prediction is likely to come true if all the necessary circumstances exist. In other cases a queen knows she is to be a queen several years before her season to reign. In still others she may not know until the Christmas preceding the Mardi Gras of her season. But there is always considerable advance notice. The debutante who is to be a queen is feted and entertained in numerous ways. Besides, a girl has to have time to prepare her wardrobe for the occasion.

How a girl is selected as queen and how a man becomes a king have always been subjects of conjecture both in the city and out of it, for even natives are often confused about the matter. There are those cynics who insist that a king simply buys his honor and that a father pays cash for the selection of his debutante daughter as queen. This isn't true, in the strictest sense. Certainly it costs a king a lot of money to be king, and someone must pay large bills for the debutante who is a queen, particularly of one of the large organizations, but the crowns are not for sale. To understand how the selections are made it is necessary to understand the mysterious functions of a carnival krewe.

These vary a little, but they are fundamentally very similar. The principal thing to remember is that although the carnival season lasts only a month or two the work of the krewes has been going on all year. Every tableau, every parade requires thought, planning, and much physical work. Krewes usually meet in April and then begin the next year's activities, some of the krewes operating under "working names" to increase the secrecy and further confound public curiosity, for all are very secret, especially in so far as their relations with each other are concerned. Even those persons who belong to more than one never tell the secrets of one to the other. None knows the subjects of any other's parades or tableaux, or who is to be king or queen. Under names like Louisiana Club, Stratford Club, School of Design, Crescent Club, and many others they gather to vote on committees who will perform certain essential duties and to decide all procedures and designs for the Mardi Gras ahead, including the costumes of the members, perhaps to elect a captain if a new one is needed.

The captain is the most powerful figure in any carnival krewe. He may be elected democratically by vote and he is subject to impeachment at any time his services are unsatisfactory, but while he holds office he is the supreme authority and sometimes a despot, for he has the responsibility for the success of the coming ball or parade and ball and he will receive the blame for anything that goes wrong. He works without pay and he works hard, often neglecting his own business and private affairs, and he does not even receive any public credit for achieving a fine ball or an unusually splendid parade, for his name must remain a secret outside of the krewe.

The captain rules the committees. He tells the committee of design what the designs will be. He decides upon the costumes and who will wear which one. In some krewes he alone selects the king and queen, choosing them from among the worthy, and from those who can afford the heavy expenses the offices carry, although this is not at all universally true. He always, however, selects his lieutenants, who will serve as dukes at the ball and in the parade, and assigns to them certain duties.

As far as the public is concerned, the king of a krewe is a very important personage. Actually he takes orders from the captain, and a king can no more break any regulation of the krewe than can any other member. The captain establishes many rules, the breaking of which means punishment or at least a fine.

In those krewes that parade the captain decides upon the place each masker will take upon a float and no deviation from his decision is permitted. Maskers arriving late at the den are fined. If they're not in their places aboard the floats when he blows his whistle or remove their masks at the ball or during the parade there are heavy fines.

And the captain has other responsibilities. Krewes like to boast that they are a sober lot, and some captains are very strict about liquor. Nevertheless universal sobriety is an unachieved dream and the captain must be careful at least that no one is too drunk to remember his dignity. Even kings have been problems in this direction, and occasionally the king must be deprived of his bottle before appearing in public. That situation has never arisen in regard to queens and maids, probably because they are too young.

The captain's main difficulty with women is keeping their mouths shut. For weeks they are required to retain the secret of their choice. The queen's mother and her sisters must remain silent, and possibly a couturier, also, who, since she must measure the queen for her royal garments, has to know of the choice. In this they are successful to an astonishing degree, everything considered.

The captain must bear with resentment, with envy, sometimes with threats of vengeance and reprisals. In the organizations of the highest social caliber there are the finest stuffed shirts—married, in many cases, to the finest unstuffed bosoms—who often harbor royal ambitions, for themselves and for their daughters, and some of them are not above using any means in their power to achieve their ambitions. Those who oppose them, including the captain, may risk business or professional injury. But the captains risk it, for they are usually men who love Mardi Gras for its own sake, not for its social implications.

Members of carnival krewes become extremely tough on occasion. One year a very powerful and influential businessman who belonged to the Boston Club and to Rex informed the officials of the organization that his daughter was going to be Queen of Carnival. If she was not, he let it be known, he would do his best to break every man who stood in his way, and he was in a position to do a lot of damage to many of them. The girl in question was not, because of the background of the family, considered worthy of the honor and she was not among those who had been considered for it. Yet so great was the power of her father that nothing could be done. So it was announced that the daughter would be queen.

When news of the selection reached Comus, however, there was relatively as much commotion as occurred at Windsor Castle when Edward told his family he was going to marry the American lady he did marry. The girl who was to reign as Comus's queen refused flatly to meet the girl who was to be Rex's queen, and as the two courts had to greet each other at the Comus Ball there was a major problem. Comus then managed a feat that touched a new depth in snobbery. The young lady who had been chosen in her cradle to be queen that year withdrew with dignity, and emissaries went into a Canal Street department store and located a salesgirl of "good family" but no money, who consented to be the queen of Comus. It was she the mate of Rex met at the Comus Ball, and ever since New Orleans society has recited with great glee the story of when the young woman who was Queen of the Carnival had to bow to a "shopgirl."

The honor of reigning over a ball sometimes remains in the same family for generations. Fathers and sons, uncles and nephews, grandfathers and grandsons have had turns at being Rex and other kings through the years. Many who have been Rex have also been kings of other krewes. Girls who are queens of the large carnival krewes are also often queens of one or more smaller ones, or members of the courts, in their cases, of course, always within the same year. The royal families of New Orleans are limited in number, and the admittance of new ones is slow indeed. In one instance a grandmother, a mother, and a daughter have each reigned as Queen of Rex in the year of her debut. On one occasion only did Rex marry his queen, however, thus bringing both crowns into the same family. Frank T. Howard and Lydia Fairchild, who ruled Mardi Gras in 1895, later married. But usually Rex is old enough to be the father of his queen.

Family remains the most important consideration among the most aristocratic clubs. There have been cases, although they are rare, when the queen of Rex, Comus, Momus, or Proteus had no money at all. All that was necessary was that some member of the family belong to one of these krewes and be able to convince the organization that the young lady was born for the honor of being queen, and that he was willing to pay the expenses involved. There have been queens who worked for a living, and through necessity, but because of their background were thought perfectly acceptable. In no other city in America would such a girl have been able to make her debut and have received such acclaim. Usually these Cinderella stories end with marriage to a rich husband too. But then, all sorts of things occur in New Orleans. There was one debutante who came out at the age of thirty-five. She had worked for years and saved up her money.

It costs a lot to be queen of a major carnival organization. What the queen's father or other sponsor spends varies, but the amount is never small. Her jewels may be furnished by the krewe, but her gown and mantle may cost anywhere between $500 and $5000, occasionally more. For the Golden Jubilee of 1924 the queen of Comus wore a mantle six and a half yards long, of gold net embroidered in rhinestones with a border of golden metallic cloth trimmed with seed pearls and leaves of silver cloth and rhinestones, and with a huge collar of gold net heavily encrusted with Strasbourg rhinestones. Her gown was of golden metallic cloth, and her gloves were dipped in fourteen-carat gold. When the queen married, the mantle was used as an altar cloth and it is now on display at the Louisiana State Museum in the old Cabildo in New Orleans, where many queens' gowns and mantles and jewels may be seen.

Formerly most of the gowns and mantles and jewels of carnival royalty were imported from France. Now most are made in New Orleans or New York. There have been famous dressmaking establishments in New Orleans in other years who have devoted almost all their skill and energy to designing and creating the costumes of carnival queens and the gowns of maids. The type of gown, mantle, and jewels is of course decided by the theme of the ball over which the queen is to reign. One year a queen had the most miserable evening of her life even in her hour of triumph, for her costume was trimmed lavishly with ostrich plumes. There were plumes on her head, at her shoulders, on her mantel, and she carried an immense fan of them. During the grand march and later the girl almost coughed, sneezed, and choked herself to death. She was allergic to feathers.

A girl will sacrifice a lot to be a carnival queen. One chosen by Comus quit Vassar to return to New Orleans to don her imitation crown. Another, invited by an aunt, who thought it all a silly business, upon a trip around the world had no hesitation in choosing to reign briefly with Proteus, although she knew the opportunity to travel in such a manner would not be likely to come to her again. It didn't.

Queens are carefully nurtured, carefully trained. Until the season she is to make her debut and thus at least be eligible for the queen role in some ball, a New Orleans young lady may run with the pack, doing all the things girls her age do and anything else she may feel inclined to do, but when that season starts a metamorphosis, guided by her mother, is begun. Heloise may no longer go out unchaperoned, even if she has been doing so since she was fourteen years of age. No longer can she ride her bicycle with her dungarees rolled above her knees. If she has been taking her bourbon straight in French Quarter night clubs without blinking an eyelash, she suddenly begins sipping light wines and champagne, and only on very special occasions, and then complains of feeling weak in the knees. She can no longer be seen being escorted by coatless young men into the Krispy Krumb and Kaffee Shoppe for midnight hamburgers. She has become a chaste young thing, all smooth, clean hair, wide, innocent eyes, and bouffant skirts, whose life is an impassioned procession of teas, receptions, dances, and parties, and breakfasts and luncheons, too, for the day Heloise eats home is a failure. Then one morning a committee arrives at her home to inform her and her proud and panting mama that she is to be queen of a carnival ball. Heloise is a success.

Now the real work begins. Besides the invitation to be

queen she is to be maid in several courts, and she must attend every ball of importance to her caste. The days become feverish ones of purchases, fittings, anxiety that all be correct and as expensive as her parents can afford, interspersed with social engagements. Heloise operates on a schedule that would be frightening and maybe fatal if she were not carried through by her own and her mama's pride and exhilaration. For her role of queen, especially if it is to be of a large krewe, there must be special training. A queen must know how to walk, how to gesture, how to bow. Often a friend who was a queen in a former year is called upon for help and advice, but only one, for the secret of her selection must be kept. The captain of the krewe issues advice, stern commands, and warnings. If it is the sort of krewe that has them, mama must plan the queen's supper which will follow the ball, when she will be hostess to her court.

If her gown for the ball over which she will reign is not to come from Paris or from New York a very special New Orleans dressmaker must be engaged. The krewe captain reveals—at least in part—the theme of the ball and Heloise's dress and mantle must fit the specifications he suggests. The material, the trimmings, the amount of money spent are up to mama.

When at last the night comes, and you see Heloise bedecked in all her regal finery, wearing her crown, waving her scepter, bowing graciously as queens bow, it is hard to believe that once you saw her climb a tree and hang by her knees from the topmost branch, or that just last year she hit her brother over the head with a milk bottle, flushed her grandmother's teeth down a toilet, and was given to screaming tantrums.

One of the most important tasks in any carnival krewe, next in importance without a doubt to that of the captain, is the artist's. He must design not only the tableaux and settings for the balls, the parades for krewes that parade, and all the costumes of the maskers, but also the invitations, the dance programs, and, in some cases, the souvenirs and favors to be given away at the balls.

Plates are designed for each float and tableau and submitted to a committee. Each plate is in full color and detail. When approved they go then to the builders, who decide whether or not the artist's conceptions can be created in the materials of which the scenery and floats are to be constructed. Sometimes modifications are necessary in order to work in papier-mâché, metallic paper, and cloth.

If all is well carpenters, painters, and decorators go to work, and in the case of parades months are spent in their construction. Floats are built upon wheeled flatcars twenty or more feet long and about eight feet wide. They cannot be more than eighteen feet high at the present time because many of the streets through which the parades pass have overhanging electric cables and telephone wires, which might break the floats or even decapitate the maskers riding upon them.

All the work is done in the secret dens in Calliope Street, to which no one who has not an official pass from the krewe captains is admitted. In some cases even krewe members are not told the theme to be used in the year to come and even they may not visit the scene of construction. Clay models of all floats are made and from these are cast plaster molds. Into these is pressed a paper pulp and glue mixture, which hardens when dried. The heavy bare floats are then supported with metal braces, and iron rods are set up in appropriate places for the support of the maskers. A light wooden framework in the design of the float is then erected; this forms the rough shapes of the figures, animals, and buildings being used. The body of the float is filled with excelsior, cotton, old newspapers, and other stuffing and covered with white canvas. Then over all is fitted the papier-mâché, the colored cloth, the tinsel, the glittering ornaments, and artists begin the final painting and trimming and decorating that transforms what had been a heap of crude materials into a chariot of ancient gods, a scene in flaming hell, or a garden filled with flowers and shells and quivering butterflies.

Distortion is necessary to attain the desired effects, and often the completed float is a far departure from the original design of the artist who conceived the ideas, for there are limitations necessitated by the size of the floats and the various materials that can be used. Too, there must be space on each float for a given number of maskers, and therefore all floats have a shell-like shape, which provides a scooped-out center in which the maskers stand. In most cases figures are cast in shapes that are grotesque and out of proportion in a deliberate effort to create the illusion of great size. Color is used in large, splashing effects for the same purpose. Delicate and shimmering objects such as flowers, birds, and brilliant insects are attached by wires that allow movement of the decorations as the floats are drawn through the streets.

The colors of day and night parades differ considerably. For those to appear at night more intense shades are used, which in daylight might be harsh and garish, but become lovely under artificial light. Day parades tend to be in pastel shades. For the night floats gold- and silver-leaf trimming is so arranged as to catch and reflect the fiery light of the flambeaux with results of astounding beauty. For the day-time parades the leaf is applied so that it will catch the rays of the sun.

As to the cost of parades, they are somewhat reduced in the cases of the older krewes because of an accumulation of properties and materials, many of which are treasured from year to year and transformed for reuse. The average cost of each of these parades today may be anywhere from

$10,000 to $20,000. A new krewe giving the identical parade, however, might have to spend about $70,000. The ball that follows each parade costs many thousands in addition. Members of the krewe, of course, contribute the money for all expenses.

Work on parades begins at once after the krewe meets in the April following the last Mardi Gras. There are workmen to be paid for nearly a year, and for the parade itself many other people must be employed. Night parades are the most costly. Hundreds of Negroes are hired to carry flambeaux, others are needed to carry the title signs for the floats and to lead the white-robed mules that draw the floats.

In all krewes, whether or not they parade, there are the maskers' costumes to be designed, made, and paid for. Each masker of course pays for his own, but he has nothing to say about its kind, color, or material. Often he does not even know what it is to be, but simply receives a number from the captain, which signifies what he is to wear, what he is to be, and what part he is to play in the fantasy. Seamstresses are provided with satin, sateen, cheesecloth, brilliants, and all the other materials from which the costumes are created. Often the krewe has an accumulation of costumes from other years, and frequently the material is used again.

Krewe favors are no longer so expensive as they once were, but the sum spent for those given call-outs runs into high figures nevertheless, each costing anywhere from one to fifteen or twenty dollars and, in the case where a masker calls out a girl whom he holds in special regard, a much larger amount.

Almost vanished now is the elaborate invitation, which used to be a most costly item. Now most of those sent are plain engraved cards, but in former years invitations to balls were magnificent affairs of every shape, size, and color, folding and unfolding into intricate designs in vivid shades. The fashion lasted until World War I. Now they are collectors' items.

Those who reign as queens and kings over a ball or a parade and a ball receive among other souvenirs hand-painted scrolls to forever remind them of their position. These are about two feet wide, three feet long, and are always framed and preserved with great pride. Each reads a little differently, depending upon the krewe. The ones presented by Rex announce:

Know all ye men: This document, duly authenticated and sealed, attests the fact that Miss ——— ——— served as Queen of the Carnival to the great delectation and supreme satisfaction of the good people of New Orleans and the welcome strangers within her gates on its glorious day of Mardi Gras in the year ———, in testimony whereof the King himself hath commanded that these presents be signed by officers of the Imperial School of Design. . . .

The Imperial School of Design is the working name of the Krewe of Rex.

Of the millions New Orleans spends for Mardi Gras each year the largest amount is, of course, spent by those outside the krewes. Much is spent by the city and by business houses, even more by individuals. It has been estimated that the women of New Orleans probably now spend from $3,000,000 to $4,000,000 for clothes, accessories, and in beauty parlors in order to attend the balls. At least $1,000,-000 goes into the costumes of street maskers. But for all that is spent there is much compensation, for most of the money is spent here in the city, and visitors spend many millions more. Furthermore, the art, literature, music and manners of the whole South have been influenced and enriched by Mardi Gras in New Orleans.

Mardi Gras is for everyone and there are krewes for everyone. There are the krewes of Creole and Garden District society and krewes for newer social groups. There are krewes for professional and businessmen. All overlap, overflow into each other, mix, blend, and intermingle, with only a few exceptions. There are krewes composed almost entirely of Italo-Americans. There are others in which most of the members' names tend to be Irish or German. And there are those that are Negro. Finally, if no krewe to your liking can be found, you can always start a new one. This is being done every year.

It seems that almost anyone can be a carnival king—or a queen—if he wants to work at it hard enough. More than one Orleanian has founded his own krewe, established himself as captain, and proceeded to make himself a king or his daughter a queen. Many captains are ambitious to be kings and it is not impossible for them to arrange that for themselves.

A captain of one large krewe was rich, influential, and determined to be Rex. He notified the Boston Club of his willingness, but he received no co-operation. It was essential to belong to the club, and he was not a member and had never been invited to become a member. Angered, he formed another krewe, elected himself captain of that, then made himself king of both his krewes in the same year. The result, however, was frustration, for his identity as king of the two balls over which he presided could not be revealed even to the members of the Boston Club, and most of them never knew it at all. At last, years later, he managed to become a Boston Club member, and then, through sheer will power and persistence, he had the satisfaction of seeing his daughter selected as Queen of the Carnival. To rise in carnival society becomes their life's ambition to an amazing number of Orleanians, who want more than anything else that Christmas Day visit from the men who on that day always bring the scrolls to those who are to head carnival courts or to serve them as maids and dukes.

SCANDAL, SKULLDUGGERY, AND SCUTTLEBUTT

*O*NCE A KING ALWAYS A KING. ONCE A QUEEN always a queen. The kings and queens of Carnival never forget it, and they never let anyone else forget it. The throne does something to those who sit upon it and they are never quite the same again.

Perhaps because it was an achievement for which they had hoped so fervently, an accomplishment that, at least in the opinion of many Orleanians, is more important than any other in the world, carnival royalty often considers itself royalty ever after. All kinds of things happen to these people, all the things that can happen to anyone in life, but not poverty nor ill-health nor anything else can take from them their little hand-painted scrolls, their rusting crown and scepter, their memory of grandeur, which to them was not mere mockery but very real, if only for a season, or a day, a night.

Those who were Rex or Rex's queen each receive a little carnival flag in the colors of purple, green, and gold and emblazoned with the crown of Rex. Each Mardi Gras after their brief reign they fly this flag above their homes. On

Scandal, Skullduggery, and Scuttlebutt

Mardi Gras you can ride through New Orleans and see the flags and you'll know that here lives a former King or Queen of Carnival. It makes no difference where they live. Some in reduced financial circumstances, old and tired, now live alone in boardinghouses, a few in worse places, but wherever they are they fly their flags—outside dingy windows, on crude little poles on roofs, from the railings of upstairs galleries. The only ones missing will be those who have left New Orleans, or left the world.

Most Mardi Gras queens marry well, for they move in a circle wherein they are likely to do so. More than a few have married into European aristocracy and have thus achieved real titles of a sort, but it is doubtful that many of them consider their new position of more social prominence than that they were awarded during a New Orleans Carnival. If they are in the United States most of them will return each year, to attend the balls and to relive *their* year with old friends. And each former queen remembers her year as the most delightful of all years before or since.

Former queens like to recall the fads and fashions of other years. This one, still fairly young, was a flapper of the 1920s. Her hair was bobbed and her sparkling gown of gold lamé stopped at her knees. Another one, much older, is certain that she dressed almost exactly like this year's queens, although she was, of course, more elaborate and elegant. Then there are the cheated queens, who missed playing their roles because of wars, but who in many cases received scrolls to attest this fact and will assure you that they were really queens after all. No matter how world-weary, how cynical or bitter an ex-queen has become, she seldom if ever jokes about this one event in her life.

The only ex-kings who can really enjoy their memories are those who were Rex, for the others are supposed to remain silent and anonymous all the rest of their lives. But these old kings who can talk dote upon their souvenirs and the scrapbook they have kept of the year they were Rex. There is one who has carried about a yellowed photograph of himself in his royal robes for years, always delighted to show it to anyone interested and to tell the story of his Mardi Gras. There is another who for many years used a small crown upon all his stationery! All fly their flags each Mardi Gras. A number have carefully treasured their crowns, jewels, and mantles, and these, together with other royal insignia, decorate their dens, their libraries, or other rooms in their homes.

Only the most extreme necessity can force a queen to part with her gown, mantle, and jewels. Most never have to, for of course those who have had extreme misfortune are in the minority, and most of the former queens (at least of the larger and prouder krewes) are the social leaders of New Orleans today, presently engaged in pushing debutante daughters into positions of importance in carnival courts. Some of these are not at all shy about their former grandeur. Only gags could keep them from talking about it and only blindfolds prevent you from seeing evidences of it in their homes.

At least one former queen displays her gown, jewels, and mantle upon a dress form in a corner of her darkened parlor. Others eventually give them or lend them—or their descendants do so at their deaths—to the Louisiana State Museum. Descendants of former rulers of Rex, and some of the ex-kings, although the latter cases are rare, also have donated their jewels and mantles to the museum. Antoine's, one of New Orleans' world-famous restaurants, has a dining room known as the Rex Room, and the glittering paraphernalia of former kings lines the walls in glass cases.

Occasionally aging carnival royalty holds reunions, and often these are dinners in Antoine's Rex Room. Here they gather for toasts and nostalgic conversation, and at least once during the evening raise their voices, no matter how quavering, in the song Lydia Thompson sang to Alexis Romanoff, "If Ever I Cease to Love." These, of course, are those who ruled over the Krewe of Rex. Those who reigned at Comus, Proteus, and Momus balls were just as proud, perhaps more so, and many a queen of a smaller organization in another year feels that her prestige is as great. This is especially true of Twelfth Night Revelers, for it is said that anyone who can receive an invitation to a Twelfth Night Reveler Ball is eligible to one for any other.

Because of the carnival system, the social climber in New Orleans has a difficult time. Yet with determination, persistence, and an infallible faith in the worthiness of his ambition, a certain amount of success is possible, provided of course that he has money.

The rising tycoon often does find a place. There are those families who would go to the guillotine rather than admit the importance of wealth, but, nevertheless, the tycoon's daughter is sometimes upon a throne before they can unroll the family trees or raise the drawbridges. If Daughter does not secure one of the major thrones, then there are smaller ones, and, if she makes this her lifework, she may, by marrying the right man, obeying all the rules, and bearing an attractive girl child, also become a queen mother, and perhaps mother of the queen of Rex. Then if her well-trained child is very careful and reasonably bright, Granddaughter may be queen of Comus. It has happened, although it is rare and unusual. Of course each generation must have the same implicit faith in the importance of it all. It is startling how many have no doubt about that importance, an odd state of mind, but beneficial to those who like Mardi Gras.

All krewes give the same reply to accusations of snobbery. They contend that since they are private clubs of paying members they have the right to invite whom they please and are under no more obligation to invite anyone else than is any other private club. In addition, they argue that they provide New Orleans with the biggest free show on earth with their street parades, which cost neither the city nor any of its citizens a penny, but rather bring large sums of money to them by attracting thousands of visitors, who spend freely and thus help every kind of business. There is an argument there.

What really goes on within the sanctums in which the committee reviews the request-for-invitation forms sent in by krewe members is also a subject for argument. Those names who have been issued invitations to the same balls year after year cause the committee no headaches, but the sight of a strange name scares some of them silly. Who is this? demands one, and all the aging heads go together in council as serious as if they were working on an improvement upon the atomic bomb or at least were searching for a new system to use at the racetrack. Smaltz. Never heard of him. There's a new man with a peculiar name, suggests one, who is something or other for that air line that's just opened. It might be he. Better find out before they make a decision. Back goes a query to the member who sent in the name.

Smaltz is his wife's second cousin from St. Louis.

Then he's not the air-line executive, reflect the committee. So sorry, but . . . They never refuse anyone whom they think may be important, or at least important according to their definition of the word. But they never risk asking the wrong sort, especially Comus, Proteus, and Momus.

Only occasionally do they make mistakes, but when they do it is thought to be a catastrophe, for it is far worse carnival etiquette to shut out someone who belongs than to admit someone who does not. Apologies come hastily. Even as recently as fifty years ago a duel might have ensued.

Rex is proud in his own way, too. The marching clubs, such as the old Jefferson City Buzzards, precede him and his parade on Mardi Gras, and many members of the krewe do not like it, but can't prevent it, since it has been going on for years. Too, it doesn't embarrass him seriously, for the small bands of walking maskers simply straggle through the street some distance ahead of the big parade. But when the Krewe of Crescent City held their first parade of trucks in 1946 and asked for permission to roll in front of Rex that was different. They advanced an argument that their decorated trucks filled with maskers would amuse the crowds waiting for Rex, who was always late anyway, without dimming the glory of the King of Carnival. But His Majesty would not have it and the city government was on the side of Rex. The Krewe of Crescent City had to take a place behind. After all, Rex is King of the Carnival.

Some of the same men have been riding on floats of the older krewes for decades. Not long ago Proteus presented a member with a gold cup for taking part in fifty parades, and without ever having a serious accident. Octogenarians are sometimes concealed beneath the brilliant costumes of the maskers on the floats, and age vanishes when they climb aboard. They dance and caper with the rest, and if they have any trouble maintaining their balance none of the spectators think they are old men. Most will, without intentional unkindness, think they are drunk, for many people think all maskers aboard floats are drunk, despite all the labor of the captains.

Spectators do get too enthusiastic at times. One year the manager of a fashionable shop on Canal Street invited a friend from New York to watch the parades from the second-story window of his shop, which was the hat department. Rex came rolling down the street and the maskers on the floats began to toss their trinkets into the crowd. The New Yorker, overcome with Mardi Gras spirit, began to pick up stacks of the shop's expensive hats and throw them into the crowd below. At least a few dozen had been dispersed before the visitor was restrained, and maskers in the street below were gleefully donning exclusive models and running away with them on their heads. "I just couldn't help it," the visitor explained to his friends. "Everybody else was throwing things and I had to do it too."

Riding a float can be dangerous, but that is only one of the troublesome aspects that are mingled with the fun. Young maskers are the sources of more difficulties, of course, than older ones. In one recent parade a man in the street tried to snatch a large bunch of strings of beads from a masker's hand. The masker jumped to the ground, swung his left, and sent the greedy spectator crashing to the pavement, then ran and reboarded his float, all without moving his mask an inch.

Maskers have been known to quarrel with each other aboard a float. Usually the reasons are simple ones, such as that one thinks the other has his position, or that he thinks the other is taking up too much room, or that the man sharing his box is throwing his trinkets into the crowd, or throwing too many, or too few. Sometimes older maskers attempt to bawl out younger ones for conduct they considered undignified. When this happens the spectators are always delighted with the sight of two men in costumes and funny or grotesque masks, balancing themselves perilously upon the rocking, vividly colored float, screaming through their masks at one another. Then a third man joins in and a fourth, and soon all the maskers on the float are in the middle of it, yelling at each other. If the captain hears of it, he wheels his horse, gallops to the rear, and settles the affair with toots on his whistle and gestures with his arms. They'll hear from him later.

A few maskers have tried to be individualists. One year one man on a float brought along his umbrella on a cloudy night and when a shower came opened it for protection. He was fined a hundred dollars.

Scandal, Skullduggery, and Scuttlebutt

Older krewe members have no patience with any of the younger generation in their family who do not share their enthusiasm, or who refuse to take Mardi Gras as seriously as they do. There have, it is rumored, been young ladies who have refused to be queens. One, when the year of her debut arrived, announced that she was going to spend that winter at an Eastern college. Her father had been Rex and her mother had been the queen of several smaller balls. Almost from the date of the girl's birth it had been considered highly probable that she would ascend some high-ranking throne, perhaps even Comus or Proteus or Momus, and she had been carefully reared toward this end. Now the family faced total defeat of all their ambitions. The father fumed and fussed, and the mother wept continuously and made remarkable statements, one of which the girl always remembered. "What good is all this education going to do you," cried Mama, "if you're not even queen of *one* carnival ball?" The parents won when Papa cut off her allowance and refused to pay the expenses for the trip and tuition, and the girl had to obey their desires and ambitions rather than her own. Begrudgingly and muttering language to herself that no queen should use, she sat upon two thrones and wore two crowns and waved two scepters. When Mardi Gras was over she boarded a train.

Then there was the case of the pregnant queen. Her delicate condition was not evident, but her mother became suspicious about a month before the night the girl was to reign over a ball, and the daughter confessed. She was secretly married, but that, if anything, made it worse rather than better. Queens must be unmarried. They're only supposed to be virgins, although it is customary to assume that they are. Mother went to bed with nerves and a trained nurse, and the father sat in his library planning his daughter's murder. The girl and her husband departed for California, from whence they mailed marriage announcements to their friends. The krewe had to substitute another queen. The parents never quite recovered from a sense of the deepest shame and never quite forgave their daughter. "If only she had waited until after Mardi Gras," her mother explains to friends, "she could have done anything she wanted! But why did she have to do it before?"

Once or twice secretly married young women have actually occupied thrones. If the krewe discovers it later they have a difficult time recovering from the shock, spend much time in attempting the almost impossible task of concealing the scandal, and take vows to strengthen their powers of investigation in future years. This is virtually impossible now in the large krewes. There must be no secrets in a girl's life.

It can be a queen's mother who causes difficulty. Upon a Christmas morning a krewe committee called at a home to present a debutante with a scroll. The girl was still asleep, but her mother was awake and very drunk. The butler admitted the men, and Mama appeared at the head of the stairs, yelling gleeful greetings down the well to the gentlemen and yodeling calls to awaken her daughter, who had more or less expected this and should have been up anyway. The gentlemen frowned, smiled, raised eyebrows, and said they would return later. But Mama would not have it. She trooped down the stairs, tripped on her negligee a few steps from the bottom, and sprawled at the feet of the mortified committee. "Madam," said one of the gentlemen as he lifted her to her feet, "you should practice your curtsy. We'll be back this afternoon." When they did return Mama was sleeping it off and Daughter awaited them, looking sweet and wide-eyed and demure.

Sons or grandsons shock their fathers now and then by their lack of enthusiasm toward membership in a carnival krewe (particularly if it is one to which the father or grandfather has belonged) and an impious attitude toward the sanctity of the whole business. One grandfather nearly wrecked his grandson's life and romance by forcing him to break all engagements with his girl during the hectic heights of the season so that he could help in decorating the Auditorium for the ball given by the krewe to which Grandfather belonged. In the cases of some krewes fathers insist that their sons join with the same determination that a parent elsewhere might use to force his son to enroll at a university he has attended. Fathers have threatened sons with disinheritance as a last resort, and every other means may be employed to undermine such stubbornness. Usually, of course, the son develops with the years the same affection for his krewe as had his father before him.

Carnival history is filled with romances that began at balls and other Mardi Gras festivities. Only one Rex married his queen, but lesser kings have married theirs, dukes have married maids and queens, and kings have married maids. Of course all the love affairs cannot be traced to the balls themselves, for almost always these people are acquainted with each other before and outside of the activities of the krewe, yet the atmosphere of a carnival ball is highly conducive to *amour*, and sometimes unsuspected affairs are either born or revealed between the grand march and the final call-out.

The king of a small krewe once divorced his wife and married the queen who had reigned with him. The irate captain asked for his resignation.

In the days when maskers presented call-outs with their gorgeous and costly mantles, a New Orleans lady once sat in the tiers of a ballroom and watched her husband, whom she recognized by his legs, fasten his mantle about the shoulders of a girl with whom he was dancing. The next day the wife asked the husband for the mantle and, not knowing his wife had recognized him, he replied that he had left it in the dressing room of the building where the ball was being held. Day after day she nagged him about it and he always pretended to have forgotten to pick it up. At last, in desperation, he managed to have a reasonable facsimile created and this he gave his wife. She accepted it as the genuine one, having decided that nothing worth worrying about existed between the man and the girl who had received the real one, but each Mardi Gras after that she reminded her husband just before the ball that she would like his mantle, and each day after the ball he took pains to place it about her.

One jealous wife at a ball of a more obscure organization waited in the call-out box for her husband's summons to dance, for it was the sort of krewe in which men call out their wives. She was not too certain of her husband's identity, but finally decided she had picked him out by his size, shape, and silk-stockinged legs and knees. At last a committeeman bawled out her name and she went into this gentleman's arms, and as soon as the music began she started, in a low but positive voice, to state exactly what was on her mind. She did not like the way he had danced with the other young women. She did not like being nearly last on his list. She did not like him. Then she delved into the past and reminded him of various other occasions when he had mistreated her. At this point the man with whom she was dancing could stand no more, and in a voice that was certainly not her husband's he explained that he and her husband had exchanged call-outs intended for their wives as a joke. That lady refused ever again to attend a ball given by that krewe, and finally succeeded in talking her husband into resigning.

One of the most humiliating things that can happen to a girl is to wait in vain for a call-out she has been promised by the little card that arrived with her invitation. This rarely happens, but accidents of one sort or another do occur. A masker may have a sudden attack of appendicitis. He may be hateful enough to fall off a float and break his leg or even his neck. Now and then he may be somewhere behind the scenery being administered black coffee and applications of ice to his head. When this happens to a New Orleans girl she is seldom ever exactly the same again. It is a stigma that may go with her to the grave. Even if a king is drunk another can be substituted and no one knows the difference, but the dowagers' eyes up in the tiers are always watching the girl who waits hopelessly for the sound of her name.

Women's krewes have their troubles too. One of these is to be certain that male call-outs show up for their ball. If there is anything worse than a lady call-out waiting for the call-out that never comes, it is a masked girl drifting around the ballroom, while a committeeman shouts a name to which there is no reply. When the music starts a female masker has only her mask for which to be thankful, if she is left standing alone. However, most male Orleanians are much too gallant to allow this to happen often.

Perhaps the most famous of romantic Mardi Gras stories that Orleanians tell is that one concerning the "ghost dinners" served each Shrove Tuesday night by a restaurant in Royal Street, when all the most delicious dishes for which the restaurant's cuisine is noted are served to empty places.

It began a long time ago, when Mardi Gras balls were held in the French Opera House. One night at Comus a young man from an Eastern city paid no attention at all to the tableaux being enacted but, instead, stared the whole time at a lovely Creole girl seated on the opposite side of the balcony. At last she looked his way, and it seemed that once their gaze met she was as powerless to look away as was he. The young man smiled and a flicker of a smile was returned. Then he rose, made some excuses to the friends he was with and strolled out into the lobby.

Mardi Gras

Later he confessed that he did not know how he was so positive, but somehow he knew the girl would join him, and in a few minutes she walked quickly through the crimson portieres, and then stood just beyond them, her face very red, for it was a period when girls still blushed.

The young man went swiftly to her side and said words he could never recall, except that among them was a suggestion that they leave together at once. The girl went with him obediently, without saying a word.

But outside she said, "You have done a very wicked thing. You made me come against my will."

"No," he said. "It was your fault."

"I was with my fiancé," she said. "You have ruined my reputation."

"If I've done that," he replied, "then I'll have to marry you, won't I? However, it might be an idea if we had supper first."

So they went into the Royal Street restaurant, and the young man told the waiter that love made him hungry and that they would have anything and everything that the waiter might suggest. And while the food piled up upon the table the couple told each other their names, all about the past of each, and what their future would be like. They sat there all night, talking and eating and drinking wine. In the morning they went together to the Ash Wednesday mass at the St. Louis Cathedral, and then they were married quietly by one of the priests, and the young woman took her husband home to her frantic family, who had searched for her all night.

A few days later the young man took his bride North, and neither of them ever saw Mardi Gras again, for before summer was over, as always happens in such romantic tales, the girl died.

Then came the most startling development of the story. A few days before the next Mardi Gras the proprietor of the restaurant where the couple had spent the morning hours after that day a year ago received a check and a strange request through the mail. The widower asked that the same table be decorated with flowers and that the same food be served in the same way it had been when the couple had sat there. This was done. The next year came another letter and another check, and they continued to come for more than twenty years after that each Mardi Gras time, and every year the owner of the restaurant complied with the request. Finally, one year, came a letter from an attorney. The man who had been buying the ghost dinners had died, but he had left a bequest in his will of a large sum of money, which was to pay for this annual commemoration of his love affair for as long as the restaurant remained in business.

Many people believe this is only a fable, but it is the story they tell, and something of the kind must have occurred, for every Mardi Gras night, if you go to this restaurant, you'll see a waiter setting places for two. There are always flowers on the table and decorations in carnival colors. Then, silently and seriously, a waiter slowly serves the fine foods and wines of an elaborate dinner for two. No one even seems to remember the name of the couple, or they won't tell you if they do, but the ritual continues year after year. It has become one of the traditions of Mardi Gras.

There have been visitors in the city who expected to find the air suffused with ether during Mardi Gras. Lucius Beebe jokingly remarked to a reporter, during one of his Mardi Gras visits, "There's probably opium around." Ether has never been used, at least not widely, during a New Orleans Mardi Gras, as it is during the Brazilian variety, and those Orleanians who smoke opium do so in private, yet there is evidence that something about it all can have startling effects upon the most staid and dignified individuals. Neither opium nor ether is needed. As proof there is what happened to a Creole spinister known to her family and friends as Tante Bébé, as are all Creole aunts who are the youngest of their generation.

Tante Bébé was the last of the eleven children in her family, and the only one unmarried. But Tante Bébé was now thirty-four and her spinsterhood had been accepted as a permanent condition by all who knew her. In her day Creole women were told to "throw their corsets on top the *armoire*" at twenty-five. No man wanted a woman that old, and the fate awaiting them was not enviable. Unless they were extremely fine seamstresses or could open little private schools for young ladies, there was almost no way they could make a living, so they became the unpaid menials in the homes of married sisters or brothers. No Creole ever let a relative want for a home, and they were usually generous and kind about taking in poor Tante Bébé, but Tante Bébé earned her keep, by helping with domestic chores, by sewing for her nephews and nieces, by what we now call baby sitting, and in a dozen other ways. She received her board and two dresses a year, but she did not have much fun.

This Tante Bébé was very unhappy. She would look into her mirror and tell herself she was thirty-four, a middle-aged woman, but she did not think she looked old. She did not feel old. But she wore dark skirts of heavy wool down to her neat square-toed shoes, crisp white blouses with collars that fastened beneath her chin with an antique pin—the one piece of the family jewelry bestowed upon the family old maid—and she pulled her black hair up into a knot on top of her head. Now and then Tante Bébé did a foolish and reckless thing. One day when the married sister with whom she lived and all her family were out, Tante Bébé stripped down to her chemise and slipped into the rustling petticoats and scarlet party dress that her niece—a girl of seventeen—had worn to a soiree the evening before. She swirled a few times before the mirror and thought she did not really look too silly at all. Then she heard the front door open and she had to change back into her own clothes in frantic haste. Her conscience ached for two weeks after that.

Another time when the family had gone out and left Tante Bébé sitting in her rocking chair on the front gallery, she broke off a spray of the rose vine that trailed over the gallery banisters, went inside, and pinned it into her hair before the pier mirror in the first parlor. It was then that a dreadful thing happened. Someone twisted the squeaky bell on the front door, and Tante Bébé went to answer it without taking the bright pink roses out of her hair. Standing there was a good friend of her sister's, a very prim and uprighteous woman, who would tolerate no foolishness. The woman looked at Tante Bébé and gasped, "Something is caught in your hair, *chère!* Take yourself to a mirror and look." Tante Bébé took herself to a mirror and threw the roses into the cold fireplace as if they were hateful things instead of so beautiful.

That was the incident that caused Tante Bébé to do what she did. The woman told her sister and brother-in-law, and they both teased Tante Bébé terribly for days, and every night she cried when she went to bed. The family forgot it as Mardi Gras approached, for the sister and brother-in-law went to balls every night and were tired the next day, but Tante Bébé, sitting home with the smaller children every evening, had time to think. As the children babbled to her of their Mardi Gras plans and as she sewed on ball and party dresses for her debutante niece, she remembered how once she had loved Mardi Gras. Now she recalled that she had always wanted to wear a costume and mask after she was grown, but her parents had forbidden this after her thirteenth birthday. They said nice young ladies did not mask and mix with the common people in the streets. Tante Bébé reflected that maybe that was what she had always wanted, and it was why she had never married. For she had had her beaux, only they were always such as her father approved, and Papa's taste and her own had never been the same.

A wicked idea came to Tante Bébé. It kept intruding itself into her thoughts and she kept pushing it away. At last she knew she could not resist it. When the children were asleep Tante Bébé stole up to the attic and rummaged in the trunks that were stored there, and finally she found what she wanted, a gypsy costume of green and red and yellow satin, a pair of bright red stockings, green shoes that laced about the ankles, a kerchief of every color in the rainbow, huge, golden hoop earrings, a little black mask. The costume had been worn by her niece a few years ago in a school play, and how the girl's father had fumed! Even for a girl of fourteen, he had said, it was indecent! Tante Bébé carried it downstairs to her room and worked on it, adding lace and bright buttons and ribbons, shortening the skirt just a little. When she heard the family returning she hid the costume in the back of her *armoire* and slipped into bed.

Mardi Gras morning Tante Bébé came downstairs for breakfast in her usual black skirt and white blouse. The family ate hurriedly, then the children got into their costumes. Her brother-in-law invited her to come with them, but Tante Bébé laughingly refused. What would an old maid like her do on Mardi Gras? she asked. They understood, and went away, and as soon as they were gone Tante Bébé hurried up to her room, pulled off her drab clothing, and took down her hair. With an iron borrowed from her niece and heated over a gas jet, she curled the ends of her thick black hair until it fell in a gleaming cascade just below her shoulders. Then she dressed, slowly pulling on the red hose, arranging her bodice, smoothing the tight skirt about her hips. Thank God her figure was good! It had not changed since she was sixteen. She applied a powder puff to her face, her throat, her bosom, so much of it exposed now

that she could hardly bear to look at herself, and knotted
the kerchief at a daring angle about her head, attached the
big earrings, took up the tambourine with its bright ribbons.
She struck the tambourine and did a little dance step before
the mirrors of her *armoire*. *Voilà!* She would do. Going
downstairs, she bit her lips hard to make the blood come. In
the hall she put on the little mask. If any neighbors saw her
go they did not recognize poor Tante Bébé. A man at the
corner did look at her legs. Let him look. She had always
known she had nice legs.

Tante Bébé went first to Canal Street and walked into
the middle of Mardi Gras. Everyone smiled at her and she
smiled back. A crowd of young people in costumes encircled
her and she walked a few blocks with them, laughing and
talking. Later a clown slipped his arm around her waist, and
she giggled, but pulled away. A youngster, dressed as a
pirate, seized her tambourine and would not give it back
until she had promised to kiss him. But she did not kiss him.
She took the tambourine and hit him on the head lightly,
and said, "Shoo! I am old enough to be your *tante*." "Aw,"
he said, "you're just a baby." She laughed, and replied,
"*Oui!* Tante Bébé."

When the parade was coming she saw her sister and
brother-in-law. At first she wanted to hurry away, but then
she changed her mind and went over to them and shook
her tambourine under her brother-in-law's nose. He laughed
and her sister smiled indulgently but frostily, and Tante
Bébé thought, "Her, she thinks I'm some woman from Basin
Street," as she danced out of their sight.

After Rex had passed, she went down Royal Street. The
crowd was so thick she had difficulty getting through, and
so many men tried to flirt, and even to seize her hand, that
she began to be a little frightened. She was having a fine
Mardi Gras, but there were risks she had not thought about
until now, and not even the public women were dressed

much more daringly than she—with her skirts nearly to her knees and her bosom so low-cut. Then the worst thing happened and a drunken sailor came up to her, and before Tante Bébé knew it she was pressed against a brick building and the breath of whisky was in her face. At that moment she even wished for her brother-in-law. But as suddenly as it had happened it was over. A hand seized hers and she was jerked away from the sailor. She went with the hand, reflecting that nothing could be worse.

It was not worse. It was much, much better. The hand was attached to an arm that was attached to a tall man who looked like a gentleman even in the costume of a red devil. She thought his eyes were nice through his mask and his mustache was fascinating. He told her she needed a drink, and Tante Bébé quivered nervously and said that perhaps a little wine would do her no harm.

In the café he removed his mask, and she liked him even more. Then she removed hers. Let him see the worst. The gentleman told her she was beautiful, and then he introduced himself by a name as Irish as Mike O'Toole. She gave him her true name, which no one ever used any more, and which was something like Marguerite, with a long Creole name behind it. They talked for hours, and soon Tante Bébé knew that she was not really old at all. Mr. O'Toole looked forty.

But as the hours passed and her eyes grew brighter from more wine than she had ever drunk before in all her life, the café became more crowded and so noisy they could hardly hear all they had to say to each other. Mike told Tante Bébé that he was from Texas and all about himself. She told him such gilded lies that she wondered if the priest would ever give her absolution if she did penance for the rest of her life. Then the inevitable occurred. A fight began in one corner of the saloon. Someone threw a chair and someone else threw a bottle. Mike tried to fight their way to the door,

but something hit him and he went down, and lay unconscious in his devil's suit at her feet. Tante Bébé began to
scream. She was still screaming when the police arrived.
That was how Tante Bébé went to jail. She was the first
member of her old and distinguished family to go to jail in
more than a hundred and fifty years.

Her brother-in-law came, of course, and took her home.
On the way he told her grimly that she had probably killed
her sister, who was prostrated. She had ruined her niece's
debut. He was contemplating suicide himself. They would
never live down this disgrace. But Tante Bébé just wept and
wondered if Mike O'Toole was dead. At last her brother-
in-law said no more, convinced her weeping was due to
shame and to the *scandale* she had caused them all.

For a week Tante Bébé remained locked up in her room.
At last she was summoned downstairs for a conference. Her
sister was better, but still pale and weak. They had plans.
A cousin in Philadelphia was willing to take Tante Bébé in
for a while, if she promised to behave herself. Perhaps she
could come back later. Her brother-in-law confessed he was
certain her mind was not quite right. An old maid her age
behaving that way! But insanity in the family was as dis-
graceful then as immorality, so he did not want his sus-
picions of her weak mind to become public gossip either.

Tante Bébé was all packed to leave the next morning
when a man came to the door and asked the colored woman
who opened it for "Miss Marguerite." The servant said
there was no "Miss Marguerite" there, for she did not know
Tante Bébé's real name. The gentleman pronounced, with
difficulty, the last name, and the Negress went for her mistress. Tante Bébé's sister was indignant, but she was too
polite to do anything but summon the Marguerite for whom
the stranger was asking.

Dressed in her severe black skirt, her shirtwaist with its
starched jabot, her little square shoes, and with her hair

done up in its stern knot, trembling from head to foot, Tante Bébé descended the stairs. Mike O'Toole went to meet her and put his arms around her, and Tante Bébé wept all over his clean shirt.

Her sister had to sit down.

Mike O'Toole then explained to Marguerite what a hard time he had had trying to find her, but at last the police had relented and given him her address.

Some of the children peered down the stair well and cried, "Tante Bébé has a beau!"

They were quite wrong, said Mike O'Toole. Tante Bébé had a husband, if she wanted one. They would have to live in Texas, but they could come back next year for Mardi Gras, and for every Mardi Gras for the rest of their lives.

CHAPTER FIFTEEN

YOU GO WHOLE HOG OR YOU GO FISHING

*Y*OU CAN DO ANYTHING IN NEW ORLEANS ON MARDI Gras, anything that is fun. You can, and you probably will, do some things you have never done before. Even little folk sayings have grown up around this fact. One of them is that if a man can't do anything he wants with a woman on Mardi Gras he'll never get anywhere with her at all.

As in the case of Tante Bébé, things happen to people on that day that they never believed could happen. It all depends on you.

Like Tante Bébé, you must give the magic of Mardi Gras a chance. It is no time for reserve or restraint or inhibition. You must become a part of the day. As Orleanians put it, you must become "a Mardi Gras." There is pleasure to be had as a spectator, but not nearly so much as when you become part of the show. This is supposed to be your farewell to the flesh, too, so make the most of it. You can do penance tomorrow. If you are not going to be a Mardi Gras, you might as well spend the day in the country.

Two things are really important—a costume and a mask.

Mardi Gras

Some people wear a costume but not a mask, which is a mistake, for the mask is the real disguise, and without it inhibitions will remain, at least with those people who have any under normal circumstances. On Mardi Gras everyone is supposed to be anonymous.

Costumes don't have to be expensive or fancy, and often the simplest ones are the best, but everyone should dress up in something and cover his face with something, and then go out to see what he can see and do what he can do. Age makes no difference, sex makes no difference. If there is the least taste for adventure there will be an adventure of some kind.

Mardi Gras has always been a wonderful time for the Tante Bébés of New Orleans and for the Tante Bébés who come to New Orleans. Not all Creole *tantes* were as daring as Mike O'Toole's girl, but New Orleans women were having one day free of the conventions long before women in other parts of the country began to take all the days off.

Years ago women went into the bars on Mardi Gras, nice women who dared to enter them on no other day. Now only the Sazerac has been intelligent enough to retain its forbidden charm, but once the respectable females of New Orleans set foot in other bars only when masked on Mardi Gras.

Nice women used to invade Basin Street. The rest of the year they scarcely ever mentioned that street, and their brothers, husbands, and sons did not mention it in their presence, but on Mardi Gras, in costumes and masks, many women from every strata of society satisfied an urge to see the palaces of sin and the women who inhabited them. The houses were always open all day, and ladies would wander in and out, whispering and giggling to each other, some who would not even have dared to attend a Ball of the Two Well-Known Gentlemen engaging the prostitutes in curious conversations, asking questions, being painfully sweet and obviously kind, and inquisitive.

The whores did not like them, but they were curious, too, and they understood why the ladies came better than did the ladies themselves. Besides, it was Mardi Gras, and they couldn't be inhospitable. And they were always discreet. They never recognized the gentlemen who might be escorting the ladies during their adventure.

When Ash Wednesday came no woman ever mentioned where she had been, not even to her husband, even though he had been her escort. It was something a lady could do on Mardi Gras, but it was not a nice subject to talk about.

Of course there have been periods when whether or not it was proper for a woman to mask on Mardi Gras has been a subject for debate. In early days women seem to have thought nothing of it. Then, in the last two or three decades of the past century and the first one of this, there arose a school of thought that considered it something for what the Creoles called the *gens du commun*—the common people. Yet the very woman who might argue against it in her parlor was likely to sneak out a back door on Mardi Gras morning, if she had an opportunity to do that. Once in the street, in complete disguise, she would have the time of her life.

There are still a few priggish and dull spirits who give lip service to the old belief that a lady should not mask, but they are few now, so few that their voices can scarcely be heard. One New Orleans social leader was terrified at the thought that the fact that she walked on Canal Street in costume and mask might be published, yet she does every year, and she has more fun than she has all the rest of the year. However, she has cousins who "consider it common to go to Canal Street at all, even to shop."

If you unmasked the people on Canal Street any year it

would be amazing to discover their identities. Perhaps even those cousins of the woman who secretly masks are there. One year a dignified and highly respected university professor and his wife danced together in the street all day long dressed as George and Martha Washington. A pair of Dalmatian coach dogs who hovered about the Boston Club entrance another year, and raised their legs each time a socialite entered the club, were a famous writer and an iconoclastic woman friend, who was of distinguished family and position and had herself been in the court of more than one carnival krewe.

Many of the famous people who come to New Orleans for Mardi Gras make no secret of their arrival, but others do conceal their presence, bringing costumes with them, so that they may have a vacation from their own personalities and be something or somebody else for a change. There is no doubt but that a sudden and general stripping of masks any Mardi Gras afternoon would uncover faces until now seen only by most Orleanians in the newspapers or on the movie screen. Not a multitude of them, of course; famous persons have a weakness for letting it be known they are around. But news did later spread that during a recent Mardi Gras one of the foremost generals of World War II romped through the streets in disguise all day, without being recognized by anyone, and without its being known that he was in the city until long after his plane had departed. Not even military rank can always be remembered on Mardi Gras. One year a lieutenant and a corporal were observed dancing together in the street. The lieutenant had borrowed a girl's hat, which consisted of a small bunch of yellow roses, worn at a rakish angle over one eye. The corporal wore a bright red Spanish hat, and he was leading.

The people's Carnival in the streets belongs to all who want to be a part of it. Everyone who is masked is a friend.

You Go Whole Hog or You Go Fishing

Strangers meet, dance together, drink together, walk along with their arms around each other's shoulders, and then separate as suddenly and impulsively as they met, and go their ways without ever knowing the identity of their companion of a few minutes or an hour or two, and certainly without caring. Here there is no rank, no caste.

Usually the most timid girl will dance with a strange man, if both are masked, and if he behaves himself—if she is the sort of girl who wants him to behave himself. When a crowd gathers in front of a small band of music in the street, or beneath a window where a phonograph has been set up, nearly everyone dances with everyone else, without introduction, of course, for it is very bad form to introduce masked persons, or even to recognize them.

There are exceptions to this informality—jealous men, or husbands and wives, who become indignant when a stranger encroaches upon their companion's time. These provide some amusement, unless they become abusive. Then they are thought to be soreheads who do not understand the spirit of Mardi Gras. Tired policemen, always around in adequate numbers, prevent most of the real trouble that could develop. If there is a fight they never allow it to amount to anything, although the jails do become a little fuller than usual toward evening on Mardi Gras. But if a gentleman merely takes a swing at another one, police and the crowd end the controversy quickly, and when a jealous woman screams at another woman she is usually laughed into moving on, with laughter that is intended as a reminder that, after all, this is Mardi Gras.

Sometimes crashing vehicles provide excitement. One year a truck filled with masked celebrants crashed into the rear of another truck also filled with maskers. A small boy, whose legs had been dangling over the back of the truck, began to cry. His mother leaped to the ground, hitching up wide hoop skirts, so she could move faster, and let loose a

223

torrent of profanity upon the occupants of the other truck.

A policeman, who had the usual disillusioned expression New Orleans police always have on Mardi Gras, went over to see what all the noise was about. He found the truck that had struck the boy pulling away. "My son's leg is broken!" cried the mother.

The policeman examined the leg. "It's just bruised," he said. "He'll be all right."

"The hell he will!" she yelled. "I say it's broken!" She rolled up a fist, reached from way back, and let the policeman have it on the nose.

"Lady!" he protested, trying to hold her arms.

Her husband came running over, and he took a swing at the cop, but missed. Then a crowd gathered, and, eventually, more police. "You all better get the hell away from here unless you want to go to jail," advised a captain.

The man and wife walked back to their truck, upon which the little boy, dressed in a monkey suit, was jumping up and down with excitement. "I tell you his leg's broken!" the mother screamed as her husband helped her to climb into the back beside her son.

"It ain't!" bellowed the indignant policeman, rubbing his aching nose.

"People on Mardi Gras!" said the police captain.

But there is a comparatively small amount of trouble on Mardi Gras now. There are almost no murders at all.

Perhaps the most prevalent crime on Mardi Gras these days is the picking of pockets. Each year via the daily newspapers police warn Orleanians and visitors to be very careful of the "whiz" and the "cannon," which in police parlance is the pickpocket. Their advice includes caution to take as little money out into the crowds as possible and that women wear no real jewelry.

The pickpocket always comes to New Orleans for Mardi Gras, along with the beggars, the pitchmen, and a hundred thousand respectable visitors. His favorite method of operation is known to police as the "fan." For the "fan" two or more of these artists work together. They crowd on both sides of their victim, one pushes him, and then offers profuse apologies. During the distraction the other operator removes the victim's wallet or roll. They usually work in crowds watching the parades or dancers or cavorting maskers, sometimes on crowded streetcars, or, if they can get into them, which is very unusual, at balls. Another form of pickpocketing is the rolling of drunks. A drunken celebrant, masked or in ordinary clothes, is likely to wander into neighborhoods or into drinking establishments where he would not ordinarily be seen. Here the criminal, sometimes in costume, finds it easy to strike up an acquaintance with a stranger, perhaps encourage him to have more drinks. The rest is very easy.

Drinking is to be expected on Mardi Gras, especially in New Orleans, where people drink more liquor all the year round than they do any place else in the country, except perhaps in New York and Hollywood. Excessive drinking is one of the few things it is a mistake to do on Mardi Gras. An alcoholic fog may become so thick that it will conceal all there is to see, and to spend Mardi Gras drunk is about the same as taking an ocean cruise for one's vacation and spending the entire time at the ship's bar. Yet there are differences of opinion as to how to have a good time, and, in spite of all this, liquor is everywhere on Mardi Gras. Maskers carry bottles through the streets and invite strangers to share them. As the parades approach, customers emerge from the crowded saloons with highball glasses and bottles of beer in their hands. By noon some celebrants are already through celebrating, and some are fast asleep, on street curbs, in quiet corners of cafés, or in doorways. By dark everyone is used to stepping over unconscious bodies in costumes, and the police are wondering if there is room for one more in the various precinct jails. The best way to handle the Mardi Gras and drinking problem is to avoid exceeding one's capacity and to remember that Mardi Gras takes place outside and not inside New Orleans bars, and that one can enjoy all the charming bars there are in the city on other days. Bartenders hate all their customers on Mardi Gras anyway.

For both resident and visitor, obtaining a Mardi Gras costume is easy in New Orleans. Lots of people make their own, and here is an opportunity for creative expression that no one should miss. Wonders can be done with old clothes, old junk, and whatever can be found in the back shed, the basement, or in Grandma's trunk in the attic. All that is needed is a minimum of materials and a maximum of imagination. At some time in his life everyone has wanted to be something that he isn't, and Mardi Gras is the time to realize that desire. The crazier the desire is the better.

For the more conventional, costume shops are plentiful in New Orleans. Some of these work all year to create costumes just for Mardi Gras. Costumes can be bought or rented. To rent them it is necessary to leave a deposit in addition to the fee charged and sometimes to furnish references. There are still a number of these places in the French Quarter, although not so many as formerly; others are located uptown, several within a few blocks on Dryades Street. In this section almost every imaginable kind of costume can be found. Special shops sell and rent wigs, and one of these has a famous window in which a group of dummy heads, which display the wigs that are offered, also at Mardi Gras wear elaborate headdresses and masks.

A visit to some of the rummage shops, which contain piles and stacks of materials, ostrich plumes, strings of beads, cards of brilliants and rhinestones, and enormous supplies of masks of every conceivable type, is in itself an adventure. Here you need neither buy nor rent a costume, but you may buy everything you will require to make your own or to have one made. There are so many possibilities to be achieved from the vast and curious stock of merchandise on display that you can, with very little trouble, be not only anything that ever was, but many things that never were.

The most famous New Orleans costume establishment of all time was Mme. Alabo's on Bourbon Street. Madame was in business for fifty years and remained in business until her death only a few years ago. Whole generations of Orleanians went into the tiny, crowded, fabulous shop each carnival season, and it is doubtful that she was ever asked for a costume she could not supply from her amazing shelves, or could not make on the shortest possible notice. One had only to step within her door to enter a fantastic world. Little paths stretched between counters and tables and shelves with all the gaudy, brilliant, beautiful paraphernalia of Mardi Gras, and led through two rooms open to each other by sliding doors. In the rear room, almost completely surrounded by boxes and more piles of material, Madame's assistant was always at work at her sewing machine. All about in both rooms were suits of armor, dummies in flowing capes, plumed hats, doublet and hose. Above, strung on wires, was an astonishing assortment of masks—animal heads, devil faces, skulls, grinning clowns. There were humorous masks, grotesque masks, hideous masks, frightening masks. New Orleans still misses Mme. Alabo.

A number of Orleanians with artistic inclinations have now turned to the making of Mardi Gras masks as a business or as a hobby. Not all of these are to be worn, but many of the mask makers specialize in huge ones to be used during Mardi Gras as decorations in restaurants, bars, theater lobbies or in homes. In some night clubs and cafés the mask is becoming increasingly popular, so that many of the places in

Mardi Gras

New Orleans where people go to play are taking on a look of Mardi Gras for the entire year.

Coaxing more people to dress up and to mask has long been a major project for all those who love New Orleans and Mardi Gras. Each year there are many maskers, but no one will be satisfied until there is not a person left in the city on that day who is not masked. Newspapers always plead with their readers to disguise themselves, and as Mardi Gras nears they editorialize on the subject.

Lyle Saxon was one of the champions of Mardi Gras throughout his life As a newspaper reporter he published article after article urging his readers to mask, and he always masked himself. He was so strict about only the masked entering the room at the St. Charles Hotel, where he held his buffet luncheons each Mardi Gras, that neither personal fame nor friendship nor social position could gain admission for the unmasked. One year a young woman was terribly upset because Saxon, an old friend, would not let her in. In sheer desperation she screamed at last, "But I have on a Lilly Daché hat!" That did her no good at all.

Whenever he could escape his guests, Saxon would sneak out into the streets, usually with Joel Harris Lawrence, who was his Mardi Gras partner for years. Once when he was a rabbit, Saxon, six feet three inches tall, then weighing well over two hundred pounds, had an accident. Another masker pulled his tail so vigorously that off came the tail and some inches of the seat of his costume. Saxon fled back to the St. Charles Hotel, but a little later returned to the streets in another costume.

Lyle Saxon loved Mardi Gras as he did all the beautiful, fantastic, and humorous traditions of New Orleans, and an active part in it was the last public role he played, when during the Mardi Gras of 1946, which was on March 5, he sat out on a balcony and described the Rex parade and the scene before him over a national radio chain. A few days later he was in a hospital, and he died on April 9.

It should be remembered that it is the very essence of Mardi Gras for all to take a part in it. To stand by and watch the parades and the maskers in the streets is ·not enough. One should give as well as receive. The pageants are beautiful, but they represent other people's fun, and although they are primarily intended to entertain the spectators as well as to amuse those who take part in them, they are also meant to stimulate those who view them.

The mask is the core of Mardi Gras. It is wonderful to dress up, but it is almost shameful not to cover the face, and to look on Mardi Gras as on any other day. On all other days it is a crime to conceal one's identity, illegal to wear a mask in the streets, dishonest to appear what one is not. But on Mardi Gras comes freedom from all this restraint. Complete escape from identity is not only possible, but it is commendable. To be something one is not is the idea, and those who try it once will do it again and again. Only the extremely conceited people of the world never weary of being themselves.

CHAPTER SIXTEEN

KING ZULU AND THE BABY DOLLS

*W*HEN JOHNNIE J. SMITH WAS KING ZULU IN 1947 he ruled with a mighty hand. "Ain't having no foolishness, just having fun," he said. "Don't send me no champagne. I'm strictly a scotch and bourbon man." Even before Mardi Gras, Negro night clubs wanted Johnnie to appear on their premises, but he postponed that. "Maybe later," he said, "but I'm too busy now. We got dates in every funeral parlor in town and a lot of other high-class places. Can't mess with that cheap stuff. It's gotta be high-class or nothing."

Weeks before Mardi Gras, Johnnie accomplished what few white carnival kings have done. He practically made himself the king. His fellow members in the Zulu Social Aid and Pleasure Club began talking about who was to be king. "Who you think?" Johnnie asked. "I'm gonna be king."

It was only fair, Johnnie argued. The year before he had been the royal witch doctor, and a mule had eaten part of his grass skirt. "A man that goes through that ought to be the king," he said.

And so it came to pass that Johnnie was king.

Days before Mardi Gras Johnnie rode around New

Orleans in a glittering limousine driven by a chauffeur, distributing the autographed coconuts that are part of the bounty always bestowed upon favorite subjects by King Zulu. Coconuts were rather scarce that year, too.

"The way them people go for my coconuts," Johnnie said, "I'd have to buy out the French Market and a couple of other places to have enough to go around, and the king's gotta have enough. People get jealous."

He bought out something, for few Zulus have been more generous. "A king's gotta advertise too," Johnnie said. "You ever meet a cheap king?"

Johnnie left his coconuts in bars, night clubs, barbershops, restaurants, funeral parlors, and private homes all over the colored sections of New Orleans. Many went to his white friends, too, who were just as eager to have them for souvenirs. One always goes to the mayor at the City Hall. "From the black mayor to the white mayor," is the way that coconut is usually inscribed. But of course not all were given away before Mardi Gras. Many were retained to be thrown from the Zulu floats during the parade. It's good luck to catch one of the Zulu's coconuts on Mardi Gras, and Johnnie wanted to spread good luck all over town.

"I'm gonna be the biggest king in Zulu history," Johnnie predicted as Mardi Gras approached. "I hear lots of people are coming from cities like Hollywood and New York to see me. They ain't gonna be disappointed. They gonna really see something."

The boastful manner of this King Zulu is part of the tradition of the ruler of Negro Mardi Gras, which has in its way just as much tradition as does the Mardi Gras of white New Orleans, and which deviates even less from its traditions year after year. Zulus will tell you that "There Never Was and Never Will Be a King Like Me!" is always their theme.

Mardi Gras

Many white Orleanians and visitors agree that there is no carnival king like Zulu, and the first thing many of them do early Mardi Gras morning is to go out to the New Basin Canal and South Claiborne Avenue to see King Zulu and his cohorts arrive on the royal barge.

In 1947 the Zulus boarded their barge, the *Lawewyn*, in the New Basin Canal at South Carrollton Avenue, some blocks from South Claiborne Avenue. King Johnnie Smith, who weighed more than two hundred pounds, was helped into a chair in the center of the barge, and his dukes, the royal witch doctor, and the Big Shot of Africa encircled him. All the Zulus wore the traditional costume of the krewe —long black underwear that covered them to wrists and ankles, grass skirts, and woolly wigs. Faces were blackened and eyes and mouths were circled with white. The royal witch doctor wore, in addition, a horned headdress and a golden ring in his nose, and carried a spiked mace. The Big Shot of Africa wore a high silk hat, a "diamond" stickpin with a stone as big as an egg blazing on the starched white dickey he wore over his black union suit, and another piece of glass of doorknob proportions on the little finger of one hand. He smoked a cigar a foot long. But the most magnificent of all, of course, was King Zulu. His Majesty wore a gold paper crown, dangling earrings, and strings of gleaming beads about his neck. His mantle was dark blue velvet trimmed in gold and edged with white rabbit fur. He carried a jeweled scepter, with which he now and then threatened the small page boy who kept pulling at his mantle. He also wore a leopard-skin vest.

As the barge moved slowly down the canal the royal prince —who always does this job—began to distribute coconuts among the crowds who lined the banks. The others held a conference with His Majesty. What about liquor? was the principal question.

"I know you all got some," said King Zulu, swinging that

232

scepter. "But I want you to hold it down, and not to be drinking too much. We got a long day ahead. There's been too much intoxication in the court and I decree it's gotta stop."

There were not too graceful movements of bulging grass skirts as attempts were made to further conceal the bottles hidden beneath them.

"All the gifts along the route come to my float," said King Zulu. "That's so I can watch what you all are doing." It is customary for saloons along the royal route to present the Zulus with bottles.

"That ain't never been done before," protested the Big Shot of Africa, who always feels he is pretty important.

"It's being done now," said King Zulu coolly. "I'm the king."

Colored girls and women along the shore began to yell greetings to His Majesty, and he waved his scepter genially, then directed the royal prince to give a special coconut to one young woman who was leaning so far over the water that she could nearly touch the barge. The royal prince obeyed, tossing it. King Zulu turned on him and berated him mildly. No coconuts were to be thrown this year, he ordered. They were to be handed. People had been hurt in other years, when Zulus had exuberantly heaved them into the crowds.

One of the dukes pulled out a bottle filled with colorless liquid and lifted it to his lips. King Zulu looked at him but said nothing. Another bottle appeared. "Okay," said His Majesty. "I told you all to hold it down. That's all I'm telling you." The bottles vanished beneath grass skirts, and no others appeared for a while. The crowd along the canal bank were in agreement that they had never seen the Zulus so sober in any year within the memory of anyone present.

The tug began to belch thick black smoke from its funnel, and the king brushed soot from his mantle. "Somebody shut that thing off," he commanded. "I'm gonna be ruined before we get started." The funnel obeyed him and stopped its annoying belching and coughing.

Someone remarked to His Majesty that during the coming year the New Basin Canal was to be filled in and that one of the oldest Zulu traditions would have to be discarded. The king snorted. "If they does that to us," he said, "they're gonna have to let us use the river, that's all. We'll just come floating down the lazy Mississippi."

When the barge docked at South Claiborne Avenue the crowd waiting on the shore, which is in the center of the most thickly populated Negro neighborhood in New Orleans, was so immense that the Zulus could scarcely see the end of it. Mostly Negro, there were, nevertheless, many white faces grinning up toward the royal entourage. About half of those who had come to view the arrival were in costume, the others in ordinary clothes. Right in front were a group of Baby Dolls, who are bands of Negresses who dress like dolls in short pleated skirts, silk bloomers, and little bonnets from which always dangle false curls of varying shades— sometimes golden blond.

The Baby Dolls shrieked at the Zulus.

"Hiyah, honey!"

"Come on, Daddy. Let's you and me go someplace!"

"Whatcha say, foots!"

"That king got it!"

Some of the dukes were impressed. "Look at them old gals," they remarked. "Man, what I couldn't do with that!"

"Shut up," said King Zulu. "Keep your mind on me!"

A Negro band, part of the parade to come, began playing, and one of the fattest of the Baby Dolls began doing a shake number. She accomplished what is called "going all the way down," lowering herself to the ground, shaking violently all the time, until she was stretched out on her back, resting upon her shoulders and feet, with her hips gyrating violently and her breasts quivering like jelly under the pink satin halter she wore above her brief skirt.

The parade began to form. One by one, the mule-drawn floats were lined up, four of them, each decorated with straw and palmetto. The band took its place in front, and then a number of Negroes dressed as policemen swung their clubs at the crowd and forced them back so that the regal maskers could board the floats. King Zulu, followed by the royal prince and the pages, climbed on the first float and sat himself carefully in the armchair in the center of the jungle that the float represented. When his mantle and crown had been arranged, someone handed him a Coca-cola highball and he raised it high and toasted the crowd. The witch doctor and several other Zulus mounted the second float. Now the witch doctor waved his mace and warned all within hearing distance that he was present to guard the health of all. "I'll cure or kill anybody that gets sick along the route," he said with a fierce expression. "If I can't find the cure I'll use the royal mace."

"Listen to him!" shouted a Baby Doll.

"I mean you too, gal!" growled the witch doctor.

The Big Shot of Africa took over the third float for himself and no one else was allowed aboard, as is the custom. The Big Shot sat himself in the armchair beneath the palmetto canopy, crossed his legs, and assumed an expression of supreme hauteur, puffing at his huge cigar and flashing his gigantic glass jewelry with exaggerated gestures and affectations.

All the rest of the Zulus crowded aboard the fourth float, and at last the parade was under way. In front were some of the dukes on horseback, surrounded by the "policemen." Then came the Young Tuxedo Brass Band, now rendering a hot number. After the floats was the property wagon, loaded with old and worn trunks labeled "Fragile, Handle with Care." What is in these trunks has always been a Zulu secret and is not to be divulged.

Mardi Gras

Negro maskers streamed behind the parade. The Baby Dolls walked the way they call "raddy," which is a strutting, sexy gait that includes much shaking and rolling of the hips. Other women imitated them. Men, both masked and unmasked, left the crowds edging the banquette and joined the women, flinging careless arms about their waists. The Baby Dolls greeted them with cordial expressions like "Hello, ugly. How you doing?" and "Man, we're gonna get it today. And I mean we're gonna get it, Papa." In front of the king's float a sign proclaimed the subject of the parade as "Let the Good Times Roll," and the good times were rolling. One of the "policemen" demanded of everyone he passed, "Gimme a drink! Gimme a drink! If somebody don't gimme a drink, I'm gonna call the wagon and send you all to the precinct for loitering around here." It was obvious that one duke had already disobeyed the royal decree of His Majesty, for he could not sit erect upon his horse, but kept sliding forward and slumping over the horse's neck, his white-painted eyelids drooping. Someone found a rope and the duke was carefully tied into his saddle to prevent an accident. But King Zulu was too busy to notice. He kept leaning down to shake hands with his subjects as the float rocked through the street, and the spectators crowded close to reach up and touch the royal palm.

"I'm the people's king," he explained. "We gotta law against being high-hat. That's one thing a Zulu can't be. I gotta be friendly to everybody."

A Baby Doll wanted to be friendly with the king, too, and she tried to climb aboard his float. "No women," said one of the "policemen," slapping her lightly on the posterior with his club. "King Zulu's too busy today."

In 1910 a group of Negroes sitting in a shed across the back yard from a saloon in Perdido Street in New Orleans agreed to found the Zulu Social Aid and Pleasure Club.

236

Negroes have always loved Mardi Gras, and even before the Civil War free people of color masked in the streets, but never had they had their own parade. This charter group decided that since the white king was supposed to come from a faraway country, their king would travel to New Orleans from Africa. He would be none other than the mighty king of the Zulus, who was the mightiest monarch in the world.

Their beginnings were humble, for they had little money. The first king, William Story, wore a lard can for a crown and carried a banana stalk as a scepter. There were no floats, so the early kings walked through the streets of the Negro sections, accompanied by a witch doctor and surrounded by warriors who carried spears and cowhide shields. A few years later King Zulu appeared in a carriage. In 1913 he wore a white linen suit and waved a scepter that was a loaf of Italian bread. The next year, however, the Zulu regalia was resumed, although King Zulu also rode in a buggy that year. By 1920 there were two floats. His Majesty then dressed much as he does now, except that he was much fiercer-looking, and wore red and yellow and green war paint and used a scepter that was a broomstick with a stuffed white rooster on the end. Two years later came the first arrival on the royal barge, which was of course a burlesque of the arrival of Rex. King Zulu was lifted, Morris chair and all, and placed upon his float. Warriors filled the other one. Another float was added in 1940, and that year the parade had its first subject, for the floats were entitled "The Pink Elephant," "Hunting the Pink Elephant," and "Capturing the Pink Elephant."

The Zulus are appropriately vigorous. They have managed to get along through the years, but not without arguments and quarrels. Considerably less reticent in regard to their ambitions, and particularly in expressing them, than are most of the members of white krewes, they wrangle incessantly over who is to be king or to hold other high office. They are even more likely to disagree over the choice of queen each year. Usually the current king chooses his own feminine companion, but seldom without dissent from officers and members who have favorite girls among their friends, or relatives with queenly ideas. Often the president of the krewe has a female friend who is nagging him incessantly about the matter, and if he holds his ground he is likely to win the crown for her, although the king has promised it to another. Love almost always plays a part in whatever choice is made, which in a way makes the Zulus more romantic than other krewes. One year, when agreement became impossible, King Zulu, who had no favorite of his own, gave the role to "Corinne," a female impersonator, who ever since has been known as "Corinne, the Queen."

Those girls who lose out as queen in any particular year become maids, for King Zulu has a full court like any carnival monarch. Mardi Gras night there is a ball, and while there is no tableau, there is a grand march and general dancing that continues well into the dawn of Ash Wednesday. Sometimes the maids wear evening gowns and carry flowers, but on other occasions they have appeared at the ball in leopard skins and little else, in imitation of Zulu women.

But the queen always wears regal robes. Her gown is usually white satin, and she is presented with a velvet and rhinestone mantle that rivals those worn by white queens. She wears a jeweled crown and carries a scepter and flowers. In most years she exchanges a champagne toast with her lord, standing with her maids on the balcony before the Geddes and Moss undertaking establishment, a Negro mortuary. After the parade passes there is a reception for the queen in the upper chambers of the undertaking parlors, and the queen has a wonderful time all afternoon. Extremely popular in her role, on several occasions it has been necessary to use actual physical restraint to prevent her from enjoying herself to excess, for she must be kept in good condition for the ball. Once she had to be locked in a room for most of the afternoon because she had become so infatuated with a male guest that she wanted to forget her duties as queen, run off with her new love, and continue her flirtation elsewhere.

The Zulus are not, for the most part, cultured or highly educated Negroes. Many of them are businessmen of a sort. One king was an undertaker. Johnnie Smith was the manager of a Negro moving picture theater. The upper class New Orleans Negroes neither like nor approve of the Zulus, however. They feel that they satirize their own race and do nothing to uplift it, and many critical Negroes are embarrassed by their antics.

But the Zulus have a lot of fun and provide a lot for others—and of every race. They pride themselves on being a people's organization, and meet the rebukes of the more haughty members of colored New Orleans with laughter, and they contend that they express a true spirit of Mardi Gras.

The Baby Dolls, the Gold Diggers, and the Zigaboos are groups of women maskers, loosely knitted together, who, like the Zulus, have become traditional parts of the Negro Mardi Gras. The Gold Diggers usually travel through the streets with male companions, who dress in masculine costumes that match those worn by the girls. The Baby Dolls and the Zigaboos always start out alone, but they never end the day that way.

Most famous of the three, the Baby Dolls were probably organized—if their group can be said to have ever really been organized—early in this century. They have usually been prostitutes, most of them living in the part of Perdido Street that is crammed with cheap Negro bars and cafés that are patronized by the lowest Negro element, and whose customers include professional burglars, murderers, fake beggars, and addicts of so many varieties of drugs that the smoking of marijuana is considered in their circle as a pastime as harmless as the chewing of gum. Baby Dolls drink a great deal of cheap sherry, take dope, and sell themselves for a dollar or less, except on Mardi Gras, when the prices go up.

Despite all this, Baby Dolls possess a keen affection for Mardi Gras, and a lot of thought and planning goes into their costumes and make-up. To be a Baby Doll they are supposed to look as innocent as possible, which may be accepted as a perfect example of altering one's personality on Mardi Gras, so they make their little skirts and bloomers out of chaste pink or virginal blue, the skirts pleated, the bloomers trimmed with ruffles and little bows. They wear waists or halters to match and bonnets that tie demurely beneath their chins. Their dusky faces, framed by long corkscrew curls of every shade, are heavily rouged and powdered. Some wear pink and blue socks, but most prefer long hose held up on their dark thighs with flashy, ruffled garters.

A Baby Doll does not act innocent, despite the demure garb. She walks "raddy," and on the slightest provocation "shakes on down." They seldom fight among themselves any more, but formerly they used to both start and cause street brawls that sometimes ended in bloodshed.

Years ago both white and colored prostitutes in New Orleans were divided into uptown and downtown groups, between which a fierce rivalry existed. The first Baby Dolls were uptown Negresses of the profession, who used to deliberately strut into the downtown Negro district on Mardi Gras, to walk "raddy" and show off in general, to tease and irritate their rivals. The culmination was usually fraught with flashing razors and flying bricks. Baby Dolls are now better behaved.

The Zigaboos are not quite so wicked a group and are not necessarily members of the same profession. They wear brief trunks and halters and fancy hats and often carry canes, which they use to effect when strutting through the streets. They walk "raddy," too, and are great favorites with Negro men, especially with the Zulus, who have a fine time calling out to them from the floats and occasionally deserting the parade for a few minutes of dancing or very public love-making. Throughout the day the Zigaboos pick up men and leave them, visit the bars and the night clubs that are always open. Like the Baby Dolls, they are usually drunk with sherry, gin, and love by dark, and are not alone.

Aside from the Zulus, the best-known Mardi Gras maskers among the colored population are the Indians. Groups of Negroes, organized into tribes, have dressed as Indians on Mardi Gras for more than a half century now. Some of these tribes have histories of which they've come to be extremely proud, and these boast of their tradition and customs quite as emotionally as do the members of the Krewe of Comus.

The clubs are formally organized. Meetings are held at regular intervals throughout the year, and members pay dues, hold elections, and plan their celebration of the Mardi Gras to come.

The real beauty of the costumes they wear often startles strangers in the city. Each is made of the richest materials available—satins, velvet, metallic cloth. Each basically consists of trousers, a shirt, a jacket, an apron that hangs down in front, elaborately beaded moccasins, a wig with long plaits, and, topping all, a gorgeous headdress of feathers. Every garment is an example of exquisite handwork of various kinds. Embroidery, beads, sequins, rhinestones, spangles, and other trimmings are used in intricate designs of the most brilliant colors. A costume of flame satin is sometimes encrusted with golden beads and rhinestones of rich blue.

Mardi Gras

Gold lamé, a favorite material, may be embellished with imitation pearls worked into a pattern of spiders and serpents. Heavy silver cloth is adorned with bright green stones and strips of white fur. Some Indians appear in snow-white costumes, with white ostrich plumes in their headdresses. Others will wear black satin, trimmed with gold, and green, black, and gold feathers. Most Indians make their own costumes, or have their wives make them, and, since they are in private life porters, cooks, servants, and shoeshine boys, a large percentage of their entire year's earnings is saved for their Mardi Gras dress. There is much competition between tribes, and even between members of tribes, and they are constantly trying to dress more elegantly than their brothers.

The oldest tribe still existing and appearing on the streets is called the Golden Blades, which is now more than thirty-five years old. There were tribes that preceded it, but they have now disbanded. Others that still appear call themselves the Wild Squa-tou-las, the Golden Eagles, the Little Red, White and Blues, the Creole Wild Wests, and the Yellow Pocahontas. Each has its chief, its chief's wife—who is very, very important—and its medicine man, the latter wearing some animal skins and horns and more terrifying facial make-up than the rest of the tribe. There are always spy boys and sometimes spy girls, who run ahead of each tribe carrying lanterns and looking for the approach of an "enemy" tribe.

Years ago they really did look upon each other as enemies, and when they met on Mardi Gras they fought. Then, too, a chief won and retained his position through physical force. When he became old and weak another and younger man took it away from him. All Orleanians can remember being warned about the "Indians," when children. White people would often go far to avoid meeting any of the tribes. Now they can hardly be called dangerous, however. They have even ceased fighting with each other. When two tribes meet they are more likely to pass around a bottle than to attack each other, and chiefs retain their high posts until they give them up of their own volition or else are voted out by the democratic process of election. Only the medicine men still try to make a fierce impression. If you approach one of them, he is likely to hop up and down, waving his arms and grimacing in a manner supposed to be terrifying, but if you persist in drawing him into conversation he usually turns out to be a quiet shoeshine boy or some equally harmless citizen.

But the Indians retain many of their old customs, some of which are strangely un-Indian and yet are not typically Negroid. They always speak to each other on Mardi Gras in a curious lingo supposed to be Indian. When chiefs meet they go through a ceremony that dates to when they did engage in combat. One chief asks, "Umba?" The other replies, "Me, no umba!" Then they dance around each other in what they conceive to be an Indian dance, in which all the tribe members sometimes join. Formerly, at the conclusion of this pistols and knives appeared, and murder was common. But now they head for the nearest saloon.

The Indians have strange songs and chants that are not at all Negro in character. These are very old and the meaning of some of them seems to have been forgotten. The best known perhaps is "Tu-Way-Pa-Ka-Way," of which there are many verses and parodies. All the tribes sing it, changing the words to suit themselves. To the accompaniment of the clapping of hands and perhaps the beating of a tambourine by the chief's wife, they'll sing:

> "The Indians are comin'!
> Tu-way-pa-ka-way.
> The Indians are comin'!
> Tu-way-pa-ka-way.

Mardi Gras

> *The Golden Blades are comin'!*
> *Tu-way-pa-ka-way.*
> *The Golden Blades are comin'!*
> *Tu-way-pa-ka-way!"*

A tribal chief often sings a solo:

> *"I'm the Big Chief!*
> *Tu-way-pa-ka-way.*
> *Of the strong Golden Blades!*
> *Tu-way-pa-ka-way.*
> *Strongest chief in the world!*
> *Tu-way-pa-ka-way.*
> *Of the fierce Golden Blades!*
> *Tu-way-pa-ka-way."*

Now he is only bragging, for most of the chiefs look like very tired old men.

Another favorite song is:

> *"Shh-bam, bang the bam.*
> *Follow me, follow me, follow me.*
> *Wha-wha-wha-follow, me,*
> *Shh-bam, bang the bam.*
> *Wha-wha-wha-follow me,*
> *Wha-wha-wha-follow me. . . ."*

That seems to be code of a sort. One tribe is directing another to follow them. If a tribe does get tough and trouble seems about to ensue, the more peaceful tribe is likely to sing:

> *"Shootin' don't make it,*
> *No, no, no, no!*
> *Shootin' don't make it,*
> *No, no, no, no!*
> *Stabbin' don't make it,*
> *No, no, no, no!*

King Zulu and the Baby Dolls

> Stabbin' don't make it,
> No, no, no, no!
> Killin' don't make it.
> No, no, no, no!
> Killin' don't make it.
> No, no, no, no!
> Fightin' don't make it.
> No, no, no, no!
> Fightin' don't make it.
> No, no, no, no!"

There are many versions of this one, all pleas for maintenance of the peace, and—with the aid and encouragement of the police—the peace is kept.

When King Zulu's parade begins there is a long day ahead. Like the white Mardi Gras monarchs, he has certain places to stop and certain streets through which he must pass, but as a whole his route is much more haphazard. During the weeks before, His Majesty has been invited to stop at a number of places, and he does his best to neglect no one. Time means nothing, for the Zulus parade all day long.

Most of the stops are at bars. In 1947 the first pause, however, was a grandstand about three blocks from the starting point, where a large crowd of subjects waited, and where His Majesty was toasted again and again. From there the parade swung neatly across the street and paused before a bar. Here bartenders brought drinks for all. After that there were stops every few blocks, and toasts at every stop.

The queen and her maids awaited their mates on a balcony in front of the Geddes and Moss undertaking parlors. Here there was a long pause, with an exchange of speeches and the presentation to His Majesty of the keys to Zululand in New Orleans. The king toasted the queen and the queen toasted the king. The queen complained later that she did not like champagne, for this was the first time she had ever tasted it, but she only made a slight grimace as she swallowed it, and otherwise performed her royal duties with grace and ease. After the toasts of the rulers, the dukes and maids also toasted each other, and then the dukes passed bottles around to the warriors on the floats, and a special one to the Big Shot of Africa, who had been comforted in his loneliness with Coca-cola highballs every time the king received another toast along the way.

Her jewels sparkling, her scepter waving graciously, Her Majesty accepted a highball from an attendant on the balcony, after the parade had moved on, and remained outside for quite a while, giving her subjects in the street below a good chance to admire her beauty. Then she went inside, where there was a large crowd who were busy having a good time drinking whisky and beer and eating sandwiches and potato salad. A corpse was laid out in a parlor downstairs, but this did not disturb the gaiety of the royal reception.

After the members of his entourage had gulped at least a dozen drinks, King Zulu began to worry again. He summoned the royal prince and issued instructions, and at the next stop the prince hopped off the king's float and ran back and forth along the sides of the others, shouting, "The king says you all drinking too much. He says hold it down." The Big Shot of Africa was the only one who chanced defiance. "The king's drinking more than me," said he. "Who's he trying to tell what?"

The Big Shot of Africa seemed to enjoy his role, and he played it to the hilt. Not once did he relax his supercilious pose. While the king was friendly and democratic, the Big Shot shook hands with no one and when the crowds whooped and hollered to attract his attention he responded only with a cool and disdainful nod. Baby Dolls gave him as much attention as they did the king, but even when they shook on down right beside his float, he usually pretended not to see them. Once he engaged in a brief conversation with an Indian, when the parade encountered a tribe, but aside from that he spoke to almost no one, but sat with crossed legs, flashing jewelry, and elegant cigar, letting all spectators know that he was superior to them all, a real big shot.

Until a comparatively few years ago the Zulus did not take their parade into the white section of New Orleans. They were particularly banned from Canal Street because of racial prejudice. Now, however, they can, and sometimes do, follow Rex. They at least always plan to do so, but they have so many stops in the Negro neighborhoods that it is not always possible to reach Canal Street before the sun goes down.

Accidents are frequent too. One year they lost the king entirely. He had climbed down from his float and gone into a saloon. Afterward he could not be found. Someone had seen him depart through a rear exit with a Baby Doll. He did show up, somewhat the worse for wear, at the ball that night, but then there was trouble again. His wife was waiting for him, so he fled the ball also and the queen had to perform the grand march alone.

The Big Shot of Africa was the victim of a mishap one year. A wheel came off his float and the Big Shot tumbled to the street. He was pretty well protected from injury by the whisky he had consumed, and he fell so like a fat rag doll that only his long underwear was torn. Somebody gave him a sack to wrap around the exposed portion of his person and the king honored him by allowing him to ride the royal float for the rest of the day, sitting at His Majesty's feet. Of course the Big Shot had lost prestige. During the balance of the parade he drooped dismally and wore a glum expression.

Mardi Gras

Probably only once has a woman rider been permitted to remain for long aboard a Zulu float. Those who climb aboard now and again throughout the parade are always pushed off before they can settle themselves for a long ride. One year, however, Louis "Satchmo" Armstrong, who is a kind of honorary member of the Zulus, and who often comes to New Orleans for Mardi Gras, brought a woman violinist along and they were allowed to ride on the king's float, and in civilian clothes. All the Zulus love "Satchmo" and he can have any concessions he wants, besides a king has to be polite to his guests, especially a mighty monarch like King Zulu.

The Zulu Ball is less formal than any of the ones given by white krewes. Almost anybody can go, and almost everybody does. "We ain't stuck up," Zulus boast.

Baby Dolls and Indians are always there. Everybody is a little tired and more than a little drunk, but somehow, when the band strikes up the grand march, fresh energy seems to come to all and a reasonable amount of sobriety returns. Soon everybody is out on the floor dancing, and how they're dressed doesn't make any difference at all. Every kind of costume is there—Mardi Gras suits, tuxedos, and sports shirts.

The king, the queen, and the Big Shot of Africa all take an active part in the dancing too. All the women want to dance with the king, and he gives as much of himself as he can. Once in a while he vanishes before the ball is over, which no one exactly approves, but which everyone understands. The queen nearly always remains until morning, but by then she has proven herself not only a beauty but a gay companion, for no one outdoes the queen in trucking and jitterbugging and in exhibiting, in general, a spirit of Mardi Gras joy. After the ball is over the queen can be fairly sure of her future, too, for during the year to come she will be as popular as any debutante.

King Zulu and the Baby Dolls

The Big Shot of Africa also leaves most of his superior air outside the ball. There are more ways than one of being a big shot, and only the king is more popular with the women during and after Mardi Gras night. Life won't be dull for a long time.

It is dawn before all go home. No one goes to work on Ash Wednesday, and even South Rampart Street is nearly empty all that day, while everyone sleeps. But when darkness comes all yesterday's Zulus and Indians and Baby Dolls emerge from their homes and congregate in the bars and night clubs for quiet beers and conversation about the day before. The king and queen—without their royal garb of course—are always around, receiving the compliments and praise of their friends. Everyone agrees it was the biggest Mardi Gras yet.

The criticism that may come now from some members of their race is lightly dismissed. The Zulus were not even annoyed, for instance, by the remarks of Dr. W. L. Russell, president of the Mobile Colored Carnival Association, when Dr. Russell complained one year that they were undignified, and, according to all the newspapers, added, "We stand by the cultural and mystical principles on which Mardi Gras was founded, and one of our very strictest rules is that there be no jitterbugging at the queen's coronation ball."

"They is jealous," explained a Zulu. "That's all what's the matter with them. You see, we Zulus know how to have fun. We get better every year. You come around and see us next Mardi Gras. Man, that's gonna be the best of all!"

CHAPTER SEVENTEEN

MARDI GRAS IN OTHER CITIES

*M*ARDI GRAS IS RETURNING TO EUROPE NOW that another war is over, and it has been revived in many places on this continent and in South America, with cities and communities holding their own versions of the annual celebration. There is a Mardi Gras as far north as Alaska, but most of them are, characteristically, in the Southern regions, for Mardi Gras is, of course, Southern in temperament and by tradition.

Shrove Tuesday is observed in many parts of Louisiana. There are parades and balls in some of the towns. Houma sometimes borrows the floats of Algiers's Chief Choctaw, who parades on the Sunday before, for their Mardi Gras parade, which is followed by a ball. Their king and queen are chosen through ballots published in the two newspapers in the town, on which readers indicate their choices and mail them in to the editors.

Elsewhere in the southwestern part of the state, where most of the natives are of French Acadian descent, there are picturesque Mardi Gras customs. Maskers stroll through the streets and along the highways and lanes of the bayou country, playing tricks on their neighbors and indulging in all sorts of foolishness and Gallic good humor. As these Cajuns put it, they "pass a good time." In another section maskers on horseback ride over the prairies in hilarious frolic on Mardi Gras. This is an old custom, called "running the Mardi Gras."

In all the Cajun country it is the men who have most of the Mardi Gras fun, for the natives are still inclined to be strict with their wives, sweethearts, and sisters, and seldom permit their women to mask. Men frequently dress in female attire, stuffing waists and skirts with rubber balls and pillows for comic effects. They dance in streets and roads and drink wine and whisky and black coffee.

Accompanied by musicians with fiddles, guitars, and other simple instruments, bands of maskers often visit from house to house, practicing the peculiar ceremony of begging for a chicken for a gumbo. When such a group arrives on the front gallery of a Cajun home the family is not supposed to recognize the maskers, even though they are often neighbors, perhaps relatives. The head of the house asks the spokesman for the maskers where they are from. The reply, which is given in song, is always that they are from England and concludes with a demand for a fat hen. The family must then supply either a hen or, should they not keep chickens, some coins. If a hen is donated it is dropped into the sack the maskers always carry. Then they usually unmask for a few minutes, amidst much laughter and joking, and drinks and refreshments are served. There are always *beignets* (doughnuts) and coffee, and frequently stronger beverages. Then, a fat hen in their sack—or with money for other refreshments added to their fund—they are off to the next house, sometimes on horseback, but as often now in festively decorated automobiles or trucks.

In the evenings there is a *fais-do-do*—a big dance of the sort Cajuns love, with all the babies sleeping in the *parc aux petits,* a small room off the dance floor, and all the *mamans* and *tantes* and *grandmères* sitting around the edges of the big room, fanning and gossiping and keeping an eye on the dancers.

Before this the delicious chicken gumbo has been prepared by the women, and the men consume bowl after bowl of the thick soup, boasting how one can eat more than the others. Later in the night those who have overcelebrated begin to pay a toll. Outside some of the men are ill. That wild Thibodeaux girl, her, she passes out and hits the floor and her *maman* takes her home, promising to beat her *go-go* good. Poor Etienne is dragged out by his wife, but *le bon Dieu* is on his side, for he cannot hear her scolding. Papa Boo falls down the stairs and he is unconscious so long that his daughter Toots starts screaming he is dead and they have to throw water on her to get her out of her fit. Numa Ledouce thrashes his wife soundly right in the middle of the *fais-do-do,* while the band plays louder so strangers outside cannot hear her piercing yells. And there are fights. Sometimes even a knife is drawn. But all will be forgiven when they meet at mass on Ash Wednesday.

There may be one major excitement on Ash Wednesday. A mother will awaken when she hears the baby crying. When she goes to the crib she takes one look and screams. This is not her baby! This is not little Patoote who she parked in the *parc aux petits* last night! Somewhere else in the community another sleepy mother, perhaps with a slight hangover, is changing a diaper. Suddenly she screams, too, and all the family comes running. *Mon Dieu! Regarde-tu!* Eugénie is now a boy!

Sometimes other *mamans* also had too much wine the night before. All rush out of their houses with bawling infants in their arms. There are rapid exchanges, until all the mistakes are corrected. Then all laugh. It just proves what a fine time they passed last night. *Mais oui,* you can always tell a good *fais-do-do* by the number of babies who get mixed up. Ever afterward when one of these children misbehaves his *maman* will tell him he is a "Mardi Gras baby." He is not hers, no, acting that way. She knows what happened. She left the right one at a Mardi Gras *fais-do-do*.

Lafayette, Louisiana, has two fine daytime parades on Shrove Tuesday and one night parade. There is a big ball, too, that night, with a king and queen, modeled very closely after the pattern of the New Orleans affairs.

There is a celebration in Opelousas with masking and costume dances. In Shreveport there is a children's Mardi Gras, as the schools celebrate the event. In the past there have been masquerade dances given by private clubs and social groups. In several Louisiana communities, such as in Monroe, only Negroes celebrate Mardi Gras. Here they dress up in comical costumes on that day and dance and strut in the streets of their partially segregated section of the town.

In other Southern states, particularly in Mississippi and Florida, there are masquerades and parties in many towns on Shrove Tuesday. There are a number of parades and other Mardi Gras events in the small cities along the coast of the Gulf of Mexico. Biloxi, for instance, has a parade and a great ball. Elsewhere observance of Mardi Gras seems to be increasing.

Outside of New Orleans the most complete and full-grown Mardi Gras in the United States is the one held in Mobile. Indeed there are citizens of Mobile who contend that their Mardi Gras is older than that of New Orleans.

This argument is a comparative one. It is true that Mobile was the first to have parades with floats, and that the float idea was brought to New Orleans from the smaller city. It is also true that the early parades of the famous Cowbellion de Rakin Society took place on New Year's Eve, not on

Mardi Gras

Mardi Gras, and that Mobile did not observe Mardi Gras with parades until 1867, long after New Orleans was doing so, long after Comus had first appeared in the Rue Royale.

On New Year's Eve, 1830, Michael Krafft was dining with Thomas Niles, Richard Coirie, Henry Daggett, Robert Roberts, Nathaniel Ledyard, and Samuel Kipp in Antoine La Tourette's café in Mobile. These gentlemen departed the restaurant a little before midnight. Apparently they were in high spirits, for when they reached Partiridge's Hardware Store they conceived of a splendid way to celebrate the New Year. In front of the store were a number of cowbells, rakes, and hoes, and the men borrowed these, took to the street again, and proceeded to arouse the town by ringing the cowbells, beating on the sides of houses with the other instruments, and singing and shouting. They did very well, for soon most of Mobile seems to have been thoroughly aroused.

They finally serenaded Mayor John Stocking, Jr., and far from being displeased, the mayor invited them in for refreshments, and there the party continued for some time. It seems to have been Mayor Stocking who suggested that the celebration be repeated the following year. Organization followed, with new members being admitted. They adopted the name Revelers, and decided upon referring to their parade as an "Escapade."

Wheeled vehicles and costumes were introduced about 1834, and as the years passed these became increasingly lavish. In 1840 the first parade with a title was introduced, this being "Heathen Gods and Goddesses," the type of subject still so often used both in Mobile and in New Orleans. This 1840 parade was the first of its kind in the United States. A member named Daniel Geary had long before this suggested the name of the Cowbellion de Rakin Society, and it was by this title that the organization was now called.

About the time of the first parade of floats and other decorated vehicles the first ball was held. After the parade the maskers would assemble in a Mobile theater. As in New Orleans, the evening's entertainment opened with tableaux, carrying out the theme of the parade. There was then a single maskers' dance, when the members danced with chosen young ladies, but after that the dancing became general. At midnight a whistle was blown to mark the arrival of the New Year, and the maskers vanished, going to a private supper, leaving the ball to their guests, who were, of course, not supposed to know the identities of their hosts.

Younger members of the Cowbellions—referred to in Mobile as the "Cows"—broke away from the parent club in 1842 and formed the Strikers' Independent Society, because most of these young men were cotton markers or "strikers." Even now their principal emblem is a marking pot and ink brush. In 1844 the T.D.S., who are sometimes called the Tea Drinkers Society, but whose correct name is The Determined Set, was organized. Until after the Civil War these three clubs held parades and balls on New Year's Eve. In the meantime, in 1857, some of Michael Krafft's friends had gone to New Orleans and founded the Mystick Krewe of Comus, and the first parades with floats in that city.

In 1865 a clerk in the market, Joe Cain, who seems to have been the town wit, staged a one-man parade in Mobile on Shrove Tuesday. Cain dressed as an Indian chief and announced his name was Slackabamirimico. There is no authentic account of his antics. One report states that he rode through the streets in a decorated charcoal wagon, playing music upon an instrument of some kind—probably a banjo or a guitar. Another has him marching on foot, playing and singing lustily. Whatever he did, it attracted attention, and Joe Cain suggested that Mobile should celebrate Mardi Gras as did New Orleans. The next year some sixteen Confederate veterans, calling themselves the Lost Cause

Minstrels and each playing a musical instrument, were out in the streets with Joe. The next year, in 1867, there appeared the first parade of the Order of Myths, with the first floats Mobile had seen on Mardi Gras. After that the clubs met and decided that all activities would be transferred from New Year's Eve to Shrove Tuesday.

New organizations formed rapidly—the Infant Mystics, the Mardi Gras Pilgrims, the Knights of Revelry, and many others—some to last only a few years, others which still exist. In 1872, the same year Louis Salomon galloped through New Orleans as Rex and the same year Duke Alexis visited that city, the first ruler of Mobile's Mardi Gras, Emperor Felix, appeared. Emperor Felix is still the Mobile equivalent of New Orleans' Rex.

Both legends have many of the same features. Emperor Felix is absent most of the year from the capital of his empire, Mobile, but each Mardi Gras he returns from his travels to his beloved city, arriving by water at noon on the Monday preceding Mardi Gras. He is received by the city officials and given a key to the city. At midnight on that Shrove Tuesday he vanishes from his ball and from Mobile for another year, departing with his queen and court in a scene of great pomp and ceremony. Like Rex, Emperor Felix is a prominent citizen, chosen during the year before. His queen is a young woman of much charm and beauty. The first queen was selected in 1893.

Carnival balls in Mobile begin on New Year's Eve night, and, as in New Orleans, there are a number of them, the last that of the Emperor Felix on Mardi Gras night. Some of the organizations boast of high social prestige, but none put as much emphasis on this as do some of the New Orleans variety. At their balls, after the tableaux and grand march, there is only one call-out dance, when the maskers dance with ladies of their selection on the floor. Then comes general dancing in which all guests may participate. Mobilians attending balls in New Orleans have been disappointed and astonished that they cannot play a more active part.

New Orleans calls herself "The Mardi Gras Capital." On the other hand, Mobile styles herself "The Mother of Mystics." Mobile's Mardi Gras is smaller and less costly than that of New Orleans, but the city is smaller. On the big day the same spirit exists in the streets of both cities.

Mobile's first parade is at the present time on the Friday evening before Mardi Gras, and there are nightly pageants through Monday. King Felix and his cohorts appear on Shrove Tuesday afternoon. That day the streets are filled with maskers, who behave exactly as do the crowds that pack the streets of New Orleans the same day. The hilarity is not quite so high in Mobile, due to the fact that the population is smaller, the liquor laws stricter, and the normal behavior of Mobilians is somewhat more restrained than that of many Orleanians. The cities have a similar background, for Mobile was Creole, too, yet the years seem to have tempered the latter more than they have New Orleans.

Mobile also now has a floral parade on Saturday afternoon, which, as yet small, is expected to grow into one of the city's most important Mardi Gras events. All Mobile parades are smaller than those in New Orleans, of course, with fewer floats in each parade. However, Mobile artists and designers have used much ingenuity and skill in the creation of their floats. Mechanical figures and moving effects are popular, and design and color also help to compensate for their smaller numbers.

Mobilians are enthusiastic maskers. They appear in many costumes as beautiful, as funny, or as grotesque as those that may been seen in New Orleans. They dance in the streets, form small parades, and ride on trucks. Social barriers between the organizations and the people are not so high, so perhaps the masker in the street feels closer to Emperor Felix and his empress and the other Mardi Gras rulers than a comparative masker would in New Orleans. It is much easier, for instance, to attend Mobile balls than it is many of the ones in New Orleans.

Emperor Felix and his knights throw trinkets from their floats and this creates exactly the same kind of excitement as occurs in New Orleans. Mobilians stretch out their hands, leap into the air, shouting with glee and begging for more. Young people form chains in the streets and run wild all day long. Parents bring out the kids, sleeping babies in rabbit suits, older devils and little girls in hoop skirts. People bring basket lunches—and some bottles. Strangers meet and talk, eat together, drink together, fight, make love. It is Mardi Gras, and anywhere there is Mardi Gras people have a wonderful time.

A MARDI GRAS CALENDAR TO THE YEAR 2000

1948	February 10	1971	February 23
1949	March 1	1972	February 15
1950	February 21	1973	March 6
1951	February 6	1974	February 26
1952	February 26	1975	February 11
1953	February 17	1976	March 2
1954	March 2	1977	February 22
1955	February 22	1978	February 7
1956	February 14	1979	February 27
1957	March 5	1980	February 19
1958	February 18	1981	March 3
1959	February 10	1982	February 23
1960	March 1	1983	February 15
1961	February 14	1984	March 6
1962	March 6	1985	February 19
1963	February 26	1986	February 11
1964	February 11	1987	March 3
1965	March 2	1988	February 16
1966	February 22	1989	February 7
1967	February 7	1990	February 27
1968	February 27	1991	February 12
1969	February 18	1992	March 3
1970	February 10	1993	February 23

Mardi Gras

1994	February 15
1995	February 28
1996	February 20
1997	February 11

1998	February 24
1999	February 16
2000	March 7

BIBLIOGRAPHY

Arthur, Stanley Clisby. *Old New Orleans*. S. W. Harmanson, New Orleans, 1936.

Asbury, Herbert. *The French Quarter*. Alfred A. Knopf, Inc., New York, 1936.

Bisland, Elizabeth. *The Life and Letters of Lafcadio Hearn*. Houghton Mifflin Co., Boston, 1906.

Cable, George W. *The Creoles of Louisiana*. Charles Scribner's Sons, New York, 1884.

Castellanos, Henry C. *New Orleans as It Was*. Graham & Son, New Orleans, 1895.

Clemens, Samuel L. (Mark Twain). *Life on the Mississippi*. Harper & Brothers, New York, 1901.

Fortier, Alcée. *History of Louisiana*. Manzi-Joyant Co., New York, 1904.

Frazer, Sir James George. *The Golden Bough*. The Macmillan Co., New York, 1922. 1 vol., abridged edition.

Gayarré, Charles Etienne Arthur. *History of Louisiana*. Hansell & Bro., Ltd., New Orleans, 1903.

Historic Sketch Book and Guide to New Orleans. W. H. Coleman, New York, 1885.

Kane, Harnett T. *The Bayous of Louisiana*. William Morrow & Co., Inc., New York, 1943.

Kendall, John S. *History of New Orleans*. Lewis Publishing Co., Chicago and New York, 1922.

Bibliography

King, Grace E. *New Orleans, the Place and the People*. The Macmillan Co., New York, 1892.

Louisiana, a Guide to the State. American Guide Series. Hastings House, New York, 1941.

Louisiana Scrap Books. Howard Tilton Library, New Orleans.

Martineau, Harriet. *Retrospect of Western Travel*. Saunders & Otley, London, 1838.

Merrick, Mrs. Caroline Elizabeth. *Old Times in Dixie Land, A Southern Matron's Memories*. Grafton Press, New York, 1901.

New Orleans City Guide. American Guide Series. Houghton Mifflin Co., Boston, 1938.

Parton, James. *General Butler in New Orleans*. Houghton Mifflin Co., Boston, 1864.

Rightor, Henry, Editor. *Standard History of New Orleans*. Lewis Publishing Co., Chicago, 1900.

Ripley, Mrs. Eliza Moore. *Social Life in Old New Orleans*. D. Appleton & Co., New York and London, 1912.

Sala, George A. H. *America Revisited*. Whittaker, Treacher, London, 1885.

Saxe-Weimar-Eisenach, Bernhard, Duke of. *Travels Through North America*. Carey, Lea & Carey, Philadelphia, 1828.

Saxon, Lyle. *Fabulous New Orleans*. Pelican Publishing Co., 1988.

Saxon, Lyle. *Old Louisiana*. Pelican Publishing Co., 1988.

Saxon, Lyle, Dreyer, Edward, and Tallant, Robert. *Gumbo Ya-Ya*. Pelican Publishing Co., 1987.

Suetonius. *The Lives of the Twelve Caesars*. Translation of Alexander Thomson, revised by T. Forester, Bell & Sons, London, 1914.

Thackeray, William Makepeace. *Roundabout Papers*. J. B. Lippincott Co., Philadelphia, 1879.

Trollope, Mrs. Frances Milton. *Domestic Manners of the Americans*. Whittaker, Treacher, London, 1832.

Wharton, George M. *New Orleans Sketch Book*. T. B. Peterson & Bros., Philadelphia, 1852.

Young, Perry. *The Mistick Krewe, Chronicles of Comus and His Kin*. Carnival Press, New Orleans, 1931.

Zacharie, James S. *New Orleans Guide*. F. F. Hansell & Bros., New Orleans, 1902.

Bibliography

Files of the following New Orleans newspapers: *Daily Delta,
Weekly Delta, Bee, New Orleans Creole, Daily Orleanian,
Daily Creole, Picayune, Courier, New Orleans Democrat,
New Orleans Times, Mascot, Times-Democrat, New Or-
leans States, Times-Picayune, Morning Tribune,* and New
Orleans *Item.*

Made in the USA